CAMP NURSE

My Adventures at Summer Camp

TILDA SHALOF

McClelland & Stewart

Library and Archives Canada Cataloguing in Publication

Shalof, Tilda
    Camp nurse / Tilda Shalof.

ISBN 978-0-7710-7984-9

    1. Shalof, Tilda. 2. Camp nursing. 3. Nurses – Canada – Biography.
I. Title.

RT120.C3S44 2009   610.73'092   C2008-904221-2

We acknowledge the financial support of the Government of Canada through the Book Publishing Industry Development Program and that of the Government of Ontario through the Ontario Media Development Corporation's Ontario Book Initiative. We further acknowledge the support of the Canada Council for the Arts and the Ontario Arts Council for our publishing program.

Typeset in Sabon by M&S, Toronto
Printed and bound in Canada

This book is printed on acid-free paper that is 100% recycled, ancient-forest friendly (100% post-consumer recycled).

McClelland & Stewart Ltd.
75 Sherbourne Street
Toronto, Ontario
M5A 2P9
www.mcclelland.com

1 2 3 4 5   13 12 11 10 09

CONTENTS

ACKNOWLEDGEMENTS

Thank you to:

Elizabeth Kribs, Marilyn Biderman, and Terri Nimmo at McClelland & Stewart, and Lynn Schellenberg.

Vanessa Herman-Landau and Allison Landau for your help with this book; Dani Kagen for her camp memories; Omri Horwitz of The Harold Wartooth for his vast knowledge of music; Dan McCaughey for his vast knowledge of the outdoors.

Anna Gersman, nursing partner and dear friend, along with nurses Cathy Dain, Annie Levitan, Donna Robins, Gert Rossman, and Ella Shapiro; doctors Ian Kitai, Leo Levin, Gary Mann, David Saslove, Eddie Wasser, and Georgina Wilcock; URJ Camp George staff, faculty, and counsellors – Deborah Cooper, former camp nurse and Chair of the Camp Steering Committee; Ellyn Freedland, Rabbi Daniel Gottlieb, Anat Hoffman, Karen Kollins, Marilyn Lidor, Rosalyn Mosko, Ron Polster, and Jeff Rose; Paul Reichenbach with the Union for Reform Judaism and the leaders of its Canadian region, the CCRJ; Gavin and Shirley Herman and Sam Reisman and family for their vision of a caring, inclusive camp community that is URJ Camp George of Parry Sound, Ontario.

With gratitude to the late, great leader Dr. Sheela Basrur, who understood how the public's health and hands-on nursing care go hand in hand.

To my campers and their families, especially Ariel and Liora Gersman, and Rachel Kreuter.

Most of all, thank you to Ivan, Harry, and Max Lewis, who remind me when I get homesick how fortunate I am to have such a loving home.

AUTHOR'S NOTE

For years, I dreamed about summer camp. Since I didn't go to camp as a child, I always had a second-hand nostalgia for my friends' camp memories: sitting round a roaring bonfire, arm in arm with friends, singing songs and enjoying gooey s'mores; the tough wilderness canoe trips, after which everyone came back bonded for life. I loved hearing about the late-night mayhem and antics of hormone-crazed counsellors. As an adult, I was a camper wannabe. So, when it came time for my own kids to go to camp, I saw a way into this happy world as a camp nurse.

This is the story of my summer odyssey, told from my dual perspectives as both a nurse and a parent. These stories are all true but in order to protect patient confidentiality and preserve the privacy and anonymity of the camps and their staff, I changed names and identifying details. In some cases, I made minor changes to the order of events for the sake of conciseness.

For the past six years, for a few weeks each summer, I've taken a break from the big-city medical centre where I care for critically ill adults, and travelled to beautiful, green Northern Ontario to tend to robustly healthy children dealing with ordinary, as well as a few extraordinary, ailments. Camp nursing has given me ways to combine my experience and intuition as a mother with my skills and knowledge as a nurse. And, just as my kids have grown up at camp, I too, have grown into being a camp nurse.

To parents, camp can feel like a secret world that we send our kids into with a mixture of trepidation and relief. In my unique position of fly (spy?) on the cabin wall, I've discovered that camp is about fun and play, learning new skills, and making friends. It is having adventures, being outdoors, and yes, making mischief. Camp is a place for children to take those first steps away from home, to connect deeply with one another, and ultimately, to create a community with their peers. Now, more than ever, kids need camp to help them connect to nature and one another.

The days are getting warmer. Soon it will be summer and time for . . . camp.

Tilda Shalof R.N.
Spring 2009

1

THE TREATMENT FOR NATURE DEFICIT DISORDER

"There's been an accident – someone's bleeding to death! Come quickly!"

Those were the first words I heard when I arrived at Camp Na-Gee-La. I had just turned in the driveway when I was greeted by this call to action from a frantic young man wearing only swimming trunks. I parked my car, grabbed my first-aid kit, and with my two sons on my heels, followed him through a thicket of trees to where his injured friend lay, also in bathing trunks, bleeding from a large, nasty gash on his knee. A pool of dark blood was spreading on the ground beside him. I was unfazed by the sight, and even my kids were calm. They were used to Mom handling emergencies. It's what I do for a living.

While I assessed the wound I asked him his name.

"It's Zack, and I'm gushing blood!"

Dripping, yes, oozing, maybe, but definitely not *gushing*. I knew exactly what to do. I took the blue-and-white beach towel still draped around Zack's neck and pressed down on the wound to staunch the bleeding.

"Ahh, not my Toronto Maple Leafs towel!" Zack looked at his knee, winced, and looked away. "Am I hemorrhaging?"

"Don't worry, you've got plenty more blood," I reassured him. In the intensive care unit (ICU) where I've worked for the past twenty-two years, I'd seen mattresses filled with blood. I'd cared for patients whose blood poured onto the floor at my feet, blood that I sloshed around in as we worked to save their lives. This was nothing.

"How did this happen?" I asked. Zack said he'd tripped while running through the forest on the way back from the lagoon. I glanced at the flip-flops he was wearing. Not the best choice of footwear. After a few minutes, the bleeding stopped. I cleaned the wound with hydrogen peroxide from my first-aid kit and bandaged it.

"You'll have to go to the hospital for stitches," I told him once I'd helped him to his feet. A deep, jagged gash like this would need stitches in order for it to heal. "When was your last tetanus shot?" I asked. Zack hadn't a clue.

"Is it really bad?" he whimpered.

"You're going to be just fine. Are you a counsellor at the camp?"

He nodded. His friend, who'd been watching anxiously from the sidelines, now stepped forward to introduce himself.

"Hi, I'm Mike, the camp director. You must be Tilda, our nurse."

Camp director? He looked more like my kids' teenaged baby-sitter. When we'd spoken on the phone, he'd seemed older than this gawky kid, still with traces of acne and a boyish grin. Mike had told me he was doing a graduate degree in political science at the University of Toronto, so I knew he had to be in his early twenties, but he looked about sixteen.

"Welcome to Camp Na-Gee-La!" Mike said. I reached out to shake his hand, but he pulled me into a hug instead. "Good thing you arrived when you did. Man, I was freaking out."

I looked around. We were deep in the wilderness of beautiful, green Northern Ontario at a "Youth-Leading-Youth Summer Camp Dedicated to Creating a Better Society with Equality and

Justice for All!" That was its motto. I was pumped, eager for my new role as camp nurse in charge of the health and safety of about a hundred children, and their teenage counsellors, too. Apparently I was already on duty.

"Breathe deeply," I had told my kids, opening up the car windows during the drive to camp. "This is *fresh* air." We were well into our three-hour trip north from our home in Toronto to Camp Na-Gee-La on the far side of Georgian Bay, long past the suburbs with their outlet malls and bedroom communities. I glanced in the rearview mirror at Harry, age eight, and Max, age six, but could see only the crowns of their heads as they hunched over their electronic games, their thumbs a-flying. "Take a look out the window. See the *countryside*."

"Are we there yet, Mom?" Harry asked, not even looking up.

They were oblivious to the glorious view, but that would soon change. Before long, they would be living outdoors in harmony with nature, singing songs around the campfire, paddling canoes, and hiking in the woods, arm in arm with their new friends. They would be campers for the first time and I, a first-time Camp Nurse. We whizzed by farmhouses, fields of crops, and cow pastures. Then, we turned off the freeway onto a single-lane highway. On both sides of the road were the massive, craggy, pink-and-grey slabs of granite rock that I'd learned about years ago in geography class: the majestic Canadian Shield.

Camp was definitely going to be an adventure – for all of us. The outdoors was a foreign world to me. I was a city girl, at home in downtown throngs, used to breathing polluted air, idling in traffic jams, and navigating the underground subway system. The natural landscape was as familiar to me as the moon's terrain, known only from pictures I'd seen in books. I had a bad case of "nature deficit disorder."

My parents considered the outdoors a wild and dangerous place, best avoided at all costs. My mother understood Nature only in an artistic way. If the subject of "trees" ever came up, she launched into rhapsodic recitation: "I think that I shall never see / A poem lovely as a tree . . . A tree that may in summer wear / A nest of robins in her hair." To my father, in theory the outdoors embodied great scientific principles, but in practice, it was merely a system of passageways to get from one book-filled interior to another.

Consequently, I spent my entire childhood indoors. I spent all my time with my parents, caring for my sick, depressed mother and listening, an audience of one, to lectures from my erudite, self-educated father. My air-conditioned summers were wiled away reading in libraries, waiting in hospital lobbies, and sitting in the cool basement of our house, surrounded by piles of books and bowls of apples for sustenance. My only activities were turning pages, staring out of windows, and daydreaming. I barely moved a muscle. And summer camp was not an option. I once suggested it to my parents, but they shot that idea down right away.

"You'll get dirty," my mother fretted.

"No, my dear," my father said. "Jews and canoes simply don't mix."

When I got married and became a mother myself, I vowed that my kids would have a different kind of childhood. I wanted them to have fun and friends their own age, to play outdoors, get dirty, and appreciate wildlife. Camp seemed like the place for all of that. My kids would learn how to make a fire, build a lean-to shelter in the woods, survive in the wilderness. They would know a toad from a frog, the bow from the stern, and the Milky Way as a galaxy rather than a chocolate bar.

For most of the long drive up to camp, it was quiet in the car, apart from the cheery, tinkly muzak of the kids' games. They were cramming in as much electronic playtime as they could. They knew that upon our arrival at Camp Na-Gee-La, I would stow their games away in the car's glove compartment, not to be touched again until our drive home, three weeks later.

Suddenly, something caught my eye on the road ahead. "Hey, guys, look at that!" Directly in front of our car, slowly making its way to the opposite lane, was a turtle with a wizened dinosaur face. I slowed down and pulled over to take a closer look. My kids were fascinated, their thumbs suspended over the keys of their games, the action on pause, as they watched and waited (and waited) for the reptile – or was it an amphibian? – to make it safely to the shoulder.

I thought about my kids. My older son, Harry, was quiet, serious, and painfully shy. I hoped camp might bring him out of his shell and boost his social skills. Max, on the other hand, was high-spirited, fiercely independent, and irrepressible. I hoped camp would give him the self-discipline and structure he needed. One thing I knew for sure: my kids were not going to merely read about the world as I had – they would *live* it, first-hand. If there were dangers involved, then so be it. I've always encouraged them to try new things and take risks – within reason.

As an adult, hearing my friends reminisce about camp, I'd felt envious, nostalgic for something I'd never even experienced: the gruelling canoe trips, the zany bunk-hopping and cabin raids, and the cozy scenes of sitting round the campfire making s'mores. My friends recall their camp days with loving wistfulness, falling into a reverie whenever that touchstone comes up:

"It changed my life. My camp friends are my closest, to this day."

"I had my first kiss at camp . . . my first slow dance. He's my husband now, and our kids go to the same camp!"

"The best was being a counsellor. Everyone knows you go to camp to get laid!"

"I lived for camp. Those summers were the best times of my life, the happiest."

I loved hearing their stories, but I had to agree with one friend who said, "If you've never been to camp, you just don't get it." Yes, I wanted my kids to be campers, and as a camp nurse, I could vicariously fulfill my wish to be one, too.

I was pulled from these thoughts by cheers coming from the back seat of the car. The turtle had made it – *a good omen*, I thought. But as I drove on, getting closer to our destination, I began to worry.

For so many years as an ICU nurse, I had taken care of patients who had serious conditions, such as multi-system organ failure, septic shock, and respiratory failure. The stakes couldn't be higher. When I had first considered the switch from the fast-paced environment of the hospital to what I imagined would be a laid-back, easy job, I had no concerns. Surely it would be a nice break from the intensity of the ICU, leaving me lots of free time for swimming in the lake, canoeing, and hiking in the forest. How hard could it be? Taking care of healthy children who had booboos, sniffles, and bug bites was a far cry from treating sick patients who had life-threatening illnesses. I had developed the typical, hard-bitten humour of nurses who toss off remarks like "any day my patient isn't in cardiac arrest is a good day." I wasn't concerned about camp nursing because, after all, these weren't *sick* kids. However, I did wonder if I'd have sufficient sympathy to offer those with everyday ailments. I realized I might have to recalibrate my "compassion-o-meter."

And there might be a few other challenges at camp that I hadn't considered. First of all I had no experience with pediatrics; I'd never taken care of children, other than my own. Also, at camp I'd be isolated and working by myself, without my ICU team to back me up. I began to wonder whether my skill set was suitable for camp. I knew what to do in the event of a cardiac arrest, but

I had never even seen a case of poison ivy. I could start an intra-venous drip, measure central venous pressure, and analyze arterial blood gases, but I'd never removed a splinter or taped a sprained ankle. Surely I could learn these things on the job? As I turned off the highway and onto a quiet country lane, the road got quite bumpy. I felt as if the dark forest of trees edging the roadway was closing in on me. I gripped the steering wheel tightly and drove on. *You can do this*, I told myself.

Then I saw the sign for Camp Na-Gee-La. As we approached the entrance gate, I tried to ease my nervousness by imagining the great times awaiting us. I thought back to my conversation with Mike, the camp director, and was reassured by his words. A few weeks ago, Mike and I had had a long talk on the phone. He'd told me about the camp, focusing mostly on its socialist philosophy. He said that Camp Na-Gee-La's name came from the Hebrew, meaning "let us rejoice." Mike had been a camper there himself every summer since the age of eight. He explained how Camp Na-Gee-La was part of a youth movement, which meant it was gov-erned by young adults. The parent council oversaw the finances and administration, but the day-to-day running of camp was done by the campers and counsellors. The parent council had voted that Mike be the camp director, and this would be his first summer in charge. He seemed eager to do a good job. He explained that it was a low-budget, no-frills camp modelled after the Israeli *kib-butzim*, or communes, of the '60s, where everything was shared, including chores, decisions, and responsibilities. It was both Zionist and pro-Palestinian, left-wing politically, and completely secular, as in no religious affiliation. "Don't worry," Mike reas-sured me, "there's no prayer hocus-pocus or anything like that."

It seemed like an important point to him, but I didn't feel one way or another about it. We were Jewish but not observant, so it seemed like Camp Na-Gee-La would suit me and my family just fine.

Mike told me more about their belief in the value of physical labour, living off the land, minimizing their ecological footprint, and "co-existing in a way that is respectful of the Planet." It all sounded good to me. Camp Na-Gee-La attracted the children of some of the country's finest artists, academics, and intellectuals, Mike said, "because of the way it inculcates humanistic values and promulgates a vision of equality and social justice."

"So, Nurse Tilda," he'd said playfully at the end of our conversation. "How about it? Are you in?"

I had taken only a moment to think it over. It certainly was flattering to be called Nurse Tilda. In the hospital, I was always called by my first name without any title. And I did admire Mike's passion for his camp. Admittedly, my kids were still young for any *inculcation* or *promulgation*, but it didn't seem that long ago that I had been young and idealistic, too. At forty-four years of age, I still felt young. Well, at least I was still idealistic. Though it scared me to think I'd be on my own without a doctor on hand and with the closest hospital a half-hour drive away, I reminded myself that I was an experienced nurse. I had handled many emergencies over my long career. *C'mon, you can do this,* I told myself. "Okay, I'm in," I said. *Bring it on!*

As I steered the car into the parking lot, I took a deep breath (of *fresh* air!) and readied myself for the plunge into The Great Outdoors.

2

BAND-AIDS, CALAMINE, AND A CAPPUCCINO TO GO

Camp Na-Gee-La was situated on an irregularly shaped piece of land made up of hills and valleys. At its hilly centre was a flagpole, from which a path sloped down to the waterfront. The mess hall was on another hill, and the infirmary was located on the highest hill of all. By the time I finished dealing with Zack's injury, it was late evening. Mike showed me to my new home, a room at the back of the infirmary. My kids would stay there with me for the night. Tomorrow, after all the other campers had arrived and camp officially began, they would join up with their cabin groups. I unpacked my things, organizing them on the wooden shelves provided, and tried to settle down my kids. We'd missed dinner, but I had brought some fruit and crackers with me, and we munched on those. They were excited but tired too, and soon fell asleep together on one of the two narrow cots in my room.

I sat down for a moment on the other cot to review some of my reasons for getting involved in this adventure in the first place. Camp fees can be expensive and I liked the idea of bartering my skills in exchange for them, but my real motivation was to get a ticket to the world of camp. It was too late for me to be a camper but this might be the next best thing. "Camp nurse" would also be my cover to spy on my own kids. I don't think of myself as an overprotective parent, but I admit I can get involved (too involved?) in my kids' worlds. I am the kind of mother who knew the adventures of Thomas the Tank Engine, and those of his sidekicks, Percy, Henry, James, and Edward, too. During the Pokémon craze, it was not every mother who could rhyme off the secret powers of Charmeleon, Squirtle, and Blastoise, but I could. Now, at camp, I could be on the inside and get the scoop on my kids' secret lives, while keeping a respectful, unobtrusive distance, of course. I could be a fly on the cabin wall. They would hardly even notice I was there.

Something else intrigued me about camp. I longed to learn the secrets of the successful campers. It was much easier for me to understand why someone might *not* like camp, what with the non-stop, exhausting activities, the noisy silliness, the bothersome bugs – not to mention the lack of books, solitude, and quiet time. I wanted to see for myself why so many loved it.

I went to check out the infirmary, down the hall. It consisted of a waiting room with a couch, a few plastic chairs, and a rattling old refrigerator. There were two other rooms, one with four beds for overnight patients and the other with an examining table and a desk. I took stock. There wasn't much in the way of equipment and the supplies looked like they'd fallen off the back of the proverbial truck. I found a dusty stethoscope, an antique blood pressure machine that belonged in a museum, a bottle of Tylenol long past its expiry date, a box of Band-Aids, a few bottles of rubbing alcohol, antiseptic, and a mystery bottle, unlabelled. All in all, this was not enough to supply a decent first-aid kit, let alone provide for an emergency. There was no airway (a tubular device to assist with breathing), no oxygen tank, no IV equipment or intravenous drugs. I had no medications to treat a seizure, a cardiac arrest, an asthma attack, or anaphylactic shock. The only thing remotely amusing about this situation was an object I discovered while rummaging in the drawer of the rickety old desk. It was a faded, cardboard disc from the 1950s called a first-aid wheel. Various injuries and ailments were listed around the perimeter of the dial. You could turn the dial and a little window revealed the treatment. I took a twirl and landed upon advice for "Choking," positioned in between the medieval-sounding "Blood-Letting" and "Dyspepsia," all seemingly equal slices of significance on the pinwheel pie:

> Loosen neckband. If object in throat, remove with finger. If child, hold upside down and slap vigorously on back. If measures fail, call doctor.

There was no mention of cardiopulmonary resuscitation (CPR), but it probably hadn't been invented when this once-useful tool had been devised. I put the first-aid wheel back in the drawer. It was a charming artifact but of little use to me.

It was getting dark, but I stood for a few moments on the porch to get a sense of the lay of the land. The campgrounds seemed rundown and shabby, but surely it would look better in the morning light?

That first night, lying on the other narrow cot in my new room, I couldn't fall asleep. All I could think of was Zack's dirty, bloody knee. I imagined it morphing into full-blown septic shock. I had seen minor wounds – even hangnails and paper cuts – develop alarmingly fast into raging infections that raced through the body at lightning speed, destroying every organ, tissue, and muscle in their way. A few of these cases had even turned out to be the devastating necrotizing fasciitis, or nec fash, as we nurses called it, generally known to the public as the flesh-eating disease. I'll never forget one patient I'd taken care of who had a swollen, inflamed toe. Within hours the infection had spread up his leg into his groin. Basically, it would have been game over if he hadn't been brought to the ICU, lickety-split.

My clinical experience was mostly treating worst-case scenarios and catastrophes. However, at least in the hospital I could anticipate them and have everything on hand I needed. Here, I had a feeling things would be simply coming at me, and I'd have none of the monitors or ICU gadgets I relied upon to know my patients' conditions and anticipate problems. My tool box was empty.

Something else threw me: When I went to make notes about Zack's injury, I couldn't find a chart or medical records. There was no record about any pre-existing medical history, allergies, or immunizations. In fact, the camp should have had detailed files for every camper and counsellor, but I only found a few health forms and most were incomplete. The nursing credo of *not documented, not done* haunted me. This place was scaring me.

I thought of all those inviting ads for camp nurses in the back of the nursing journals I subscribed to. "Have a fun-tastic, fun-nomenal summer with your kids!" they promised. The best was: "Get paid to have fun!" They had lured me in but now that I was here I felt out of my depth and way beyond my comfort zone. This place was more like a *danger* zone. What had I gotten myself into?

I was still tossing and turning later that night when music started blasting out from the mess hall. I got up, threw on my clothes, and went out to see what was happening. I stood on the mess hall porch and peered through the window. It was Party Central in there! The counsellors were bringing down the house with a full-blown rave. Techno music was pouring out of a portable CD player and bodies were swaying and undulating to the pounding, hypnotic beat. On the table were bottles of beer and wine coolers.

Two guys rushed in past me, arm in arm, shouting, "Let's par-tay! It's our last chance before the kids get here."

Were these counsellor-kids the ones going to be responsible for the camper-kids? When I was sixteen, seventeen, and eighteen, I definitely didn't have the maturity to be a counsellor – and I was beginning to wonder if they did either. As camp nurse, was it my role to put an end to their fun? Probably. But it wasn't much of a stretch to dial up my own inner teenager and remember what I was like. I, too, had loved to cut loose and be wild. A part of me wanted to join in on the fun with them, but reluctantly, I headed back to my cabin and slept for what seemed like a few minutes.

The next thing I knew it was morning. The sun was blazing and music blared from scratchy speakers that had been placed in the trees. I stood on the porch of the infirmary to get a daytime overview of the camp from my vantage point on top of the hill. I'd been wrong: in the clear morning light of day, the place looked worse, much worse. It was a dump. The cabins were ram-shackle and the mess hall, with its caved-in roof and crumbling porch, looked like a condemned building. There was garbage and empty beer bottles littered all over the ground from the party the night before. The campers' wood cabins were rundown, dilapidated shacks spread out helter-skelter in a valley. The "Nature Shack" was wind-blown, and the arts-and-crafts tent appeared to be sinking into the mud. Down, down the entire camp slumped to the one jewel of the place: the waterfront. With Camp Na-Gee-La situated on beautiful Lost Loon Lake with its sandy beach and protected cove, it made me wonder why Zack and Mike had been swimming in a pond in the backwoods.

On the porch outside the mess hall, a counsellor was strum-ming "Stairway to Heaven" and singing soulfully. It was way too early in the day for that intense song, but preferable, I supposed, to last night's head-banging lullabies. Other counsellors were on the grass, tossing Frisbees, and unbelievably, a few counsellors were stretched out on the lawn, covered in baby oil, "catching some early morning rays," they told me. I made a note to self to talk with them later about sun safety practices. Meanwhile, Harry and Max were amusing themselves while we all waited for breakfast.

Mike came over. "Hey, Nurse Tilda. Rough night? You look wrecked. Not a good look for you – no offence! That was your last chance to rest. The kids arrive this afternoon, so you'd better pace yourself. Did you manage to get any sleep?"

I shook my head.

"Ahh, that sucks."

"Is there coffee?" I asked.

Mike led me to the kitchen for a cup of hot tap water poured over instant decaffeinated crystals. He introduced me to the cook, a man who was a bit older than the others, which put him in his mid-twenties. He had a scruffy beard and spiky, geometric tattoos depicting daggers and jagged wires along his arms. "You must be the nurse dude," he said. "My name is Gord, but everyone calls me Sarge."

I looked around Sarge's kitchen. A young woman in a do-rag, wearing an inside-out T-shirt and tattered jeans, stood at the stove, breaking eggs into an industrial-sized frying pan with one hand and flipping pancakes with the other. Two gas burners were blazing with nothing on them. On the counter in the direct sunlight was an open bottle of mayonnaise. On the floor in front of the stove, glistening in the rays of sun, was a puddle of melted butter. Beside the puddle were two huge vats, one filled to the brim with peanut butter and the other with strawberry jam, over which bees were noisily buzzing. This place was a death trap if anyone had any life-threatening allergies. I would have to talk with Sarge about the hazards in his kitchen. Maybe I could also tactfully drop hints about hygiene, especially hand washing, for food handlers.

"Hey, I bet you're the nurse! Wassup?" A tall, lanky guy came over and brushed the hair out of his eyes to get a look at me. He pointed at himself. "The name's Jake but everyone calls me Wheels." He told me he was the camp driver. "I run the kids into town to the hospital and pick up supplies. I know everything about camp, so whatever you need, call on me – no explanation necessary." He hiked up his baggy pants that were slipping off his hips.

I suddenly realized how they all knew I was the nurse. I was, by far, the oldest person at Camp Na-Gee-La. My only competition for this dubious title was Anderson, a middle-aged maintenance man I'd been hearing about, who would visit the camp from time to time to do repairs. After breakfast, I left the mess hall and noticed Sarge sitting on the stoop out the back of the kitchen, sur-rounded by overflowing garbage cans, smoking a cigarette. I waved at him. "Hey Sarge, thanks for breakfast." He grunted in response. "What's for lunch?" I asked.

"Don't talk to me when I'm in my Zen garden," he snapped, but then added, less rudely, "Don't worry, it'll be something edible."

As I made my way back to the infirmary, I happened to meet Anderson. I found him leaning against a tree, just outside the mess hall, observing something with the focused gaze of a scientist.

"I've been standing here for twenty minutes," he said. "See that?" He pointed to a bottle of ketchup lying directly in the path of counsellors filing out of the dining hall after breakfast. They were stepping around or over it. "They won't pick it up. No one gives a rat's ass about this shit hole." He shook his head in disgust. "Nothing worse than rich socialists."

Suddenly, I heard laughter and the pounding of running feet. "They're here! The kids are here!" The sun worshippers, Frisbee-tossers, and soulful guitar-player whooped, and raced to the flagpole, the central spot in camp, where the buses were arriving and unloading the campers. As they tumbled out, each child was greeted and hugged by a counsellor. Most of them looked happy to be there, but I quickly spotted two little ones, a girl about ten and her younger brother, who seemed bewil-dered. In no time, the little boy found his counsellor from last year and ran to him. The counsellor picked him up, threw him in the air, caught him and spun him around and around. His sister looked on the verge of tears, but then she too was found by her counsellor and gently coaxed away to her cabin. Max eagerly went off to the youngest cabin, the "Friends," and Harry went off with the "Fellows." The next group, the thirteen- and fourteen-year-olds, were the "Comrades," and the oldest campers, the fifteen- and sixteen-year-olds, who stood off in a group by themselves, were "Counsellors in Training," or CITs.

I returned to the infirmary to wait for "business" to arrive.

They came. Children lined up to hand in their meds, and in no time I was inundated with plastic baggies filled with pills, capsules, and tablets; meds in film canisters, old cosmetic bags, and Tupperware containers. Someone handed me a mysterious herbal mixture that came in an empty jewellery box. I received a box full of tiny bottles of homeopathic remedies, some to be given in the event of "feelings of unease" and others for "disorientation." In a bottle decorated with Strawberry Shortcake and Winnie-the-Pooh stickers were tablets that looked like Advil but labelled amoxicillin, an antibiotic. One child handed me a large business envelope containing black-and-white capsules and red-and-white tablets, all mixed together. In an empty M&M's box, I found ten tablets of what appeared to be Tylenol with thirty milligrams of codeine, a heavy-duty narcotic. "They're my T3s," the young child told me, not too pleased to have to turn them in to me.

Mike popped by to say "hey" and inform me that the first day of camp was known as Safe Day. "Everyone can hand over any contraband to you," he explained. "You know, like booze, smokes, or drugs."

The whole scene was unnerving: I, who was used to the precise and controlled hospital environment where I had administered drugs in micrograms or titrated medications in milligrams or millilitres, was now expected to dispense unknown tablets by the handful?

I read through the explanatory notes some parents sent:

Jay is in tune with his body. He will let you know which pills he needs and when.

Madison experiences strange sensations at times. She'll tell you when this happens.

Phillip sometimes complains of depression, but he loves camp. Just talk him through it if it happens or if he says the "bad feelings" are coming over him.

In the hospital, I couldn't give an Aspirin without a doctor's order, but suddenly, here at camp, it seemed like anything went.

Kids kept coming. After lunch, they continued to line up on the infirmary steps and then spilled onto the grass outside, waiting to hand in their meds or discuss something with me.

"Hi, are you the nurse?" A pretty little girl pushed to the front of the line. She was barefoot, in a bathing suit, her long hair wet from a dip in the lake. "Hi, I'm Micaela and I'm going to be a doctor, an interventional neuroradiologist. My mother is a microbiologist and she put me on a drug holiday for camp. I normally take a cocktail of meds, but she thought I should have a break. Hey, what's that?" She sniffed the air. "It smells like our kitchen after my mom mops the floor."

"It's the trees. Your mom must use pine-scented cleaner."

Micaela handed me a note from her mom, entitled "Presenting . . . Micaela Brown." It explained that Micaela had a "touch" of attention deficit disorder and hyperactivity but was a "free spirit who needs to be allowed to do her own thing."

"I've never actually been *fond* of camp," Micaela said, "but my *hypothesis* was I would like this one because it's unique." She glanced at me to see if I was keeping up with her. "I know, I know, I use lots of *polysyllabic* words. Everyone tells me that. I've been tested, and verbally, I'm right off the charts! I'm in the ninety-ninth percentile for my age, which is twelve, going on twenty, as my mom always says."

"Have you ever been to camp before?" I said to try to interrupt the torrent of words.

"Oh, I've been going to camp, like, *forever*. Well, for the past three years, but not this camp. Now, I *live* for camp. At first, I didn't want to come, but then my mother found this place. She decided I should take a break from my meds, because it's not like school where I *need* them. My mother says nature has a calming effect, but I don't like nature. Well, I don't mind nature, per se, just the bugs."

"Where's your counsellor?" I looked around for someone to take her away, eyeing the line of kids stretching on into the afternoon.

"She knows I'm here. I love to visit the nurse. Hey, do you have ibuprofen? I get bad headaches and my head explodes. I get an aura with *scintillating scotoma*, you know, that wiggly, jiggly flashiness?" She drew a wavy picture in the air with her hands.

She was wearing me out. "Micaela, I have to see the other kids."

"I'm sorry! Sometimes I give *too much information*. Am I TMI comin' at ya? I know I talk a lot, but what can I do? My mom says I'm a turbo-talker."

For someone with attention deficit, it seemed she had an amazing ability to focus – at least, on things that interested her.

That first evening there was a singsong for all the campers around a roaring bonfire. Zack, or Moon Doggie as he was called at camp (and who hadn't, by the way, come to the infirmary to get his wound cleaned, as I had instructed), played the guitar while the kids sang "We Shall Overcome," "Give Peace a Chance," "My Song Is My Weapon" and other protest songs about the evils of materialism, the triumph of the working class, and the fight for freedom.

"That's what bugs me about Beethoven and those other old-school guys," I heard one kid say to his friend. "No lyrics." Then he caught sight of me and gave me a pitying look. "Your era must have been so boring," he said. "No cellphones, videos, or computers. What did you do all day long?"

I stifled a laugh. "It was rough, but we managed."

While the kids roasted marshmallows, Mike gave a rousing speech.

"Camp Na-Gee-La is a special place," he said. "Here we learn about sharing and caring for each other, for our community, and for Mother Earth. We are striving toward a society of equality and justice for all. For example, take candy. Any candy you have must be shared equally. Don't forget, because next week we have a trip to the jellybean factory.

"We are youth leading youth!" he called out and a great cheering roar rose up.

"We have a dream of a better world!"

"Yay! Yay!" The crowd clapped and whistled.

"Justice and freedom for all oppressed people!"

When the roar died down, Mike said, "Tomorrow you will be assigned your chores, and I expect everyone to work to the best of their ability, whether it's kitchen duty or cleaning the toilets."

"Ewww . . . pee-yoo!" they groaned.

"Remember, 'from each according to his ability, to each according to his needs'! *Hers*, too." He grinned.

After hugs all around, the younger campers headed to bed while the teenagers got busy with high-energy games of skateboard b-ball and gladiator dodge ball. Watching them, I remembered being their age and that feeling of boundless energy. It was fun seeing kids engaged in sports that didn't involve a coach, uniforms, schedules, and a drive to and from the event, not to mention trophies handed out for just showing up. Meanwhile, the oldest group, the CITs, went off to their evening program, which involved all of them, boys and girls together, going into the forest that surrounded the camp and staying there for over an hour. Mike called it a social mixer, a way to break the ice so that everyone would get to know each other fast. "When you're in the dark and can't see your way, you have to lean on each other. It builds trust," he explained. These goings-on weren't building any trust in me. They could be having an orgy in there for all I knew. I can't say for sure what did go on out there in the woods, but when they finally emerged, rumpled and dazed, they looked pretty pleased with themselves.

While all of this activity was taking place, counsellors who had the night off snuck away and headed for a "romp in the swamp," which included, rumour had it, skinny-dipping. Later, after it seemed that almost everyone else had gone off to get some sleep and I headed to my cabin and bed, walking past the tripping shed where they kept the paddles, canoes, and kayaks, I heard soft moans coming from inside. Two pairs of flip-flops were lying haphazardly just outside the door. I had to smile.

By the second day I felt as if I'd been there a week. I took a stroll around the grounds. In no time, I was in a scene from a "What's Wrong With This Picture?" puzzle. Wherever I looked, I saw a potential hazard, something about to break down or an accident waiting to happen. There was broken glass on the ground left from the counsellors' party. At the waterfront, I found rusty nails protruding from the dock and no sign of a lifeguard anywhere. Later that day, I cornered Mike.

"I have some concerns, things that need your immediate attention."

"I hear you, but give it time. I know it's crazy-busy at first, but trust the process." He tucked his clipboard into the crook of his arm in order to take my hands in his. "You can do it, Nurse Tilda. Be positive!"

Over those first few days I realized that if I was going to last, I'd need a daily routine. But when I tried to set infirmary hours, the kids still came and knocked on my door whenever they liked, day or night. During the brief intervals of quiet, I locked up and walked around camp. I liked to watch the activities because everyone seemed so happy, even doing their chores. My own kids were having a great time, too. Harry found a snake and kept it in a jar beside his bed, along with a pile of flat skimming stones he was collecting. Max discovered the joys of peeing in the forest, climbing trees, and hanging out with his new pal, Wheels, the camp driver, who took him for rides around camp on his BMX bike.

Why couldn't I just relax, enjoy it like everyone else?

By the third day, the flow of traffic in the infirmary had not slowed and the nights were still full of interruptions. By day the campers came; at night, it was the counsellors. At the end of each day I was exhausted but I learned that there was no point going to bed before midnight because I would only get woken up. One night, for some strange reason (sisterly bonding?), there was a run of gynecological problems. Long after midnight, a counsellor woke me up about a menstrual problem.

"I'm losing all my blood," she wailed. "It's extreme."

"How long has this been going on?"

"Weeks and weeks," she moaned.

"Is it worse tonight? Why did you decide to come to me now, so late at night?"

"I was walking past and saw your light was on."

I had taken to leaving a little light on in the hallway to help me as I fumbled around for my flashlight and jeans when I got woken up. I made a note to self to remember to turn it off. I handed her pads and tampons and promised to book her an appointment with a doctor tomorrow. "It's not easy being a girl," I commiserated.

Shortly after that girl left, another one came to the door with a "quick question" about itchiness and burning, "down there." *Doesn't anyone ever sleep at this place?* I offered to obtain the treatment for a possible yeast infection the next day.

"Okay, but if I take it, how soon after can I, you know, be with my boyfriend?"

"The over-the-counter treatment takes three nights. After that, you should be okay."

"We can't wait that long!" She burst into tears.

"Goodbye!" I showed her the door.

I would never talk to a hospital patient like this, but here, it seemed the way to go.

I dozed off, but around four in the morning, I woke up and turned on the light. *Something is not right*, I thought. Just then, Wheels carried Micaela into the infirmary. She was crying and scared. Wheels's tough-guy image and usual bluster were gone. He was gentle, holding her close and stroking her hair.

"I hate camp," Micaela said. "I am sooooo homesick. I want to go home."

"Is there anything you like about camp?" I asked.

"I only like hanging out with you in the infirmary."

"You seem happy during the day. You have lots of friends."

"It's an act. I'm faking it all the time."

She sat up, now wide awake. "Do you want to play chess?" she asked Wheels, putting her arm around his shoulder.

"Listen, Micaela, it's late. Can we discuss this in the morning?"

She nodded. I put her to bed in the infirmary, just down the hall, and she seemed pleased with that.

The late nights, the broken sleep, and my daytime worries were getting to me, and there were still two and a half weeks to go. I cornered Mike after breakfast the next day. "We need to talk," I said.

"Are you having a hard time, Nurse Tilda? You look like you could use a hug."

I dodged him and continued. "There are a few problems that need your immediate attention."

"Lay it on me, sister," he said, patting my back.

I gave him my top-ten list of what needed to be done to make the camp safer.

"Whoa!" Mike said, holding up his hands. "You're stressing out for nothing. You know what, Nurse Tilda? These are awesome suggestions. Maybe you should come to a staff meeting. We don't usually allow parental involvement because we're self-governing, but we might make an exception in your case. I'll run it by the others, put it to a vote, and if they're okay with it, you can join us tomorrow, after breakfast. Sound like a plan?" He put his arm around me. "Hang in there, Nurse Tilda."

What choice did I have?

From time to time, I checked on my kids, but there really was no need. At least *they* were enjoying camp. Harry was particularly impressed with the lake. He thought its warm currents were from an underwater heating system. I didn't correct him but did dispel the camp myth that was scaring him and the others about poisonous rainbow frogs that ate little kids' toes. As for Max, he loved everything.

"Where's Max?" I asked his counsellor one day when I was down at the lake. The counsellor was stretched out, belly up, on the dock, a towel over his face.

"No idea," he mumbled from under the towel. He looked like he was taking a nap. *Was he the lifeguard?* Did I have to supervise the waterfront too? I clenched my teeth. Mothers probably made the best lifeguards, anyway, I thought as I scanned the beach for Max.

"Nurse Tilda!" someone called. "You're needed in the infirmary." Okay, but where was Max? He was a bit of a wanderer, and though he always found his way back, I was worried. I could see kids gathering outside the infirmary at the top of the hill, waiting for me, so I headed back. *Max'll show up*, I told myself.

Just then, Wheels on his BMX bike came barrelling down the hill toward me at top speed. "Yo, Nurse! Comin' through!"

He had a passenger. Perched on the handlebars, his bare feet jutting out in front, was Max! "Boo-ya! Step off!" Wheels called out. I jumped out of the way just in time. Wheels slammed on the brakes, Max tumbled off and stood up, giggling madly.

No helmet or protective pads? I scolded Wheels.

By the time I got back to the infirmary, the place was packed. The ceramics instructor who often had just "one quick question" now had "just one more." A little girl was pale and feeling "yucky." Another kid claimed to have been attacked by a swarm of killer bees. There was a boy with a scraped arm, and a CIT who was complaining about a wart he'd had for the past three months. Zack was there, too. After my daily nagging, he'd finally showed up so I could clean his wound. (He hadn't gotten sutures and now it was far too late.)

I did what any nurse would do: triage. Mentally, I prioritized them from life-threatening conditions to emergencies, to potential serious problems, to everything else. With that logic in mind, I took the bee boy first, just in case he really had been swarmed and might be having an allergic reaction. But I couldn't find any stingers and decided the small raised bump on his arm was merely a mosquito bite. (I most definitely did not follow the advice from the first-aid wheel: *For insect stings: Remove stinger and wick the poison out with wet tobacco leaves.*) I put some soothing cream on the spot and sent him on his way. Then, I let the little girl who was feeling yucky lie down on a cot while I disinfected the boy's scraped arm. A few of his friends had by now joined him, all of them trolling for Band-Aids. I tended to be stingy with Band-Aids and doled them out seldom and reluctantly. I preferred to leave small abrasions open to air. Band-Aids seemed useless and I dreaded coming upon soggy ones in the sand or clogging up the shower drain. "I'll give you one," I told the boy with the scraped arm, "but only if you promise to dispose of it in a garbage can when you take it off." I told the CIT with the wart to wait till he got home to get treatment. Finally, I turned to Zack's knee. Although it was the most serious problem, it would take the longest to treat. The moment I saw it, red and inflamed around the open edges, oozing with thick, sticky pus, I knew it was infected. He would have to see a doctor for antibiotics. I was furious. This infection was totally preventable.

"Why didn't you come to me earlier to have this wound cleaned? This happened almost a week ago! You're a counsellor. You should know better."

Zack didn't argue. He looked sheepish. Just then, a tough-looking kid wearing purple-brown fingernail polish and filthy jeans with heavy chains hanging out of the pocket burst into the waiting room.

"Hey, do you have anything for depression?" he called out, as nonchalantly as if he was asking for a cough drop. "But please don't call my parents," he begged me. "They'll have a cow."

He wasn't homesick, he said, he loved camp, but kept having these "bad thoughts." Zack used the distraction to beat a hasty retreat, promising he'd come back again to follow up about his knee. By then, the girl who had been lying down had recovered and returned to her cabin with her counsellor, and the ceramics instructor who had only a "quick question" had gotten impatient and left, so Phillip and I had some privacy.

"Phillip, I want to call your parents. This may be something serious, something you need help for."

"Ahh, do you have to? I wouldn't have told you if I knew you'd rat on me. Don't you have a pill I could take right now, to help me sleep?"

"Come with me, let's go out." I'd learned the best way to get my own sons to talk was to get them moving. In motion, the words came. As we walked, Phillip agreed to let me contact his parents and restart his antidepressant meds if that's what they decided he needed. He promised he'd come back to talk with me again.

The next morning after breakfast, I went to the staff lounge, where the senior staff members held their morning meeting. They were lying on the filthy old couches, sinking into the deep indents made by many previous weary bodies. The guys were stretched out, their heads in the girls' laps; girls lay back with their heads in other guys' laps. Slumped into each other, the whole mess of them looked like rows of wayward dominoes. I pulled up a metal folding chair and launched into my list of concerns: waterfront safety, the importance of sunscreen, fluids to avoid dehydration, general hygiene, and foot care.

Mike stifled a yawn.

Wheels got up and walked out. "Catch ya later, Nurse Tilda!"

Carly, the head of culture and education, who everyone called Gidget and was hooked up with Moon Doggie (I figured out that their nicknames were a reference to an old TV sitcom), had been paying attention at first, but soon I lost her too. I'd already had a run-in with her the day before when she asked me to check her and her campers, but I didn't find the lice that she swore her

entire cabin of little girls was infested with. She sat there, sul-
lenly, fiddling nervously with her nose ring or else poking her
fingers into her Afro, checking for lice when she thought no one
was looking.

One by one, as if felled by a sedative, they tuned me out or
drifted off to sleep. There was only the sound of my voice droning
on about sun hats and closed-toe shoes, especially on long hikes,
but no one was listening. Mike was actually snoring softly.

Let me out of here! I thought, but there was no escape.
Young people usually have to inhabit the adult world, accommodate to our tastes, timetables, and rules. Here, at camp I was
stuck, having to put up with their preference for late-night
parties, their predilection for mac and cheese, watery hot
chocolate, and ramen noodles with MSG broth, and being
exposed to their unfamiliar music. I was held captive, trapped
in the lonely chasm of the generation gap. Before I came here
I'd thought of myself as young and hip, but now I felt like an
old lady, nagging, scolding, and complaining. I was wearing
jeans and a top from Old Navy but to them it was as if I was
wearing polyester stretch pants, bifocals on a string around my
neck, and hobbling along with a walker. I crumpled up my list
and angrily lobbed it into a garbage can. Mike woke up with a
start. "Hey, save a tree! Use the recycling bin," he said. He was
right but I wasn't in the mood.

After the meeting, Mike came over. "Nurse Tilda, you look
like you need a hug."

I stepped back. "No one was paying attention, Mike," I complained. "This is important stuff."

"Camp Na-Gee-La is all about process. We're a community
of shared governance. We don't come down heavy with rules.
Everyone has their say."

"Not when it comes to health and safety."

"That nurse needs to chill," someone said as I walked away.

"Yeah," her friend agreed. "She should take anger management."

Meanwhile, everyone else seemed to be having a grand old time. My own kids loved camp. Phillip was feeling a lot better after his outburst in the infirmary and our walk and talk and there were no more Micaela meltdowns. In fact, as I strolled around camp, all I ever heard were the sounds of laughter, of gleeful kids at play. I was the only miserable one. Even on rainy days, when they stayed in their cabins and had a bunk day indoors, they entertained themselves by singing funny cheers, performing silly skits, and playing board games and rock, paper, scissors, for hours. It was nice to see how content they could be, whatever the weather, managing quite well without parental intervention, technology, or toys. Of course, there were many days when they got into lots of mischief, plotting and carrying out pranks such as panty raids, cabin-hopping (when they invaded another cabin or sometimes even switched over all the furniture and camper belongings), and toilet seat-greasing. One afternoon, a posse of boys burst into the infirmary, begging to borrow the stretchers and bandages so they could dress up like accident victims. They took pictures of each other to send to their parents.

But I didn't give up trying to bring them in line with what was important to me: health and safety. After they returned from a five-kilometre hike into town to buy (and, of course, share) candy, they were flushed and happy, but their arms and faces were badly sunburned and their feet were sore and blistered. Again, my lecture to the counsellors fell on deaf ears.

I noticed that the organic vegetable patch, which they called "The Farm," wasn't thriving; in fact, it was completely overgrown with weeds. During my phone interview with Mike, he had said that the garden would be used to feed the camp and the surplus would be shared with the local food bank. I doubted it would yield enough vegetables for one meal. And that wasn't the only thing being neglected. Chores around camp were done sloppily or not at all.

It wasn't because they were too busy. After the long, intense lectures the kids endured each morning on Socialism or Political Activism 101, they had lots of free fun time on their hands. Though the camp didn't own much in the way of equipment – the sports department consisted of one soccer ball and one basketball – they played a lot of the "old-school" games, as they called them, like capture the flag and hide and go seek. They also had interest groups, like folk dancing (dances of oppressed nations, only), extreme Frisbee, a rock 'n' roll club, stressbusters, a yo-yo workshop, dream interpretation classes, and the very popular Hippie Club. I wondered what they did in *that* club – smoke weed, drop acid, have sit-ins, and let the sunshine in?

"What goes on in that one?" I asked Gidget, who organized the interest groups.

"Hackey-sack, cornrow braiding, and macramé-flower pot holders."

"What about the Fear Factor Cookout?" I asked.

"Well, today they cooked up a batch of fake snot."

"What's the recipe?" I asked, half kidding.

"Gelatin, green and yellow food colouring, corn starch."

There was even a handstand class. "Not enough propulsion and you can't get your legs up. Too forceful and you'll flip right over," the instructor cautioned the kids.

I asked Mike about the daily routine. "It's a creative schedule," he explained. "We try not to impose a lot of rules. We believe kids have a right to make their own decisions about how to spend their time. We don't want to stress them out. If they want to do nothing, that's okay, too. They need downtime."

"We need more safety practices," I said. "There have been too many accidents and preventable injuries."

He seemed worried. "You're not going to bail on us, are you, Nurse Tilda?" At that moment he looked like he did on that first day, a scared boy at the gate, waiting for a mother to save the day. He must have sensed how frustrated I was feeling in this chaotic, lawless place because he tried to win me over. "You're the best nurse we've ever had." It wasn't his flattery that made me stay; there was simply no way out. I didn't know how I was going to last two more weeks, but I was a nurse and would never abandon my patients.

I returned to the infirmary and sat down at the desk. For amusement, I took another whirl on the first-aid dial, my own little wheel of misfortune.

Electric Shock: Call doctor. Start artificial respiration at once. If victim is burned, apply wet baking soda or strongly brewed tea leaves to affected area.

Yeah, right, someone gets hit by lightning and I'm going to put on the kettle for tea! I tossed the wheel into the garbage . . . then fished it out again. Its comic relief might come in handy. I took a look at my growing shopping list. I needed a thermometer, bottles of sun block, a jar of aloe vera gel for sunburns, electrolyte replacement powder for dehydration. The days were hot and no one was drinking enough water or wearing a hat. Already a kitchen worker had fainted from heat exhaustion. I'd had to hose him down and pack him in ice.

The next time I saw Wheels, I handed him my list. He took a glance and gave it back to me. "It's all up here." He pointed to his noggin. "My memory is perfect. I hear something once and remember it for life – no explanation necessary. But I won't drive to town for just a small errand. I don't sweat the small stuff."

"So, let me get this straight," I said, exasperated. "You'll make a run to the hospital if it's an emergency and only a trip to town if it . . ."

"I need a real reason. Like, if a kid is in a coma or having a dying spell, then, obviously, I'll go. That's a no-brainer. No explanation necessary."

"I see," I said, gritting my teeth.

We didn't have to wait long for a "real" reason. Later that afternoon, Owen, a tall, tanned counsellor, rushed in with a female counsellor cradled in his arms.

"Becky fell," he said and laid her down gently on the couch. "She banged up her arm." Becky cradled her right arm close to her chest. She bit her lip as tears streamed down her cheeks, but managed to tell me what happened while I gently examined her.

"I was showing the kids tricks on Wheels's BMX and did a 360 into the bushes and landed on my hands. My arm broke my fall." She gasped with the pain.

Wheels appeared on the scene. I had to give him credit, he was always reliable in an emergency.

"Here's your second reason to go to town," I told him. "Becky has to be taken to the hospital for an X-ray and probably a cast." I turned to her. "What's your job at camp?"

"I'm a swim instructor."

Swim instruction? As far as I could tell, swimming consisted of a counsellor standing on the beach, bellowing into a mega-phone: "Everyone into the lake!" I still hadn't even seen an alert lifeguard at the swim docks.

Becky was shivering with the pain. She was going into shock. I wrapped a blanket around her. She was about to vomit and I handed her a basin and held her hair back. "I think you've broken your arm," I told her as I created a splint out of a rolled-up newspaper. I ripped up a bed sheet and fashioned a sling to support the weight of her arm.

We loaded Becky into the van. Owen, her boyfriend, hovered over her, looking worried. He hugged and kissed her. "You're going to be all right, Becks."

"They couldn't run this place without me," Wheels said cheerfully to me, revving up the motor and turning on the car radio.

"I'm quite sure," I muttered.

"Hey, look at that!" Wheels admired my handiwork on Becky's arm. "You're more of a DIYer than I thought. You rock, Nurse Tilda! Maybe you don't need all that stuff from the drugstore after all."

"Get everything I asked for!" I practically shouted at him. "And drive carefully," I added. I wondered if I should go with them, but Becky's condition was stable and I was reluctant to leave the camp on its own if I didn't have to. I hoped my makeshift arm splint would keep Becky's bones sufficiently immobilized on the bumpy drive to the hospital.

Something else was on my mind. "Wheels, is there a coffee shop in town? Could you bring me a cappuccino?" I handed him a few bills and as I watched him drive away, I hummed the first few bars of that corny song, "Hello Muddah, Hello Faddah, here I am at Camp Grenada . . ." I started counting down the minutes to their return. I desperately needed a jolt of real java.

3

DANGEROUS FUN

Things got worse. Every day, the waiting room filled up and the line of kids wanting to see me snaked out the door. There were noisy coughs, stuffy noses, assorted stomach aches, and a fever that went away after a day. Two CITs were made to stay overnight in the infirmary because the camp council decided this would be a suitable punishment for their streaking through camp. However, their stay in the infirmary ended up punishing me more. Their raunchy jokes and raucous laughter kept me awake all night.

When I wasn't busy treating children in the infirmary, I was running around camp, doling out pills, bandaging wounds, or taping up sprained joints "in the field." I was either offering Band-Aids, or band-aid type solutions. I was constantly putting out fires, both figurative and literal ones. Yes, a real fire broke out. It happened in the kitchen. Sarge couldn't find the fire extinguisher, though he swore he had one . . . somewhere. I heard the commotion from the infirmary and rushed over, grabbed a box of baking soda, and poured it on the greasy flames that had been ignited by a splattering, overfilled deep-fryer.

So far, nothing had come up that I couldn't handle, but the sheer volume and insistence of both the campers and the counsellors' round-the-clock demands kept me hopping. The infirmary had also become a social gathering place. At first I assumed it was because of the cans of Coke I kept in the refrigerator, but the kids kept hanging out in the waiting room, long after those had been guzzled. At times, I took a breather and sat in my office with the door closed, eavesdropping on the conversations going on in the next room.

"My dad makes toilets," one girl was saying. "He taught me everything. I can work my way around a toilet like that." She snapped her fingers.

I might need her skills. Anderson still hadn't unclogged my toilet that got blocked after some kids snuck in to use it. I had caught one boy who'd forgotten to flush the evidence, just as he was making his getaway.

"Use your own!" I shouted at him.

"Yours is cleaner!" he shot back.

One day the waiting room was quiet. *Too* quiet. I went out and found a bunch of kids painting their finger- and toenails with yellow and turquoise polish, the girls doing their own nails and then polishing the boys' and talking quietly among themselves.

"Isn't camp awesome this summer?" I heard one say.

"Yeah, at home we'd never get away with half the stuff we do here," another said. I was glad I didn't know what "stuff" he was talking about. I went back to my room and spun my first-aid wheel and chuckled to myself.

Gunshot Wounds: Call doctor immediately. Such wounds may cause lockjaw.

At least I didn't have to deal with that kind of injury, but there were some serious cases, and I made sure to keep detailed notes on them. Becky's arm had a serious fracture and she needed surgery. She came back from the hospital with a cast up to her elbow and left the next day to recuperate at home. Owen, her boyfriend, trailed off after her. He was the camp's tripper so that effectively put an end to all canoe trips. A roar of "hurray" rose up because no one wanted to go anyway.

One fourteen-year-old boy suffered a mild concussion.

"My teeth got shoved into a guy's shoulder," he told me. "We were playing tackle football and I was wide receiver. The other guys forgot about the ball and one went for my stomach and the other went for my head. I'm feeling dizzy and I just threw up." He did seem a bit spaced out. That night, I set my alarm clock for every two hours to perform neurological checks on him. At first, I was tempted to ask the counsellor to help me out, but he was so dopey, I wondered if I should be doing neurological checks on him, too. It wasn't easy differentiating between a coma and a teenage stupor, but the kid at least was fine in the morning.

Then a situation came up that I'd never encountered before, and it stumped me. A twelve-year-old from Michigan needed an x-ray. (Mike had mentioned we had a few American campers, attracted by our forests and clean lakes.) The problem was, the boy was unhappy about going to the doctor and the possibility of having an x-ray.

"My mother can't afford the medical bills," he explained.

The same thing happened with a camper who had a severe stomach ache. After twelve hours the pain still hadn't abated, so I sent him to the hospital to rule out appendicitis. He was seen, blood work was drawn, an x-ray and ultrasound were done, but then he threw up and felt better. His mother was angry because she had had to pay for a hospital visit that turned out to be unnecessary.

I was uneasy when health care and business mixed. Growing up and working in Canada, I hadn't worried about the cost of health care. As a nurse I'd always been guided by what was best for patients, not by their ability to pay. Call me naive – or just call me Canadian – but that situation left me flummoxed. In over twenty years of practice, I had never had a patient who couldn't receive medical attention because of lack of funds. I'd never even seen a hospital bill.

Unfortunately, I had no one to talk to about such issues, or about anything for that matter. I was getting lonely. Overhearing the constant counsellor chatter on the walkie-talkies made me feel even more alienated because I couldn't follow the fast volley of conversation filled with private jokes, secret references, abbreviations, and codes. What I missed most of all was adult conversation and companionship, my husband's, Ivan's, especially. I called him one night to complain that I was homesick. He listened and encouraged me to tough it out. I knew I had to stay till the end. I had only been there a little over a week and there were still two weeks to go, but already I was thoroughly exhausted and frustrated. In some ways the work here was more demanding than in the ICU. There, at least, emergencies only took you by surprise if you hadn't prepared yourself ahead of time – something we nurses were trained to do. Almost everything that could happen to our patients was predictable. For example, if I noticed early signs of congestive heart failure, I would slow my patient's IV fluids to minimize his fluid intake and thus reduce the load on his heart. At the same time, I'd have a vial of a diuretic ready to boost the urine output if he became "wet," meaning if his lungs filled with fluid. If I was worried that pneumonia was brewing in my patient's chest, I could step up the chest physiotherapy to mobilize secretions in the lungs and maximize lung expansion. But here, I was simultaneously bombarded with the serious and the significant, the preventable and the accidental. All I could do was react on the fly.

"Lots of stuff coming at ya, Nurse Tilda?" Wheels sympathized one morning.

"You got that right," I said, sipping my coffee, back to instant after the one glorious cappuccino interlude.

He had to be tired, too. The revelry went on every night, way past midnight. Just the evening before, the counsellors were involved in some wild pagan ritual in the mess hall revolving around Wheels himself. I had peeked in to see him standing at the centre of a circle, holding up a flaming torch, surrounded by female counsellors in various states of undress and wearing crowns of dandelions and rainbow scarves wrapped around their necks and waists. They were swaying and offering up bowls of fruits and vegetables (from their rotting garden?) onto an altar. One of them was holding out a chalice of what I hoped was merely red juice.

"All hail King Wheels, God of Camp Na-Gee-La, Lord of the Lagoon!" they chanted. "Bow down to Wheels, God of camp!" they chanted.*

They said later it was a celebration of the summer solstice, but from what I could tell it was all part of their insatiable need to lose themselves in group fun. By day they looked after their campers, but the nights belonged to them.

After hours, whenever they could, they snuck off to the lagoon in the forest. Once, on an evening stroll further afield, I stumbled upon the hidden path. I followed it, led by the sounds of laughter and singing. Soon, I came to a mucky-looking pond around which male and female counsellors were whooping it up, dancing topless beside a campfire, smoking, and swigging from bottles of "hard lemonade." I stood back, out of view, wondering again if I should put an end to their fun and do everything possible to have this dangerous place closed down. But I didn't want to take on the role of morality police, and besides, the campers were safe in their cabins with counsellors who were on duty. I looked up at the sky and stars for answers. A shimmering sound, clear and bright, vibrating in the night, came from the lake, then it sounded again. Was it an echo or the call and answer

---

* I don't make this stuff up.

of two birds singing to each other? I turned back to the infirmary.

The late-night merriment was definitely taking its toll on the counsellors. They were rundown, getting colds, sore throats, and headaches. Whoever was in charge of the morning wake-up music was getting to it later and later and choosing more mellow selections, such as "Dream Weaver." With its ethereal synthesized plea about closing your eyes, getting through the night, and making it to the morning light, it was not a tune to rouse anyone out of their slumber. It seemed that the frenetic energy of the first two weeks was now starting to peter out, just as we were heading into the final stretch – the third (and my final – ever!) week at Camp Na-Gee-La.

Most evenings, there was a campfire. I went but made sure to stay back and sit just outside the circle, so as not to intrude on the intimate gathering around the fire. It felt like the campers' private space and I didn't belong. However, one evening they gave a concert at the campfire. Counsellors performed folk songs on banjos, guitars, a harmonica, and a set of drums. They played old Pete Seeger songs, Arlo and Woody Guthrie numbers, and Bob Dylan. I loved it, but I heard grumbles among the kids.

"This music is so yesterday," someone complained.

Soon the musicians switched to more modern songs about peace, many alternating between Hebrew and Arabic. There was one in particular they all loved that kept repeating the words "Peace," "Shalom," and "Salaam" over and over.

They are good kids, I thought. *Their hearts are in the right place.*

I was worried about Sarge. He didn't look well, and late at night, in his cabin at the back of the kitchen, I heard him coughing uncontrollably. I made him come to the infirmary and the moment I placed my stethoscope on his chest, I could hear high-pitched wheezes as he breathed in and out. "Do you have asthma, Sarge?"

In between hacking fits, he glowered at my question.

"Do you use an inhaler?" I asked.

In answer he pulled one out of his pocket and huffed into it a few times.

"Sarge, has anyone ever shown you how to use it properly?"

"I know how to use it."

"You're blowing out the medicine. Try it again."

He did it again, the same old way. "The medicine is going out into the room, not your lungs," I told him. He tried again but was getting frustrated. Then I had a hunch what might work.

"Pretend it's a joint, Sarge. Toke on it. Just suck it in and hold it."

He grinned. Now he got it.

I shook his inhaler. It was almost empty. "Do you have another?" He looked away. "This one's almost finished, Sarge. You should never be without it." He still didn't respond. "I'm going to get you a new one." He walked to the door and turned back, keeping his eyes on the ground. "Okay, but send the bill to my welfare case worker," he said, "not my foster parents. They have no more money to spend on me."

I tried to not look sympathetic because I knew Sarge wouldn't want my pity. "Okay. Will do," I said, as if what he'd just mentioned was a simple matter of account-keeping.

"Thanks, I owe you one, Nurse Dude."

"Okay, then, why don't you just tell me what's for dinner."

"Food," he snapped, back to his usual irritable self. "Ood-fay," he added in pig Latin. "Eye of newt. Mystery meat! Toxic tuna with arsenic thrown in. Are you happy, now? Didja ever wonder why the infirmary is next to the mess hall? That's so when the kids get food poisoning, they can go straight to you."

"Why won't you ever tell me what you're cooking?"
"No chef likes that question."

With the third week came even more wonky headaches, irritated rashes, queasy stomachs, scratchy throats, and assorted bumps and bruises. It seemed like everyone at camp had one complaint or another. I did what I could to make things better, and luckily the problems were fairly minor. Nothing turned into pneumonia or septic shock, and certainly not flesh-eating disease. I handed out a panoply of over-the-counter painkillers. I sang the corny old song about "black flies pickin' at my bones in North On-tar-i-o," but of course they didn't find it the least bit amusing. Sometimes, as a private joke, I put ordinary Vaseline on their bites and they walked out, satisfied and cured; it soothed them just as well as the expensive ointments, which wasn't much.* Sometimes all the kids needed was a hug, a few moments of attention, an explanation, a short rest, distraction, encouragement, or reassurance, all of which I could easily give.

Sometimes my nurse-patient consultations took place in the mess hall. Hardly a meal went by when I didn't feel a tap on my shoulder. I'd be mid-bite and a camper or counsellor would bend down to show me some sore part of their body or divulge a private matter. "Come see me later," I begged, "during office hours!"

An unusual dish was served up at one meal. When girls at a nearby table started jumping up and shrieking, I went over to investigate. It turned out the hot dog lunch was the inspiration for one boy to place his penis inside a bun and offer it to them on a plate. "Who wants to lick off the ketchup?" I heard him say.

"Put that back where it belongs immediately!" I shouted, but

---

* One resourceful counsellor took his itchy kids to the kitchen to find a banana. He rubbed the inside of the peel on their bites and that seemed to work well, too!

no one could hear me over the roar of laughter of the entire camp.

Sometimes they came to me with problems that might actually be serious. A disturbing disclosure was made over the veggie stir-fry one time.

"I've missed my period," said a counsellor, plopping down on the bench beside me. "It's been two weeks. Should I be worried?"

"Yes!"

The sluggish, overweight ceramics instructor who always had a "quick question" for me finally got my attention when she happened to mention in passing that she'd recently been diagnosed with diabetes. "My blood sugar rate is around 2.1 or maybe it's 21? I can't remember. Which is worse?"

"You need to see a doctor," I told her. "It could be serious."

"My diet doctor ordered vitamin B_{12} shots. He said you'd give them to me."

"We don't stock that in the infirmary." I dreaded making another request of Wheels. "You'll have to get it yourself."

"What about two B_6? Do you have those?"

"It doesn't work like that . . ."

I was often stumped by the kids' problems. You have to know a patient's medical history and personality in order to determine the best approach and method, and I had very little to go on. I was operating on a strictly need-to-know basis.

As for my own kids, I hadn't seen them in days. One morning, I headed down to the cabins in search of Max. His cabin was quiet and I assumed the campers were out at their activities, but I knocked first. (I didn't want a repeat of the scene when I'd walked into what I thought was an empty cabin and found two counsellors in bed, making out.) No one answered, so I opened the door and stepped into the darkened room. A burly, hairy guy was lying in Max's bed, naked under a sheet that fortunately covered up his private parts. He squinted at me and shielded his eyes against the light from the open door. "Who are *you*?" I asked.

"Who are *you*?" he grunted. "You woke me up."

"I'm the nurse. Why are you sleeping in my son's bed? Where is Max?"

"Who's Max?" Without waiting for an answer, he turned over, and settled in for more shut-eye. I slammed the door behind me and set off in search of Mike. It was a shame they'd never gotten around to giving me a walkie-talkie because I was ready to scream at the whole camp. Imagine, this scary thug, sleeping in a child's bed!

I found Mike in the staff lounge, lying back on the couch, listening to music with his girlfriend, Shona, who was draped over him, her head resting in his lap. He chuckled when I told him about the intruder. "Oh, that's Spleen. He's a legend around here." He shook his head in recollection of past heroic Spleen antics. "Spleen – what a guy! Hey, don't look so worried. He's harmless. He's buddies with Quade, Max's counsellor. Spleen's out on parole – I mean, on *vacation*. He's staying with us for a few days before he moves on."

"*Out on parole?*"

Shona giggled and turned away to hide her amusement.

"He was convicted of a B and E but I swear, he didn't do it! Spleen is awesome with kids. We're lucky to have him at camp."

I guess I didn't look reassured.

"He's not a serial killer or a child molester, I promise you that."

I wiped my brow in an exaggerated gesture of relief.

Eventually, at the waterfront I found my kids. Harry was swimming with his friends, watched over by a dopey-looking lifeguard. Max was happily playing with his gang on the beach, building sandcastles and smashing them down. I returned to the infirmary. There I found a raging, pacing Carly. She had buzzed off her 'fro and her almost-bald head was covered in a bandana do-rag.

"There are more cases of lice infestation!" she snapped at me.

"There's an epidemic going on around here and you're doing nothing about it."

"I examined your campers' heads. I didn't find a single lice – I mean louse."

"I showed you those white thingies in Sasha's hair."

"That's dandruff. Nits stick to the shaft of the hair follicle. You can't flick them off. I'm not going to treat a kid who doesn't have lice."

"Well, Wheels has already gone to town to buy me lice shampoo!"

"So, you are going to put chemicals on your scalp that you don't need?"

"My head is so itchy. I've been up all night. This is so freaking me out."

Everyone runs around barefoot, sunscreen bottles haven't been opened, your own boyfriend won't take care of the dripping, festering wound on his knee, and you're worried about harmless head lice?

"This is a serious hygiene problem," she said.

"Lice are a nuisance, not a disease. Besides, no one here has lice," I told her.

I wanted to lock the door and barricade myself in there, but of course, there were no locks on any doors in this place. I put a sign on the door that I was going for a walk. First I stopped at the mess hall to fill up my water bottle at the fountain. As I was doing that, I noticed a little rivulet on the floor of what looked like . . . blood! I followed the stream to a large puddle that was being fed by a continuous drip from the unplugged refrigerator. *Was there a body in there?* I yelled for Sarge. He came running.

Packages of frozen meat had been placed in the fridge to slowly defrost, but instead had melted into warm, oozing messes. When Sarge saw the bloody puddles on the floor and then the soft, grey meat he threw down his dishrag and cursed. "Damn kids! They unplug the fridge for their music at night and then forget to plug it back in again afterwards."

I looked down at the meat blood. "When was the last party?"

He stopped to think. "Not last night, but the night before. I think."

"Do not use this meat, Sarge. Throw it out immediately."

I stood back trying not to retch at the smell of warm meat blood. "It's rotten. It's been out more than twenty-four hours." I watched him thinking this over. He prided himself on his frugality and recycling. (I'd seen him make soup out of potato and carrot peelings.) Sarge didn't take suggestions about his cooking at the best of times, but this was serious. However, he wouldn't promise to dispose of it, and I stomped away, frustrated again.

In sheer desperation, I called Ivan to tell him my troubles, but he was out. I left a pathetic message, one that would make him feel sorry for me having such a terrible time while he was probably living it up, eating out at restaurants, and enjoying the single life, temporarily unfettered by any responsibilities. I returned to the infirmary to spin my first aid "Wheel of Fortune," hoping for some sage advice to miraculously appear.

I landed on "Toothache: See your dentist."

Thanks a lot! I spun it again.

Foreign Body Obstruction in Airway: If patient swallows a sharp object, get him to eat mashed potatoes to surround object. For further treatment, call doctor.

I was laughing my head off at that one when Mike burst in, the screen door banging behind him. "Hey, Nurse Tilda! Someone's on the phone from the public health department for you. Something about the water supply. Sounds majorly important."

I closed my eyes for a moment, taking in this fresh disaster.

The inspector explained that there was run-off from the septic tank leeching into the reservoir – the lagoon – at the back of the camp. The underground spring that supplied drinking water to the camp was contaminated with unsafe levels of bacteria.

"What a bummer," Mike said when I got off the phone and told him what was wrong.

I got up slowly, thinking rapidly. "From this moment on there will be no drinking water from the tap or the lake. Swimming and showering are banned. The water supply has to be turned off."

"Hey, does that include swimming in the lagoon?"

"It's a cesspool!" I glared at him. "This camp should be shut down," I muttered.

"If there are problems, we will form a task force to address them," said Mike.

"No committees! No meetings!" I thundered at him. "This is a deadly situation!"

"Watch out, guys," he warned his pals who'd gathered around us. "The nurse is going ape."

I grabbed his walkie-talkie and screamed into it. "Listen up! To everyone at Camp Na-Gee-La, there is no drinking water until further notice." I held it close to my mouth and repeated the warning. I turned back to Mike, who now looked ready to comply.

"We'll put up signs all around camp," he said.

"That's not good enough! Call Anderson! The water supply has to be shut off."

"Can it wait? He's busy fixing the roof. It's been leaking."

"No!" I stormed at him.

"Don't stress out, we're dealing with it."

"People can get seriously ill and die from contaminated water," I told him. Mike looked shocked. Was I finally getting through to him? "I want you to order a truckload of bottled water and tell Sarge to boil all water before using it for cooking or washing. This is an emergency."

At that, Mike stood there, thinking. "Does this mean the carnival is cancelled?"

I lunged forward to strangle him, but he must have thought I was zeroing in for a hug. Once again we ended up in another tangle of misunderstanding. I pulled away. No one was taking me seriously, but at least I could try to save my own kids. I raced to find them and warn them not to drink the water. I barged right into Max's cabin, and plowed through a sludge of wet towels and bathing suits, piles of grubby clothes and scattered candy wrappers. The kids were all there, a couple of them up high in the rafters, climbing the beams and swinging like monkeys. A few kids were gathered on the floor in the corner of the cabin, feeding potato chips to a family of mice. I happened to notice a nine-year-old boy wearing a dress, with his hair in pigtails and ribbons, but there was no time to inquire about that. Quade and a few other counsellors were playing poker with Spleen, while Max sat on the jailbird's shoulders, doing flips backward onto the bed, giggling helplessly each time. (Fleetingly, I had to wonder if the gambling winnings would be divvied up equitably in true socialist form.) I interrupted the game to give them the warning.

"Hey, first you tell us to drink more water and now you're telling us not to drink the water at all? I don't get it," Quade said. "Make up your mind. What's your bottom line?"

"Yeah, what gives?" Spleen said without looking up from his hand.

No time to explain! I ran out and continued to spread the word. Rain started coming down, a heavy but pleasant downpour that broke the heat wave. By late afternoon, it was still coming down. The roof was leaking in the mess hall and Anderson and Wheels were up there, trying to patch the holes. The water had been shut off and bottled water had arrived. Meanwhile, all around camp, the valleys were filling up. Two enterprising counsellors hauled up canoes from the shed near the lake and were paddling on the newly forming ponds of knee-deep water. The kids piled into the boats and others started jumping into the water with their clothes on. Kids dragged the vinyl mattresses from their beds and used them as rafts or to slide off the mess hall porch into the middle of a huge pile of mud. Pretty soon, just about everyone was deep in the mud, wearing their bathing suits or else stripped down to their under-wear. I caught sight of my own kids. Max was running through the mud barefoot, looking like a feral child, while Harry was drifting around contentedly in one of the canoes, his white, mosquito-bitten arms splattered with mud. Everyone was deliri-ous with joy! It was Woodstock, but without the drugs or music. But then someone realized that music was exactly what was missing from this scene and ran to bring the boom box from the mess hall. Soon the valley resounded with garage band grunge from what sounded like a homemade tape.

Mike joined me and gazed at the scene appreciatively. "The fun never stops around here, does it, Nurse Tilda?"

Please, make it stop! Just then I noticed that the live electrical cord running from the mess hall was lying in a foot of water and I ran off to put the kibosh on the music.

Later on, after the water emergency ended and the mud bac-chanal died down, and after I'd finished treating the cuts and twisted ankles from kids slipping and sliding in the mud, there was still Zack's knee and Sarge's lungs to worry about. I had nabbed Zack at lunch, but he couldn't understand why I wouldn't examine his knee right then and there (he'd placed it right beside my tuna-fish sandwich).

"Bring this knee of yours to the infirmary after lunch," I'd barked at him, nudging it off the table. He didn't show up until much later. Immediately I saw that his knee was even worse. The wound was now wide open, smelly, and mushy – all signs of infection. "Okay, that's it. You're going to a doctor. This could have been prevented but now you need a deep debridement to clean all that out and antibiotics, too."

"You mean pills?"

I nodded.

He backed off. "I have issues with pills."

"How so?"

"I don't take medicine."

"You can't swallow pills? I'll crush them into applesauce for you." I was losing patience.

"My mother's a Scientologist," he said. "She doesn't want me taking pills. She believes in the body's natural healing powers."

Just then Sarge arrived, right at dinner time. "I came for my breath-a-lyzer," he said, his usual cryptic self. His lungs sounded better now that he was using his medication properly. I handed him the new inhaler I'd bought and had charged to the camp. I had him in my corner so I tried again. "What's for dinner, Sarge? Hope you saved me something tasty!"

"Spaghetti," he said, and, like the true gonzo chef he was, added, grinning sadistically, "with *meat* sauce."

4

ESCAPE FROM UTOPIA

Sarge wasn't joking. He had cooked up the rotten meat and served it for dinner.

All I could do was retreat to my room and wait for the victims to start staggering in. I hunkered down in bed under the covers, hiding from them all, and braced myself for the impending food-poisoning disaster. I left the light on in my room all night, and I stayed in my clothes so I'd be able to jump up and react even faster. I studied my textbooks, reviewing the signs of salmonella and staphylococcal food-borne infections. "Botulism," I read, "starts with diarrhea and vomiting, eventually leading to paralysis of the eyes, mouth and throat, and respiratory system." Ultimately, they would all go into cardiac arrest! Let the outbreak begin: I was ready.*

The funny thing was, that night everyone slept more soundly than ever before. It was the first night I wasn't disturbed. No one even came for an antacid tablet. The only thing I ended up nursing was my own resentment and fatigue. In spite of the ominous events, things actually improved over the next few days. Mike had gotten Anderson to board up the entrance to the lagoon in the woods. Plumbers were called in to repair the leak

---

* I was only marginally aware that I was losing it.

in the septic system. The camp's water supply was shut down and the public health authorities disinfected the system. We drank bottled water for three days and then the water was re-tested, deemed safe to drink, and the advisory lifted. The weather had turned sunny and hot, so I returned to my previous harangue about drinking lots of water to avoid dehydration and heat stroke.

I knew for sure that the camp's spirit was back to normal the morning when the wake-up music was "Walkin' on Sunshine."

There were only a few days left until the end of my tour of duty. I still fantasized about fleeing, but I was determined to see it to the bitter end. Mike and I had even become buddies.

"The buzz around camp is we're thinking of inviting you back next year," he told me. "You should take it as a compliment."

"The only buzz I'm aware of is from the mosquitoes," I shot back grumpily (though I was secretly pleased).

I had to admit, there were some delightful moments at Camp Na-Gee-La. One day I watched a group of twelve-year-old girls and boys on kitchen duty. The music was blaring, and the kids, all in their bathing suits, were laughing and dancing, spraying each other with the hand-held ceiling nozzles. They were having such fun – their wet, shining faces so joyful as they threw gobs of bubbly suds at one another. I tried to not notice the slippery floor, the piles of food residue in the sink, and the partially rinsed dishes.

I also enjoyed observing the CIT "activities of leadership development." One activity was a game called "Which Would You Rather?" that posed thought-provoking questions such as: Would you rather see into the future or communicate with animals? Would you rather be famous or smart? Their Truth or Dare game must have been abandoned hastily because I kept coming upon the cards strewn all over the campgrounds, blown around by the wind.

Truth: What do you do when you really want to punish your
        parents?
Dare: Remove your top or eat a bug.
Truth: What's a more important political issue: poverty or the
        environment?
Dare: Perform your best "sick" routine you do to punk the nurse.

Another leadership session started off well but soon erupted
in a messy food fight. They were making a map of the Middle
East, with gumdrops for Egypt, raisins for Jordan, popcorn for
Israel, and licorice sticks for the West Bank, when suddenly, they
started hurtling gobs of chocolate pudding (the Mediterranean
Sea) and blobs of green Jell-O (Sea of Galilee) at one another.
Well, one look at that scene and anyone could see why there'd
never be peace in that region!

On one of my last nights at camp there was an emergency. It
was the most terrifying situation I'd ever faced as a nurse – not
because I didn't know what to do, but because I had to face it
totally alone and completely ill-equipped to treat it properly.
  Mike banged at my window in the middle of the night during
a rainstorm, shouting, "Hey, Nurse Tilda! Wake up! Come
quickly! Someone's having a seizure!" I jumped out of bed, fortunately still in my clothes, and charged out the door. My heart
was pounding as we raced to one of the Comrades cabins. I had
no idea what to expect. I ran in and found thirteen-year-old
Amanda lying on the floor in the midst of violent convulsions.
This was a true full-blown or grand mal seizure. The other girls
and the counsellors were gathered around her, terrified, and I
pushed them aside to get to her. I knelt down and turned Amanda
on her side and cleared the space around her of people, furniture, and obstacles. Had we been in the hospital, I would have

given her a shot of Valium and called a "code," to summon the resuscitation team, but here, all I could do was try to keep her safe while we waited it out. After a few long minutes, the seizure eased up and she lay there, unmoving and unconscious but breathing, slowly and deeply. I took her pulse; it was steady but rapid. Wheels was already waiting outside the cabin in the van. I thought about calling for an ambulance, in case Amanda deteriorated on the way to the hospital, but I let myself be persuaded by Wheels that he could get us there faster. He came in and helped carry her to the car. We laid her on the back seat and I crouched on the floor, next to her.

As we drove to the hospital the rainstorm turned into a raging electrical thunderstorm of biblical proportions. Visibility was poor, even with the high-beam headlights on. There were no streetlights on those winding country roads and it was only during the intermittent split seconds when the sky cracked open in a burst of light that we could see where we were going.

I thought through all the possible scenarios. What if Amanda went into cardiac arrest? Mentally, I prepared myself to perform CPR. What if her airway became obstructed? If that happened, she would need an emergency tracheostomy; I'd have to cut into her windpipe and breathe air into her lungs. I didn't even have a scalpel or an airway with which to perform such surgery, much less the qualifications or the guts to actually do it. But if I didn't make an airway, she'd have no oxygen flow to her vital organs. I noticed a plastic straw on the floor of the back seat, probably from someone's trip to the Dairy Queen. I picked it up. Mentally, I landmarked her neck for the cricothyroid membrane, the place I'd have to slice open with a scalpel (if I had one) and then insert the dirty straw to make an airway for her. In the hospital, I had assisted in hundreds of these procedures on my patients, both emergency ones and planned ones, but under completely different conditions! I held on tightly to the crumpled straw in one hand and to Amanda's hand with my other. *Oh, why did I listen to Wheels? I should have called for an ambulance!*

Amanda continued to breathe. I shone a flashlight into her eyes to check the response of her pupils. They were equal and reactive, which was a good sign, but when I pressed down on her breastbone, there was only a minimal response to that painful stimulus, indicating that she was still deeply unconscious.

Oh, hurry, hurry, get us to the hospital. Wheels had to drive slower than usual because it was so dark and treacherous.

"Wow, it's like Jurassic Park," he said as another bolt of lightning turned night into day and then back to night again.

"It's like a horror movie, except we're in it," I said gloomily from the back seat. What was I doing here? *I wish I was back at home, in my bed, safe with Ivan.*

"Hey, Nurse Tilda, don't be stressed. Amanda seems better, now."

"She is seriously ill."

"Oh, I've seen worse, much worse."

"This has the potential to be worse."

"Oh, well, the *potential.*"

Although she didn't appear to be seizing, I was afraid Amanda might be in a state of an underlying seizure, called *status epilepticus*, which could cause permanent brain damage. "Amanda! Wake up," I shouted at her, fruitlessly.

"She's tired, let her sleep," Wheels suggested.

"She's not asleep, she's unconscious," I said. *You fool.*

"I've brought kids to the hospital who were in way worse shape than this. Last year we had this kid who fell through a window and, like, lost almost all of his blood. I sat with him for hours in the ER. They just bandaged him up and sent us packing. Most of the people waiting in the ER don't even need to be there," he said cheerfully. "You practically have to be having a dying spell before they admit ya, these days. I'm sure they'll send us right back to camp. You'll see, she'll be back at camp tonight."

"She is staying in the hospital, and then she's going home."

"Listen, Camp Na-Gee-La has a perfect record. We've never sent a camper home. Besides, do you know who her parents are?" He told me their names, a politician mother and movie producer father. By that time we had arrived at the hospital. He pulled into the parking lot, straight into the reserved spot of Dr. McNab, Chief of Surgery. "Don't worry. He knows me. No explanation necessary." He hitched up his pants, scooped Amanda into his arms, and carried her into the emergency department.

The triage nurse took her immediately. The doctor examined her and quickly administered an intravenous drug to try to break the seizure. By then, Amanda was beginning to wake up, but was groggy and confused. She had no recollection of what had happened. They admitted her for further tests, including a CT scan of her brain. It was three in the morning, and I had to call Amanda's parents. Shocked and distraught as they were, they said they would be leaving shortly from Toronto to be with her. I went back out to the waiting room, which was indeed full, as Wheels had predicted.

"Boo!" Wheels jumped out at me from behind a plastic decorative tree. "See, what'd I tell you? Half these people don't even need to be here. Where's Amanda? Did she have a good nap?"

I gritted my teeth in response.

I tried to snooze on the drive back to camp, but Wheels played the radio and chattered non-stop. Rain was still coming down, but the heavy storm had blown over.

"I've been at plenty of other camps but this one's the best. I used to go to this Johnny Appleseed–type place, run by real Native people who were trying to take back their culture. They said Thanksgiving prayers to the trees and the wind – you know, like 'I thank the Lord for the birds and the bees and the apple trees.'" He took his hands off the wheel, clasped them, and closed his eyes in fake prayer. "Me? I'm more a rub-a-dub-dub-thanks-for-the-grub Yayyy, Ggggod! kind of guy, but hey, whatever floats your boat. That place was wild! We got to go to their sweat lodge and smoke the peace pipe."

"Keep your hands on the wheel!" I sat up to shout at him. "Watch the road!"

"Yup, my parents always sent me off to camps. I guess they needed a break from me, no explanation necessary there, ha ha . . . Oh, I've been told I'm a handful. They tried to put me on meds, but I don't need them any more. Obviously, I can deal."

Just get us back safely, I prayed.

"Once they sent me to one of those 4H camps in the States. You know, all that head, heart, hands, and health stuff – it made me puke. So goody-goody! Yeah, right! One summer the nurse came up with her daughter who was a counsellor and they were both sleeping with the same counsellor. Can you believe it? Hey, anyone you dig at camp?"

At that moment, I was grateful to see the entrance to camp, thus ending Wheels's monologue.

"Good night," I said as he let me out in front of the infirmary. I was ready for bed but by now the rain had stopped, the sun was up, and it was almost time to dole out the morning meds.

Later that day, I spoke with Amanda's doctor in the hospital. The brain scan had showed a small cerebral bleed, a tiny stroke, that likely caused the seizure. She would be going home to Toronto to be examined by a neurologist and undergo more tests. She would definitely not be coming back to camp. I never found out how she was after that. It was often like that in the ICU too. We got our patients through a life-threatening situation and stabilized them. Once they progressed to the floor, they went

home and we never heard how they fared. Our job was to get
them through the crisis.

There were only three more days left at camp and it looked like I
was going to make it! I sat reviewing my notes and making sure
they were in order. I had written them one quiet day when all
activities had suddenly been cancelled. (I soon found out why:
The latest Harry Potter tome had arrived and everyone who
could lay their hands on a copy was busy reading.)

Freddie A. Eleven-year-old with sore finger, painful after
two days, improved after x-ray and ice cream cone.

Daliah C. Camper claims to have been bitten by a rat-
tlesnake. States she heard "rattles." On examination, no
findings. Possible insect bite? Camper kept overnight for
observation in infirmary. Vital signs taken every four
hours. Condition stable. Slept well. No signs of neuro-
toxic venom poisoning.

Zack D. Counsellor. Knee wound still infected. Edges are
macerated and red, still not approximating and very little
granulation tissue. Appointments made with a doctor in
town, but he refuses to go.

Allan E. CIT. Canoe dropped on big toe, left foot. Large
blood bubble under the nail. Very painful. Ice applied and
drainage with sterile, sharp object.

I left it at that short note for Allan E., but I'd never forget that
toe! It must have throbbed, but he tried not to let on just how
painful it was, though his eyes teared up and his fists were

clenched. I knew what I had to do after reading about this very thing in my first-aid book. "This is going to seem scary," I warned him, "but it will relieve the pressure." With Sarge's cigarette lighter, I heated a needle to a high temperature and inserted it into the centre of the blood spot. The hot needle melted the nail, the blood spurted out, and the pain was immediately relieved. Allan smiled, which was the biggest reward. It's so much easier to inflict discomfort when you focus on the fact that it will make things better in the end.

It was my last night at camp. There was an outdoor barbeque, but Sarge's cooking had turned me into a temporary vegetarian. (At dinner one evening, not long after the rotten meat fiasco, I had decided to take a chance on beef stew à la Sarge. My fork slid down into a decidedly un-stew-like object. I dug around and pulled out a used Band-Aid.) Eating Sarge's food was *my* "Fear Factor." So, at the barbeque, I played it safe. As I munched on a condiment burger made of ketchup, relish, mustard, pickles, and lettuce piled on a bun, Mike came over to say goodbye and graciously thank me. "Will you be back next summer, Nurse Tilda?"

No chance! I shook my head no.

"It was wild at times," he admitted, "but that's camp. I hope you felt the love. Anyway, the main thing is that everyone had fun. You had *fun*, didn't you, Nurse Tilda?" Mike asked.

I couldn't answer him right then because I was choked up with emotions. It was a mixture of relief, pent-up frustration, and gratitude that it hadn't been any worse – and it could have been so much worse. Fun was not enough for me. I needed safety measures in place, a semblance of order, and . . . well, something else. Overriding all of my emotions was a nagging disappointment. I had come to camp to get outdoors but had spent most of my time indoors. I wanted to understand the appeal of camp, yet I now understood it less. Worst of all, I hadn't connected with a single person there, and despite all the hijinks and hilarity going on around me, I'd been lonely and stressed out the entire time. My kids had had a great time, but I knew we wouldn't be coming back here again.

That night there was a farewell campfire. It was chilly and the kids were wrapped in blankets and huddled close around the fire. I stayed just outside the circle where I could still feel the heat and watch the flames work their magic.

Afterwards I walked back to the infirmary to pack my stuff. We were leaving first thing in the morning. The door to the infirmary was closed and the screen door barricaded shut with a chair on the inside. I knocked on the door and rattled the door knob. Eventually, Gidget and Moon Doggie came out, dishevelled and flushed, their arms draped about each other. I should have known. I'd seen rumpled sheets in there before. I guess I should have been turning down the blanket and leaving condoms on the pillow like chocolate mints!

"She ruined our fun," I heard them say outside my window, "but what a great little love nest while it lasted."

They left me some poetic graffiti on the cabin wall:

We made beautiful music in here.
Gidget played the meat flute and Moon Doggie hummed
*   on her harmonica!*

The next morning, my kids were sad to be leaving. I tempted them with the promise of bubble baths, unlimited television, gourmet meals – some of the things *I'd* been missing. "When we get home, I'm going to give you kids the royal treatment," I told them.

"Mom, *you're* the royal treatment," Max said, his eyes twinkling with mirth.

The three of us were quiet as we drove out of camp. The boys looked out the windows and didn't even ask for the return of their electronic games. As I glanced into the rearview mirror and bid a silent farewell to Camp Na-Gee-La, I noticed that the recent storm had blown away the sign at the gate.

I returned my gaze to the road ahead and we got started on the drive home.

5

THE BUSINESS OF FUN

By the time January rolled around (and a bitterly cold one, at that) the unavoidable bugaboo topic came up among the mothers in the school playground. "What about summer vacation?" we asked each other. "What are you doing with your kids? Have you decided about camp?"

I came up with a radical idea and told them about it. I proposed to spend the summer at home with my kids. We'd go on fabulous excursions around town and drives out to the country. We'd equip ourselves with all the supplies needed to build Popsicle-stick picture frames, lanyards, papier mâché masks, and clay pots. We'd do everything it took to stave off the dreaded "b" word.* I'd call it Camp Mom.

"You'll never pull it off," they said.

My kids were not pleased – to say the least. They loved camp. Play dates with Mom were not going to cut it. Besides, it wasn't *my* companionship they craved. They wanted to be with their own kind, other children – and that's probably the way it should be.

I thought about sending them to camp by themselves like most parents did. It wasn't as if my kids needed, or even wanted, me

---

* There are many bad "b" words, but there's only one I can't bear and have banned from our household, and that is "bored."

there. As camp nurse, I'd have to be on call at night, face the daily mess hall feeding frenzy, and deal with attitude from rude teenagers. The freebie of the barter arrangement wasn't worth it for the work and aggravation it entailed. Still, I had this fantasy of being that iconic camp nurse, hardy, youthful, and adored by all the kids. I wasn't ready to give up my dream.

Spring came quickly and I had to make plans. I perused camp brochures and advertisements. One day I found a camp that looked like it might suit my kids, and me, too.

Camp Carson seemed in every way to be the exact opposite from dangerous, fly-by-night, bare-bones, Camp Na-Gee-La. It was an established, accredited, well-organized camp that offered every conceivable activity and amenity. At first, the name caught my attention. I assumed it was in homage to Rachel Carson, author of *Silent Spring*, a book my father loved and had given me when I was twelve. Back in the 1960s, Carson had been one of the first environmentalists and had raised the alarm about pesticides, acid rain, and the depletion of the ozone layer. I imagined Camp Carson would be a back-to-nature sort of place with homespun values. However, I soon met the camp director, *Bruce* Carson, no relation. *Oh well.*

Still, Camp Carson's glossy brochure was enticing. It was filled with photographs of smiling campers kayaking, canoeing, waterskiing, windsurfing and wakeboarding, doing arts and crafts, and horseback riding. There were also a few features I couldn't have even imagined, such as a ropes course (including a "climbing wall" and a "trust bridge"), an extreme skateboard park, a video production studio, cyber-arts workshop, and state-of-the-art music studio where kids could record their own compositions, even make a demo.

"Camp Carson – a place where friendships are formed and memories are made," was the camp slogan.

How beautiful is that?

"Providing a safe and fun summer experience for your child."
What could be better?

"A place where every child can have a *wow* experience."
Yes, wow, by all means!

In the letter to parents that accompanied the brochure, the directors stated the camp's philosophy: "Each child is unique and special. We will do everything possible to accommodate your child's individual needs. Our mature and nurturing counsellors will keep your child safe and happy. We aim to please!"

I met with Coach Carson, as he liked to be called, and his wife, Wendy, who were the owners and camp directors, for a job interview in their swanky office in downtown Toronto. "Are you ready for a fantastic summer?" Coach Carson asked me. He was a toned and tanned marathon-running man in his mid-fifties who spoke so animatedly, it was as if he were about to break into a camp cheer at any moment. "So far, we have a record-breaking eight hundred campers enrolled, which means we're filled to capacity. We even have a wait list!"

Coach Carson explained that he'd worked in the corporate world for many years, but as a "people person" and a lifelong camper, it was as a camp director that he felt he'd finally found his true calling: the "business of fun."

"*Safe* fun," Wendy interjected.

My ears perked up at this.

"Camp is in my blood," he said. "I'll never grow up. Camp keeps me young." He grinned and shrugged, raising his arms in a helpless what-can-you-do gesture.

My face was beginning to ache from excessive smiling in response, but then his tone dropped down to deep concern. "Kids these days are anxious and stressed." He shook his head sadly. "More than ever, kids need camp to escape pressures at home and at school. Camp is no longer a luxury. It's an absolute necessity."

He invited me to a screening room to view a video he'd pro-
duced, "Welcome to Camp Carson – a Cutting Edge Camp."
While he was setting it up, I studied a map of the camp and surrounding area, displayed on the wall. On the map the camp was
located on Stormy Lake, but in the brochure, it was called Lake
Serenity.

"We changed the name," he explained, "so as not to cause
undue alarm. It's a gorgeous property! Hollywood celebrities have
built stunning cottages right across the lake from us. If you're
lucky you'll catch a glimpse of one or two over the summer."

A secretary placed a plate of Rivi's Guilt Free Cookies along
with bottles of mineral water on his desk. I sank into an over-
stuffed leather couch to watch the video. It opened with a
friendly, rockin' medley of popular tunes in a peppy soundtrack
over a kaleidoscope filmstrip collage of happy children's faces –
flushed, glowing, covered in face paint or theatrical makeup,
smudged with pottery clay, all with huge smiles grinning out at
the camera. Everyone seemed to be having the time of their lives.

"Did that *wow* you? Are these great visuals or what?" he asked
as a perfect sunset stretched across the sky and a silhouette of
kids sitting around a campfire faded out in the final frame.

Next, I sat down with Wendy, who was the coordinator of the
camp's Medical Centre, or MC. She and Bruce met at Camp
Carson many years ago, when it was run by Bruce's father.
Wendy was fit, blonde, and pretty, decked out in stretchy yoga
wear with a pearl necklace. I couldn't imagine her getting down
and dirty at camp and she readily admitted she didn't. "I'm
mostly in the office, but all the kids know me. They call me the
'The Tiger Lady,'" she said with a chuckle. "They say I'm tough,
but they know I love 'em and the parents know their kids are
safe with us."

After a review of my qualifications, Wendy Carson laid down
the law.

"Drugs, cigarettes, and alcohol are strictly prohibited. Any counsellor or staff member under the influence or found using any of these substances on campgrounds will be immediately dismissed." She looked at me to check if I was okay with that, which I was. "As for sex . . ." She paused to let this new subject register. "Sex is forbidden."

For a second, I paused, too. Did that apply to me? I guess it didn't really matter since Ivan wasn't planning any conjugal visits. He was looking forward to yet another carefree break from his wife and kids. I nodded my agreement.

". . . as for PDA – that's what the kids call it, Public Displays of Affection – we have the four-hand rule. They must keep their hands to themselves. For example, if you see them around the campfire and suspect they're getting into mischief, tell them you have to see four hands at all times. Oh, you have to keep an eye on them. After one CIT canoe trip, we found two sleeping bags zipped together!"

Next, we turned to the medical files. "I'm a nurse, too," Wendy said, "but now I head up the office administration, marketing, risk management and disaster planning."

Such as, what, hostage-taking, bomb threats, biological warfare? Any searches for Weapons of Mass Destruction? These guys were certainly thorough!

"We have a doctor on staff and two nurses," Wendy continued. "I don't do any hands-on nursing any more but they all come to me for hugs." She opened her arms wide to show just how welcoming those hugs were. "I know them all by name. I was the camp nurse when their parents were campers."

As I scanned the camper medical files, Wendy explained their policies about medications. "First and foremost, all drugs will be kept locked up at all times, except at meals when you take what you need to the dining hall. Only asthma inhalers and EpiPens may be kept with the camper in a fanny pack.

"Another thing," she continued, "we encourage parents to dis-
close everything about their children's health on the forms, but
occasionally you'll find they leave out key information, perhaps
out of fear their child will be rejected, which, by the way, would
never happen. As you can appreciate, we like to know as much
as possible ahead of time. Now, with your vast nursing experience, I'm quite certain none of their medications will faze you."

Oh no, believe me, I *was* fazed, all right. Many children were
on long lists of medications, as many meds as I'd seen on some
of my very sick hospital patients. There were children on antidepressants, and anti-anxiety drugs, some that they took daily
and others on an as-needed basis. There were kids on a variety
of drugs for attention deficit disorder (ADD), hyperactivity, or
"oppositional behaviour." Some children who were on these
drugs were also on nighttime sedation to counteract the stimu-
lating effects of their daytime meds. (Technically, these drugs
were stimulants, but for children with ADD they had a calming
effect.) In addition, some of these children required liquid nutri-
tional supplements because the ADD drugs decreased their
appetite and they didn't take in sufficient calories. Other
children – and by no means only the youngest ones – had problems with bedwetting and they took a dose of a drug called
desmopressin before bed. It was a synthetic version of a natural
hormone and I was familiar with it from the ICU. There, I'd given
it intravenously to brain-dead organ donors to curb their urine
production prior to transplantation. I hadn't known that as an
antidiuretic it could also be used to treat bedwetting.

In addition to those meds, many children were on allergy pills
and asthma puffers and inhalers. Parents also sent their kids with
bottles of non-prescription drugs, over-the-counter painkillers
and anti-inflammatories, along with vitamin and mineral supplements. Then there was a huge range of natural products I'd only
heard of but had never administered, such as anti-oxidants,

immune-system boosters, and products that contained St. John's wort for "mood disturbances," tryptophan and melatonin to "regulate the sleep cycle," and ginseng and kava-kava for "energy boosts." Given all the medications they were on, I wondered if the kids were sickly, but as I read through their health forms, I noted that they were all robustly healthy. Many were high achievers – athletes, musicians, child actors, and award-winning students.

"I'm not familiar with some of these medications," I admitted, "but I'll read up on them before camp."

Then we went through the special diets, food restrictions, and dietary requests. Some children needed wheat-free, gluten-free, and/or dairy-free meals. Some were strictly or flexibly vegetarian, including one whose mother stated her child didn't eat anything that "had parents"; some just didn't eat red meat, and one camper stated she ate everything except mammals. Some requested kosher food, but others were okay with "kosher-style," which meant no bacon or cheeseburgers. There were kids with life-threatening food allergies to peanuts or tree nuts. Others merely had nut sensitivities. There were allergies to fish or eggs or to common fruits, such as apples or pears, or to more exotic fruits such as kiwi and persimmon. Some children would eat no vegetables at all. Many parents mentioned their children's food dislikes in lists that included beets, broccoli, and sardines – no surprises there – but one mother wrote a lengthy letter stating that her daughter was on a sugar-free diet, with no caffeine or carbonated drinks, and was "highly allergic to chocolate." Her insistent tone made me wonder if she simply didn't want her child to have those treats.

I asked how the kitchen staff coped with so many requests and Wendy explained.

"Trish is the Five-Star General and Johnny, her husband, is her Commander-in-Chief. Our kitchen is run like a military operation. Trish makes the place tick like clockwork. Each task is timed. Kitchen workers know they will be fired if they work too slowly or inefficiently. It has to be this way. Don't forget, we are feeding three meals a day to 800 campers, plus 320 staff members. By the way, kitchen staff are strictly forbidden from socializing with the campers."

That sounded like a strange rule but Wendy's authoritative tone didn't invite discussion.

Coach Carson and Wendy offered me the job on the spot. I figured if I was going to work so hard, I might as well do it in exchange for a camp that offered so many activities and such luxurious facilities. However, just before I signed the contract, Wendy asked me something that did give me pause.

"It's important that our nurses get involved in the life of camp, such as the singsongs and campfires. Our nurses must be *fun-loving*. Would that describe you?"

"What a question!" I said and plastered a big smile on my face.

A fleet of air-conditioned coach buses was lined up in the parking lot of a shopping mall, ready to transport the campers on the three-hour drive to cottage country, the clean, green, Haliburton Highlands of Ontario with its abundance of beautiful lakes, forests, and rocks. The children's duffel bags had been sent ahead earlier so that the counsellors could unpack their clothes and have their beds made up for them by the time they arrived. (I hoped they wouldn't notice I hadn't sent anywhere near the ten pairs of shorts and eight pairs of pants the clothing list dictated. My kids would have to use the camp laundry.)

I was stationed at the Medical Centre van, clipboard in hand, wearing the extra-large T-shirt Coach Carson issued me, with the Carson logo in blue, green, and gold. My job was to receive the campers' meds and ensure they were properly labelled.

Afterward, I would drive the van up to camp on my own. My kids
were going with the other campers, because, as Coach Carson
explained, "camp starts on the bus." They went according to
their groups: Max, age seven, was a Hawthorne in the Wildflower
Unit, and Harry, at nine, was a Polaris in the Constellation Unit.

During the intake of camper meds, I collected a huge pile of
epinephrine syringes – EpiPens for short – in a large plastic
laundry bin. They were the emergency treatment for those children who had allergic reactions so strong that they could go into
anaphylactic shock, a life-threatening situation. These campers
had to bring along extra EpiPens because for every one of them
two pens were kept in the Medical Centre, another in their cabin,
and a few others in strategic positions all around camp; as well,
each camper carried a pen at all times. I couldn't help but reflect
that in this plastic bin there was more standby epinephrine* than
the total amount I'd given in treating all of my hospital patients
during the hundreds of cardiac arrest cases I had participated in
over the years. It was one of the first drugs we reached for when
a patient's heart rate dropped dangerously low and it was used
in almost every cardiac arrest. Well, we'd certainly be prepared
for any cases of anaphylactic shock that might arise, but I
couldn't help but wonder if a few of these EpiPens were sent
"just to be on the safe side." Peanut allergies were certainly on
the rise, but were all of these truly lethal allergies? I had a feeling
there was also a component of parental anxiety – completely
understandable when the issue is a life-threatening condition.

Along with meds, I received other items from parents. One
father handed me a heavy knapsack filled with textbooks. He'd
requested that a counsellor tutor his twelve-year-old, "to give him
a head start on next year's material. I want him to have that edge."

_____

* Synthetic adrenalin, a powerful emergency drug to shock the heart back into a
normal rhythm and create a blood pressure.

A mother gave me an insulated food jar containing a hard-boiled egg rolling around in it. "Please give this to Justin when he arrives at camp," she said. "He needs protein after the long bus ride."

While the campers and parents said their goodbyes, I stood browsing through a growing pile of letters addressed "Attention: Camp Nurse."

Connor stutters and kids pick on him a lot. Has a hard time with letter-writing (no spell-check at camp!) so counsellors, please help. Also, very sensitive to many things, especially loud noise and flashing lights. Please, no strobe lights!

Shawna is afraid of snakes. Please ensure that she has no contact with snakes. <u>NO SNAKES</u>.

Wayne doesn't like to be touched. Please give him a warning if you want to hug him or pat him on the back. Must carry bug spray with him at all times. He worries about West Nile Virus. He tends to be quiet, prefers to sleep in his clothes and will not change them unless forced to by counsellors. Gets a rash if he sits around in wet bathing suit for too long. Can't handle lack of privacy. Does not respond to a sarcastic tone. He doesn't like to swim in cold water (takes a long time to get in), but drinks only cold water.

Melanie is a gifted singer. Please tell the musical director she must have a decent part in the camp play. She was overlooked last year. A HUGE mistake. It's been bad for her self-esteem!

Josh can play soccer, but not as goalie. [Was that offered as a health advisory or a game strategy?]

Shane is not officially gifted but tested VERY *close.*

If Brian can't sleep, give him two Tylenols to settle him down. Has some anger issues. Is working on controlling his temper.

Mandy has a wheat and dairy intolerance and is allergic to peas, tree nuts, and all legumes. May also be allergic to poopy [sic] *seeds? Has never had a reaction but must carry EpiPen with her at all times.*

Some notes were alarming, all the more so because of their cryptic matter-of-factness.

Darren had an isolated episode of hysterical blindness but has experienced a complete cure. Stress-related.

Michael and Jenna's father died a few months ago (suicide) and I'm hoping camp will help them take their mind off of things.

Deanna's father and I have divorced recently. She needs to be with other children of divorced parents to talk things over. Has hay fever and is in a complicated love triangle with her parents. Vomits easily and likes things organized. High anxiety if there is disorder.

Please keep an eye on Samantha. She was recently hospitalized due to weight loss. She's fine now, but FYI.

Megan recently gained fifteen pounds and needs to lose it!
We're praying she'll lose weight at camp. Please make sure
she doesn't lie on her bed reading all summer and weigh
her once a week.

I need to be informed of everything. Notify me if you
intend on giving Chad anything, even a Tylenol.

Reading these notes and seeing the parents say their goodbyes made me realize how hard it must be for parents to give up control and entrust their children to the care of strangers. It brought home how huge my responsibilities would be with the children in the weeks to come and how important it would be for me to be that reassuring voice on the phone to their parents.

Most kids were handling the goodbyes fairly well, even the boy who was jumping up and down just before getting on the bus. He explained, "I'm trying to get rid of everything I learned at school." He pulled at his scalp in an attempt to expel the offending material. The kids were coping, but the parents, not so well. I was just about to pack up my car when a mother in tears ran over and threw herself on me. "Please look after my darling babies!" She grasped my shoulders and pulled me close.

"What are your children's names?" *So I'll know which ones to avoid.*

"My daughter is Alexa Rose and she happens to be the prettiest girl at camp! She's a Scorpio and her brother, Thomas Carl, is an Aries." She handed me a bottle of pills called Ativan, a sedative. "Give Alexa Rose one at night for separation anxiety and T.C. can have one too. Oh, and give them a few drops of Rescue Remedy." She handed me a small brown glass bottle containing a clear liquid. It was a tincture of distilled flowers that contained a touch of grape alcohol. She clutched her children before tearing herself away.

Just before the campers boarded the buses, they all reluctantly handed over their electronic games, cellphones, and portable computers. Turning in their hardware was the signal to say goodbye. Now, all each of them carried was a hefty tool chest (like the one Anderson had toted around at Camp Na-Gee-La but rarely used), as if they were carpenters, going off to a job site. These tool boxes were filled not with nails and screwdrivers but with bulk candy: bags of Nerds, jawbreakers, Sour Warheads, Cherry Blasters, Fuzzy Peaches, SweetTarts, and Skittles. The junk food policy at Camp Carson seemed to be to bring as much as you could possibly cram into the most gargantuan tool box you could find.

Alexa Rose's mother came back to me. "I feel like I'm abandoning them," she said as she dabbed at her tears. "This is so hard on me. I wish I was going, too." She wrung her hands as she gazed at the departing buses. She gave herself a few drops of Rescue Remedy from her own bottle. "It's hard to believe they can survive in that wilderness without me there to protect them." As the buses began to pull out of the parking lot, she ran alongside, waving at her children, now beyond her reach.

Camp Carson was every bit as impressive as the video showed, but what it hadn't conveyed was the exclusive, country club atmosphere. Even with Coach Carson's warm welcome and private tour, I felt uncomfortably like an outsider. I focused on the beautiful surroundings and learning my way around the vast property.

The camp was built on an oval, sparkling lake. All of the facilities were situated on manicured lawns spread out over sprawling grounds. First, Coach Carson took me to the Lodge, where there was a staff lounge with a TV, video games, an indoor pool, and billiard and ping-pong tables. Next, we made a loop out to the camp's periphery to see the campers' cabins. They were

modern wood-and-log structures that had been freshly painted
in forest-green, maroon, or navy-blue to denote the various
units. Inside, the walls, ceiling, and rafters were made of unvar-
nished, light pine wood. There were eight single cots and four
bunk beds, so there was space for sixteen people, usually twelve
campers and four counsellors, two of whom were swim or water-
ski specialists, for example, and only slept in the cabin. Each
cabin had its own showers and bathrooms.

We walked back to the centre of camp where the dining hall
was located. It was a long, grand rectangular room with several
entrances and a balcony that ran right around the outside, offering breathtaking views of Lake Serenity whichever direction you
looked. It was decorated in expensive-looking, but rustic,
cottage-type décor, with a stuffed moose over the stone fireplace
and polished pine floors. All over the walls hung bright plaques
and banners from Colour War battles and victories of days gone
by, all signed by campers, many of whom were probably parents
of children now attending Camp Carson.

Next, Coach Carson took me to meet Trish and Johnny and see
the kitchen. It was as scrupulously clean as any operating room
I'd ever been in, right down to its chilled ambient temperature,
white tiles, and large spotless stainless-steel tables for food preparation. A counter the full length of one wall separated the kitchen
from the dining hall. Kitchen staff handed out platters of food,
pitchers of "bug juice" – the ubiquitous, flavoured sugar water
that was the standard camp beverage – and condiments across the
counter. The kitchen workers seemed to be between sixteen and
eighteen, around the same age as the counsellors. They lived in
trailers at the back of the campgrounds. I wondered how they felt
about working and waiting on their city counterparts whose work
in comparison looked more like playing and partying.

Coach Carson pointed out the office, a modern, well-equipped
log cabin, where he, Wendy, and their staff worked. Just outside

of camp, down the road a short distance, was a cabin where the
Carsons lived, and another for the camp doctor and his wife. To
end our tour, Coach Carson showed me the Playhouse, which
had a surround-sound system and plush seats. With great pride
he told me about his son, Eric, who was the camp's head of
drama and would be directing the camp play.

"See, I knew when you saw the camp, you'd go *wow*! So, what
do you say?"

What could I say but "wow"?

We had lunch, which we inhaled at a pace that I'd come to
know as camp tempo. It was a breakneck gobble of submarines-
tomato-soup-Rice-Krispie-squares. Afterward, Coach Carson
went up to the podium and welcomed both returning and new
campers to Camp Carson, now in its thirty-fourth year. At that
first lunch, I was introduced to Dr. Don Kitchen, whom everyone called "Kitch," and his wife, Marg. Kitch was a general
practitioner who took his summer vacation at camp. He called
it a working holiday. He'd been the camp doctor for years and
knew all the kids. He and Marg had three kids who had grown
up at the camp and were now counsellors. Kitch told me that
every morning after breakfast, he would hold a clinic. After
that, Caitlin, a newly graduated nurse in her early twenties, and
I were to be available to the campers and staff at all times. We
could consult with him over the phone if we had any questions.
He was only a few minutes away and promised to come for
emergencies. After lunch, Kitch got up and gave a stern lecture
to everyone about the dangers of the sun. His words carried a
lot more weight than mine ever had, but probably the scary
mention of premature aging and deadly skin cancers made
them listen up.

The Medical Centre was a centrally located, cozy wood
cabin nestled in a grove of pine trees. There was a large, comfortable waiting room, plus a well-equipped doctor's office,

two examining rooms, and one room with six beds for girls across from another room with six beds for boys. There was also a small isolation room that had one bed in the case of a patient with an infectious disease. At the back were two small bedrooms, one for me and one for Caitlin, who had worked at the camp the year before when she was still a student nurse. After dinner that first night, Caitlin and I got to work setting up and organizing the supplies and medications. I pointed out to Wendy that some of the meds left over from the previous summer were now past their expiry date.

"Pack them up," she said, "and we'll send them off to some Third World country along with any outdated equipment. They're grateful for whatever they can get."

Caitlin lowered her voice. "The Tiger Lady is tough. She runs a tight ship with supplies and stuff and freaks out if something goes missing. She's always worried a parent might sue them for something. But she's such an old-fashioned nurse when it comes to treating the children. It's basically, *suck it up*. Like, a kid's arm could be falling right off and she'll say, 'go, have a drink of water,' or something, and it makes them laugh their heads off and forget about whatever was bothering them."

I laughed, too. *Once a nurse, always a nurse.*

The days started off with pleasant wake-up music. It was usually a selection from a mainstream repertoire, like the Barenaked Ladies, the Steve Miller Band, or the Red Hot Chili Peppers. Breakfast was at 8:00 a.m., during which Caitlin and I were on pill call duty for campers on meds. When we arrived at the dining hall, they would come at us in a mad rush. Caitlin usually stayed on "crowd control" while I gave out pills from a big picnic basket. I had to laugh as I imagined myself skipping in like Little Red Riding Hood with that straw basket over my arm!

Caitlin and I did our best to get to everyone at breakfast, or else we'd have to go hiking all around camp to track down kids who had missed their pills. If a pill accidentally dropped, the kids were quick to remind me of the five-second rule, the interval in which a dropped pill was still okay to take. (Funny, that was never covered in my pharmacology course!) After receiving their meds, the kids returned to their seats and slouched back down on the benches, beside their cabin mates, comfy in their baggy flannel plaid pants, faces hidden deep inside cozy hoodies, their feet in thick, grey woolly socks shoved into Birkenstocks.

The roar in the dining hall at meals was deafening. Conversation was impossible so I worked at reading lips and deciphering the sign language of "Please pass the Cheerios" or "More bug juice?" The food was delicious and plentiful.

After each meal, there were amusing skits and announcements about things like the swim marathon or tryouts for the camp play. Since that first week of camp fell over both July 1, Canada Day, and July 4, Independence Day in the United States, there were moments of patriotism, too. While the majority of campers were Canadian, there were some Americans. (There were few differences between the kids except the Americans referred to the tuck shop as the "canteen" and they liked to imitate the Canadians use of "eh.") On July 1, the camp dutifully sang "O Canada." But a few days later we listened to the much more enthusiastic belting out of "The Star-Spangled Banner" by the handful of Yankee campers and staff, who waved their flag and held their hands over their hearts as they sang. Our much more subdued show of national pride made me wonder if a *lack* of patriotism was one thing Canada *was* known for.

There was a definite hierarchy at this camp and you saw it clearly in the dining hall seating. The camp directors, the doctor, his wife, and their friends sat at a head table, presiding over the crowd, like at a wedding. The unit heads, who were in charge of the various age groupings, had their own tables, and the various heads of specialties such as pottery, art and crafts (A and C), or sail, sat at other tables. Counsellors sat with their campers, which was necessary so they could keep an eye on their kids and also rise up as a group when called upon, to chant in unison their own cabin's cheer. Caitlin and I sat wherever we could squeeze in. I was usually at the overflow table of swim staff, and she would angle for a spot at the trippers' table.

After an embarrassing gaffe when I mistook a camper for a counsellor and another when I mistook a counsellor for a camper, I made a concerted effort to get to know the names of the counsellors and where they sat. Soon, I also knew where each specialty was located. At the table of dance and drama instructors – known as "Divas and Drama Queens" – there were entertaining scenes featuring hysterical laughter or uncontrollable weeping over various comedies or tragedies, inevitably ending with someone getting up and stomping away. They would cry at a moment's notice and burst into song at another. They were super careful about what they ate and never took seconds. It was known that anyone scrounging for extra desserts could help themselves freely at that table.

The long table near the outside wall, right beside the balcony overlooking Lake Serenity, was where the group of trippers, most of them male, seated themselves. They would be taking the children out on hikes and four- or five-day canoe trips in the wilderness of Algonquin Park. With their scruffy beards and wearing do-rags, tight muscle shirts, and hiking boots that seemed suited to scaling Mount Kilimanjaro, they got up frequently during meals to swagger about like conquering Vikings, stretch their legs, strut along the balcony and hork spitballs over the edge onto the lawn. They were buff and stunning specimens of young male beauty. Ah, the macho glory of the trippers! They had big reputations to maintain and glorious traditions to uphold. In the camp pantheon, the trippers were at the pinnacle. But their reputations, both on and off duty, were well-earned, or so they claimed.

"We work hard, but when we're off, we're off," Jordan, the head tripper, told me.

"They're pretty hard-core party animals," Caitlin said when she saw me gazing at them. "Enjoy the eye candy while it lasts," Caitlin advised. "They are only at camp in between trips. That's when they get to lounge around and take up a lot of space being beautiful – which they do so very well, don't they?"

"Not too hard on the eyes," I said, trying not to let my admiration of the trippers' good looks be too obvious.

After lunch on the first full day of camp, Caitlin and I went from cabin to cabin, checking each camper for lice. It was the standard, first-day practice, Caitlin said. We worked steadily all afternoon and managed to get to all eight hundred heads, thanks to assistance from a fastidious counsellor from the Constellation cabin who was known as a champion nit-picker. "My whole family had lice. I know what to look for. They call me Miami, as in Miami Lice." But as it turned out, I was the one who discovered the only cases – two sisters – and felt oddly triumphant at this weird accomplishment. Camp policy dictated that they would have to be sent home and allowed back only after being treated and deemed "clear." Treating them at camp would be too time-consuming and tedious (after a few minutes of that work you have a new understanding of the phrase "nit-picking") and the risk of spread to other campers was great. Kitch explained the sensitive matter to the crushed parents on the phone.

That day, the whole camp was abuzz with excitement and jitters about the swim test that everyone had to undergo before being allowed to participate in any water sports. I had been surprised when I learned that Camp Carson had an indoor pool, situated as it was on such a beautiful, calm lake, but Coach Carson explained that it was for rainy days and those kids who couldn't get used to the weeds, the rocks, and the cool water. The Carsons had, it seemed, anticipated every possible risk of a risk and prepared for it.

For safety's sake, the Carsons also had many rules that were exactingly enforced. First, all campers had to undergo swim testing. Each child had to jump into the lake fully dressed, crawl into a canoe, tip it, swim a few lengths, and then tread water while a member of the swim staff observed and made notes about his or her swimming form. It seemed like everyone at camp, even the strong and confident swimmers and those who took private swimming lessons all year round, was nervous and on edge until they received the coveted green bracelet signifying they could participate in all waterfront activities. (They even made me take the swim test. I passed – phew!) The embarrassing yellow bracelet meant the swimmer had a conditional pass, and the red bracelets "were for losers," as one kid told me. The head of the swim staff explained to me that the red bracelet was to alert them to the kids who needed closer supervision around and in the water. That made perfect sense and it was quite a change from the non-competitive "everyone's a winner" attitude at Camp Na-Gee-La. Yet, recognition only for the star performers didn't seem right, either. How to strike a balance?

The next day was still slow in the MC so I went down to the waterfront to watch the proceedings. I've always loved being near the water but, truth be told, I was also hoping to sneak a peek at my own kids to see how they were doing on the swim test. Max had already passed it and was playing with his friends on the beach. Harry was in the midst of it. The lake was warm and now, at the age of nine, he knew that its warm currents came from the sun, not an underwater heating system.

When the swim instructors saw me near my kids, they shooed me away, so I went over to watch other kids. Most were jumping in gleefully. The few who weren't used to swimming in cold lakes were slower to jump in, but soon they too were happily splashing about. My attention was quickly drawn to Wayne, a boy I recognized from Max's cabin.

"First, I have to get psyched," I heard him saying to his swim instructor, nicknamed Cargo (her name was Carla Gordon), who was coaxing him into the water. Wayne had a high-pitched, squeaky voice. He wore glasses and had hair that was stiff and straight-up, as if he was perpetually shocked. His skinny chest showed his ribs with each breath.

"Now, Wayne, we're not going to go through this again this summer, are we? Your mom said you had lots of swimming lessons," Cargo told him. "Go for it! Jump in." Her clipboard at her waist, she was poised to tick off his swimming skills as soon as he demonstrated them to her. He was just about to jump in, then hesitated.

"Are there sharks?" His voice was higher and squeakier. "What about leeches?"

"Wayne! I'm waiting . . ." She took his glasses from him. "You're going in!"

Again, he made moves as if he would take the plunge, then stopped himself. "I know how to swim," he said, "just not in the deep end." He squinted out at the lake. "Which is the deep end?"

"You're stalling, Wayne!" Cargo said, her clipboard at the ready.

He stared down into the water. "It's dark in there." He looked out across the lake under a flattened hand at his brow. "Is this lake polluted? Last year, something slimy swam between my legs. Are there fish in this lake?"

"Probably, but they're harmless," Cargo answered. She tapped her foot.

"Are they endangered fish?"

"Wayne, I can't wait any longer. Just jump in. Let's see what you can do."

He stood there, thinking. "What about goldfish? Are goldfish endangered?"

"Come on!" She was getting exasperated. "The water's warm today!"

An older boy yelled out, "Hey, Waynester, watch out for the snapping turtles! They'll bite off your toes!"

"Turtles?" he gulped.

"Do a cannonball! Go for it!" someone else called out.

"Wayne, we've wasted so much time! Swim period is over!" Cargo shouted. She blew the whistle, signalling the campers to get out of the water. Wayne's ordeal was over, at least for now.

"You made it past them today," I said to him sympathetically as I wrapped his sun-warmed towel around his dry, shivering body, "but how are you going to get out of it tomorrow?" He gave a weak grin and ambled off to find his cabin.

"Who's that?" I asked Cargo, pointing to a teenaged girl sitting under a tree in the shade in her clothes, jeans and a long-sleeved shirt on this hot day.

"That's Samantha. She's weird this summer. She was here last year. She's actually a decent swimmer, but she says she's got her period."

I returned to the beach the next day after morning clinic, to see how these situations were going to pan out. I must have looked concerned because the head of the swim staff came over to talk to me again.

"It's all about safety," he said. "Kids have to learn how to swim. They have to get into the water. It has to be this way."

"It seems harsh with kids who are afraid. Kids have been coming to me, begging for swim excuse notes."

"We can't mess around. Everyone has to swim and we need to know who's safe in the water and who's not."

Fair enough, I agreed, but did they have to use such commando tactics?

Again, today, Samantha was under the tree, huddled there, clutching her knees, looking out at the lake. It was another hot, sunny day and she still wore heavy clothes. Her long sleeves were pulled down over her hands, almost to her fingertips, as if she was cold. From her sad, resolute expression, swimming seemed like the last thing she was prepared to do. I wondered how this strong-arm approach was going to work on her.

By the third day, Wayne still hadn't gotten into the water.

"You're going to rock that swim test today, buddy," Cargo said with a playful punch on his shoulder.

That day he was wearing his prescription goggles, so maybe his improved eyesight would give him the confidence he needed. He wrapped his arms around himself, then made a few diving poses as if he might really go through with it.

"Okay, Wayne," Cargo said briskly. "I talked to your mom and she says you *have* to go in. She says she spent lots of money on your swim lessons and she knows you can do it. We can't fool around with this any more. You're going in, buddy."

"No, no, no!" he shouted, digging his toes in between the cracks of the wooden boards of the dock as she pulled at him and he pushed back at her. *Splash!* Wayne was in the water, within Cargo's tight grip. She tried to get him to ride on her back like a dolphin but he remained absolutely rigid and terrified.

Mission accomplished, but whose mission and what accomplishment? It made me especially grateful that Max and Harry weren't afraid of the water. I hadn't talked with them much, but from what I could tell, they were enjoying camp. Harry tended to avoid me and slunk away, the hood on his sweatshirt suddenly up, when he saw me coming. He never liked to be singled out for attention. At first, Max bounced over every morning for a hug or to share his opinion of the meal, but his counsellors quickly came to retrieve him. They told me that seeing Max with his mother made the other kids miss theirs. I saw their point, but I also think they were having a hard time with Max and his tendency to wander off, so were trying to keep him close.

Evening pill call at the MC was much more relaxed than the mad rush at breakfast and lunch, because it was the end of a long and busy day and there were fewer pills. Mostly it was the time when the kids came for their evening sedation or antidepressants. A few teenaged girls shyly and discreetly came to receive their birth control pills (for medical reasons other than birth control, they made a point of telling me). Just before bedtime, campers came for their pills to prevent bedwetting. (The pills mostly worked, but not always, so the counsellors were expected to check the beds each morning and change the sheets if necessary while the kids were at breakfast, so as to avoid embarrassment.) I had to admire the sheer aplomb of the ten-year-old boy who told me, "Sure I wet the bed. Is there something wrong with that?"

Evening also seemed to be the time that homesickness came out. Wendy made rounds to all of the younger cabins, tucking the kids in and reading them stories. Surprisingly, it wasn't the youngest kids at camp who were the most homesick, it was the eleven- and twelve-year-olds, and frequently the teenagers. Most just needed a hug or a distraction to get them through a difficult moment, but a few kids had a bad case of it.

"Whatever you do, don't let them call home," Kitch had instructed me. "It always makes things worse."

Alexa Rose, the girl I'd met in the parking lot along with her mother, had been coming to us every bedtime in her pyjamas and furry Ugg boots, each evening more miserable than the last. She was an eleven-year-old Wildflower, a Lupin (not to mention Scorpio). Every evening I gave her a few drops of Rescue Remedy that promised on the label "to comfort and reassure" and sat with her while she sobbed.

"Can I call home?" she asked.

"It's not a good idea."

"My mother said I could call if I wanted."

"It's a camp policy. We don't let campers call home."

Phone calls home were rarely allowed and only with Coach Carson's agreement.

"But that's for everyone else. My mother said I could call home if I wanted to and if I got really homesick, she said she'd come get me."

"Does your brother know how unhappy you are?"

"He doesn't know I exist. I haven't even seen him." She tugged at her furry boots. "He's having an amazing time, so he doesn't understand me."

"Aren't you hot in those boots?" I asked, trying to distract her.

She stared back at me like I was an idiot: to her, they were the exact right temperature: cool. I looked at her forlorn face and knew exactly how she felt. For a moment, I was taken back to when I was her age and felt homesick, right in my own home. My mother was sick and depressed and my father preoccupied with her care. I was always angling to be a guest in other peoples' homes. I softened my approach. "This is only the third day of camp. Maybe give it a few more days?" I wheedled.

"Can't I just call them? If I just speak to them, I'll feel better."

"No, but you could write to your parents and tell them how you feel," I suggested.

"I feel terrible!"

"Then mention the things you *do* like about camp."

"But I don't like anything!"

"I'm sure you could think of something you like," I said, knowing I was not following Kitch's advice, which was to redirect children who were homesick rather than talk with them about it. My strategy was to try to get her to focus on the positives. It wasn't working. In between sobs, she managed to tell me all the things that were troubling her. "I'm the new girl and I don't know anyone except this one girl I know from school. We used to be BFFs, but we're so not any more. Now, I don't have a best friend at camp and everyone else does, except me. Anyway, she's jealous of me because of my stuff. She touches everything. She used my shampoo and said it was by mistake, but I mean, my nanny labelled everything, so she had to have seen my name. She knew it wasn't hers."

Perusing Alexa Rose's chart, I noted that she disliked dogs and that got me thinking. I could understand being afraid of lightning storms, or even monsters under the bed, but dogs? If forcing children to swim was a way to get over fear of the water, could playing with a friendly dog give her the courage to conquer that fear? Perhaps a dog could even help Alexa Rose with her homesickness? I had seen first-hand the comfort animals could bring. I knew a wheaten terrier who took his work as a therapy pet seriously. He helped people cope with the grief of losing a loved one. I had been impressed by the therapeutic influence of Merlin, a miniature collie who paid regular visits to residents of a nursing home. And I would never forget a dying woman in our ICU and her nurse who granted her patient's last wish to see her horse. She had wheeled her patient down to the back of the hospital, IV poles on one side of the stretcher, oxygen tank on the other. The horse was led down the ramp of the unloading docks straight to where the patient lay. He looked at her, whinnied, and stamped his hoof, as if in recognition. I don't think the patient had the energy to cry, but those of us gathered there to witness the moment did.

I looked at Alexa Rose's miserable face. "What about a dog to cuddle?"

"I hate dogs," Alexa Rose said. "They have rabies."

She didn't like any animals, she said, not even ones in the zoo. I wondered how she was going to cope at the camp's Eco

Zone with its rabbits and guinea pigs, as well as the Carsons' poodle, Skippy. "Maybe a dog could help you with your homesickness? What if I bring Skippy on a leash? You can see how gentle she is."

"No way! That's so not happening." She folded her arms across her chest and looked away. She seemed ready to return with her counsellor who'd been waiting patiently. At least I'd managed to distract her. It's hard enough to overcome a fear you want to overcome, much less one that you don't.

Early each morning, Caitlin got up, did yoga stretches, and at seven o'clock knocked on my door. "Wakey, wakey, girlfriend. Let's go!" she'd say and would drag me out of bed for a brisk morning walk on a trail through the woods. Right before setting out, she'd apply a layer of fruity lip gloss. "I'm addicted to this stuff," she'd say, slipping the tube into her vest pocket for another fix along the way. Then, she clipped the walkie-talkie we shared to the back of her jogging pants and off we went. With her ponytail pulled through her baseball cap, swinging back and forth with the pumping of her muscular legs, Caitlin set a brisk pace and I did my best to keep up.

She had grown up in a small Ontario farming town and was used to the beauty of nature, so it didn't dazzle her as it did me. She was impatient when I'd stop to ooh and aah over various sights. One morning, a deer stepped out of the forest on the side of the road and paused in front of us. I paused, too, but Caitlin bypassed it without a break in her stride. "Keep up the pace," she called back over her shoulder.

Feeling so alive and healthy on those walks, I experienced walking for the sake of being outdoors, breathing the fresh morning air, and moving vigorously. In the woods, I allowed myself to take in the sights around me, especially the exotic (to me) patches of brilliant yellow, purple, and white flowers. (Caitlin pointed out that they were weeds – buttercup, loosestrife, and Queen Anne's Lace – but I still thought they were pretty.)

Caitlin was interested in hearing about my work in the ICU but was taken aback when I told her how long I'd been at the same job.

"Twenty years?" She looked at me with pity. "Isn't it time to move on? Haven't you had enough of the bedside?"

No, I explained, I loved taking care of patients, found my work challenging and fascinating, and felt that I still had a lot more to learn. She said she might be interested in critical care one day, once she got more experience under her belt, but it sounded stressful and depressing. "And what's with the twelve-hour night shifts and working weekends?" she asked, shaking her head. "I don't think so, I want to have a life."

But she must have been intrigued by my stories of the ICU because she kept asking me for more. For the first time, I found it strange to talk about that work I loved so much with all of the pain, suffering, and sadness it entailed, out there in that beauti-ful, natural setting and with the new lightheartedness I was feeling. Should I tell her about the patient I'd cared for on my last shift, a young man who had cystic fibrosis and was awaiting a lung transplant? He struggled with every breath and his family stayed at his side all day and night, waiting for news that would save his life. I had to leave at the end of my shift without ever finding out whether he'd received a new pair of lungs or not. Caitlin shuddered and seemed upset when I told her about such sad things and so I veered onto lighter topics. My two nursing worlds never felt so far apart.

That first week went smoothly. As far as I could tell – from a distance – my kids were content. I was enjoying myself too, finding lots of time to get out and participate in activities around camp. I'd spoken on the phone with Ivan a few times and although he didn't say it, I had the distinct feeling he was missing me, which wasn't such a bad thing.

Toward the end of the first week, after lunch, Coach Carson announced it was letter-writing day. "Tell your parents about the fun you're having, your new friends, and how delicious the grilled cheese sandwiches are," he prompted them.

At first they balked, then he told them that a letter home was their meal ticket for dinner. They found letter writing and the idea of snail mail amusing.

"Wow! Stamps!" many exclaimed. "Cool."

"Letters take, like, forever," one kid grumbled, "three or four days or something. My news will be old by the time they get it."

"It's weird not to be able to text my parents," one kid told me, "but I don't miss messaging my friends 'cause I'm here with them 24/7."

Understandably, they were used to instant contact whenever the whim hit. Did they even know how to write by hand? Would they pepper their letters with electronic language like LOL for "laugh out loud," or "Camp is kewl! Camp is GR8!"*

Coach Carson told me that the lack of Internet access was problematic for parents who wanted contact with their kids. He was looking into setting it up at camp for the following summer, but in the meantime, all they had was old-fashioned pen and paper. I was curious to see how the kids would manage.

That night, at dinnertime, Coach Carson looked worried.

"Whaddup?" I asked, trying out the new lingo I was learning.

"The kids' letters have gone home."

"And your point is?"

"Brace yourself."

---

* I'd like to remind younger readers that my generation had its share of codes too. There was 2ysur, 2ysub, I CUR 2Ys4ME and SWAK for "Sealed With a Kiss" and DDDD for "Deliver De-letter De-Sooner De-Better," so don't feel sorry for us!

"For what?"

"You'll see," he said grimly.

A few days later, I understood the reason for Coach Carson's ominous tone. The campers' letters had finally made their way home. Overnight the camp telephone answering machine and e-mail box filled up with calls and urgent messages from parents.

6

ARTS AND CRAFTS NURSE

A boy ran up to me. "Hey, Nurse! Did ya hear? All the toilets have been stolen!"

"Is that so?"

"Yeah, the police are investigating but they have nothing to *go on*. Get it?"

"Very funny."

"Hey, Nurse," he said, now looking serious. "Did you know your wenis is showing?"

"My what?"

"Your *wenis!*"

How hilarious. This joke – which I didn't get – was on me.

"You got punk'd, girlfriend!" squealed Caitlin when I told her. Kitch had heard that one before. "Wenis is the medical term for the flabby skin on the elbow," he said. In the MC waiting room I stood in front of the mirror, fingering my wenis. Flabby, was it? I felt young at heart but they didn't see my heart, only my age. Mature, maternal Nurse Mom next to young, youthful Nurse Caitlin was not a pretty picture. What I needed was not street, but camp, cred. So, I told Caitlin it was time to kick up our morning hike a few notches. I was ready to shift into high gear! I joined an afternoon hip hop class and in no time, was poppin', lockin', and slidin' along with the rest of them. "Work it, girl!"

The dance instructor offered encouragement as I did my best to ignore the few "what's she doing here?" looks. *I'll show them who's cool!*

By the end of the first week of camp I knew most of the campers by name and the meds they were on. A few kids stumped me, such as the identical twin brothers, Michael and Martin, each on different meds. They got annoyed when I kept asking who was who until one day I noticed that one of them, Michael, had a mole. Some kids stood grinning at me, making me guess their names. Others gave me fake names or only their first names. I guess I could have always just shouted out Michael ChristopherMatthewJoshuaNicholasAndrewDanielBradley or AshleyJessicaSarahBrittanyEmilySamanthaAmandaStephanie Nicole and *someone* would have come forward for something! The other problem was they often dragged their heels, coming late for their meds, or not showing up at all. Then I had to go after them.

"Here comes da nurse, here comes da nurse!" a CIT called out when he saw me approach with my pill basket. "Run, kids! Hide from the nurse!"

I managed to nab one camper, then I trapped another fugitive at the tennis court.

"They're just vitamins," she told me scornfully. "I don't really need them."

"Yes, but your parents want you to have them."

I hunted down one boy in his cabin who had a pretty good comeback. "Sorry!" He slapped his forehead. "I was stuck in traffic all morning."

"Here comes my connection," I heard one kid tell his friend. "She's my drug dealer. The pill pusher."

"You're not making it easy for me," I scolded another kid.

"That's why they pay you the big bucks," he quipped. "Ka-ching! Ka-ching!"

Because of these delays, the after-breakfast clinic got pushed back later and later. Kitch was understanding because he knew how many meds we had to give out. He'd calculated that roughly a third of the entire camp was on meds of one kind or another. "That's fairly typical, these days," he told me on an especially busy morning.

"It's always such a mad rush," I complained. "Are all these pills necessary?"

"Many of the kids with ADD wouldn't be able to come to camp at all without them." He disagreed with parents who put their kids on a "drug holiday" because in his experience, kids were happier staying on their meds. "Camp is a busy, structured place and they cope better if they can follow directions, wait their turn, and organize their belongings, things they can't do if they're not on their meds. Their behaviour is better and they get along with their cabin mates and therefore enjoy themselves more."

It was time to get to work. While Kitch sat in his office perusing medical journals, Caitlin and I went out to the crowded waiting room to assess the kids' problems and decide in what order they would be seen. At camp, triage wasn't strictly a matter of the severity of their medical problems. There were other factors to consider. The loudness of the whining, persuasiveness of pleading, and forcefulness of pestering didn't get anywhere with *me* – nor their "pedigree" of influential or wealthy parents – but it did influence Kitch and Caitlin, who tended to treat the high-maintenance or high-profile ones first. In my own triage system, when all medical issues were equal, campers came before counsellors and politeness was the only effective grease. I complimented one boy on his exceptionally good manners.

"Don't think I behave this well at home," he cautioned me.

For some children, it was a badge of honour how many times they frequented the MC, and for others it was more of an achievement to avoid coming altogether. I often wondered what prompted one child to rush for attention and treatment for a single mosquito bite and another to tough it out, even when covered in bug bites. Usually, I had little time to ponder such questions. Sometimes, when the waiting room was full, I asked them to write down the reason they came. It kept them momentarily occupied, but their notes weren't usually all that helpful:

Can something be done about my freckles?

Feeling crappy!

Ate evil hamburger last night. Might have Mad Cow Disease.

Eye?

Bug bite. Check it out – there's a planet on my neck!

Knee falling off [accompanied by sketch of knee, labelled with "ouch" and arrow].

In and out of consciousness.

Kitch saw each child who visited the Medical Centre, even the ones with splinters and mosquito bites that I could treat myself. At first, I assumed it was his thoroughness, or to catch something I may have missed, but Wendy explained the real reason.

"Our parents feel better knowing that a doctor has seen their child. It's what they expect. Besides, the doctor can bill for his services. He doesn't get paid if the nurse treats the child." Wendy went on to explain another situation where health care and commerce converged. "As for the American campers, it's problematic since he can't bill for his services but is still exposed legally. He takes care of them out of the goodness of his heart."

It was a pleasure working with Kitch and I had a lot to learn from him. Also, it was a relief to have him be the "enforcer." When a twelve-year-old boy needed stitches for a cut on his head, Kitch forbade him to swim until they were removed. The boy sulked, argued, and went swimming anyway. When the cut got mildly infected, Kitch stepped up to be the bad guy who scolded him. But Kitch also had the advantage of knowing the kids better than I did from having been at the camp for so many years. He could see through fabricated excuses to get out of going on a tough canoe trip. He uncovered a case of self-sabotage, when a child damaged his own braces to nab a few days home to visit the orthodontist! He was exceptionally good at identifying faked (whether consciously or not) ailments. One morning, a group of girls, all from the same cabin, showed up together with identical headaches and stomach aches. He checked their schedule and discovered they were supposed to be doing the climbing wall. He knew they didn't like that activity so he prescribed pottery class for them instead. When the dance or drama instructors came in with various injuries or muscle strains – or simply a case of rattled nerves – they often requested painkillers or something to help them relax. Kitch managed to calm them down just by sitting with them and giving them attention. He spent a lot of time talking and, perhaps more importantly, listening, to them. One day he went out to the crowded waiting room and brought in one little girl right away. "This is an MID," he told me. "A muffin in distress. All she needs is a hug."

I envied his mastery of the art and the craft – not just the science – of healing children. "So much of what I do is explaining, reassuring, and consoling," he said with a shrug, as if it were nothing.

These skills were a big part of my nursing practice, too. In the hospital I always made note of when I offered my patient "comfort measures." At camp, I recorded my intervention as

"TLC." How well I've learned that Tender Loving Care can be just as effective as a medication.

I learned a lot about sore throats from Kitch after we started to see a run on them for a few days. "More than ninety percent of sore throats are viral and therefore do not require an antibiotic. It's unlikely to be strep throat if the patient has a runny nose, stuffy ears, cough, but you can't rule it out altogether. Strep throat is worrisome because of dire complications that can develop if left untreated, such as throat abscesses, kidney inflammation, or the main one, rheumatic fever. Prudent medicine would dictate that a swab be sent for each and every sore throat, but it's not always feasible to do so." He then told me about one summer when a mysterious sore throat went around camp. The mystery was that out of one hundred and seventy-five swabs that were sent to the lab, only one came back positive and that child wasn't even symptomatic. He then had to start an antibiotic on a child who felt perfectly well.

"The question to always ask is: Is it viral, bacterial, or allergic? The answer will guide your approach," he said.

As for earaches, they always need to be examined, he explained, but few patients needed antibiotics, only painkillers to ease the discomfort, then follow-up. Most resolve by themselves. Under Kitch's tutelage, I improved my examination of the tympanic membrane inside the ear canal. We examined each child and compared notes.

"Hey, you get to see a part of me that I'll never see," one kid said, as I peered into his ear. "My eyes, too. I'll never see my own eyes, except in a mirror."

"You're right," I said. "I hadn't thought of it that way before."

There were lots of skin ailments I'd never encountered. Kitch taught me how to diagnose eczema, athlete's foot (an infection not always found on the foot), heat rash, and others, such as ringworm (which is not a worm, but a fungus). And I no longer worried that every red and swollen mosquito bite would turn into infective cellulitis or the dastardly flesh-eating disease. Nonetheless, I did a careful examination, demarcated the reddened area with a marker so I could track its progress, took baseline vital signs, gave an antihistamine, and followed up the next day.

One time I discovered a galloping skin infection by accident. I happened to bend down to pick up a dropped pill (within the allowable five seconds, of course!) and noticed a big, red, wet sore on the back of the leg of a boy named Wesley.

"Oh, that," he said. "It's nothing."

But on closer inspection, I found another sore, and then, further up his leg, a few more. His other leg was also covered in these sores.

"They're mosquito bites," he said. "They don't bother me."

"They bother *me*!" I started him on antibiotic ointment, but even so, they quickly spread onto his arms and chest. Within a few days, an entire cabin of eleven-year-old boys all had unsightly, open sores all over their bodies. Kitch took a quick glance at one of them, scanned the others, said one word – impetigo – and started them all on a ten-day course of antibiotics. "Skin infections like these are unavoidable in close quarters. We have to eradicate it – preferably before Visitor's Day," he said with a wink.

Kitch taught me a lot of practical skills. One evening after dinner, a bench fell on a young camper's foot. *Ouch!* It was bleeding under the nail and swelling up fast. "It's a subungual hematoma," Kitch said. I prepared a sterile field and assisted Kitch to perform an incision in the nail to release the blood under the nail. I didn't dare tell him about the makeshift procedure I had performed at Camp Na-Gee-La using a needle heated up by a cigarette lighter, with a first-aid book at my side.

Another skill I learned from Kitch was removing ticks. These pesky little insects got entrenched on the skin and held on fast. Together we removed a bunch of them from a young boy's legs.

"You want to make the tick squirm but not squeeze it, 'cause you'll leave the pincers embedded in the skin. Gently coax the tick to let go." He explained the importance of getting it in its entirety so as to avoid the patient contracting Lyme disease or Rocky Mountain Spotted Fever, rare infections, to be sure, but possibilities all the same.

Splinters had to be extricated with even more delicacy. A Ph.D. thesis could be written on the topic of splinter extraction! What a world of difference there was in each child's reaction to those irritating, teeny tiny logs of wood embedded in their tender skin. Some kids ignored them while others picked at them quite savagely. Another group of kids, admittedly a *splinter* group, cried so much and became hysterical at even the prospect of removing them that Kitch would apply a topical anaesthetic cream, scrub in, and perform mini-surgery while I comforted the sobbing children. Personally, I found removing splinters a very satisfying experience. I was deft with the needle and I loved seeing the pride children felt after overcoming their fear. When a child asked, "Will it hurt?" I told the truth: "Yes, it will, but I know you can handle the pain," or "Yes, but I'll help you get through it."

Headaches were very common. Kitch believed they were often stress-related and usually ran in the family. "You do a little digging and it turns out the parents have headaches too and everyone in the family is stressed out. They've all been to specialists and have had specialized scans and tests, but there are no findings. The parents are disappointed in the lack of diagnosis, but not every feeling of being unwell can be diagnosed, especially in children," he said. "Sometimes children experience a collection of vague, transient symptoms for which no particular illness can be identified. Often, they resolve with time, through no intervention whatsoever."

Stomach aches were another common problem. Often it was the same child, over and over again, complaining of them. "Most stomach aches turn out to be nothing," Kitch said, "but you always have to be vigilant for the signs of something serious like appendicitis. Ask the kid to jump. If the kid can't jump, you know for sure the pain is severe. Another thing to remember is that the farther the pain from the belly button, the more likely it's something serious like a bowel obstruction. Always keep in mind that pain that wakes a kid up during the night almost always has a cause."

He summed it all up with an insight that captured so much about medicine and nursing, too: "You have to know what you are looking for. You only see what you know to look for." That struck me as true about many things in life.

One day, Kitch called me out on my cover-up job. He noticed that I often waved off kids who stopped by for Band-Aids for minor scrapes or cuts. I usually sent them packing without their trophy.

"Studies have come out recently proving that covering a wound helps promote healing and prevents scarring," he said.

Oh, well, evidence-based practice must prevail! I had a new respect for Band-Aids after that.

Kitch also cited scientific evidence that helped me understand another medical issue I'd been wondering about. I had asked him about the excessive number of EpiPens that had accompanied so many children to camp. "There has been an alarming increase in peanut allergies among North American children over the past few years, but I agree with you that there's probably a percentage of EpiPens that are sent purely out of parental anxiety and doctors' fear of liability. Normally, it wouldn't be a problem, but overreaction is causing a lot of anxiety in children who worry unnecessarily about dying from anaphylactic shock. Problem is, if the parents don't know for sure, they err on the side of caution and send up the drug." He shrugged his shoulders. "Who can blame them?"

Kitch was always ready to share with me his vast knowledge and grasp of the most up-to-date scientific findings, tempered by his years of hands-on, real-life work with children. He was particularly skilled when it came to treating their bones, limbs, and joints.

"I'm quite certain the locals aren't running off for x-rays as frequently as our city kids," Kitch said with a chuckle. "Our kids simply aren't used to walking outdoors. They walk in shopping malls and on paved sidewalks. They're not nimble-footed around rocks and their eyes aren't attuned to twigs or roots sticking up out of the ground."

Again, it's about seeing what you know, I thought.

"Either they don't have as many injuries as we do, or they do but suck it up and allow nature, rest, and time to heal their injuries, as they usually do, anyway. Personally, I prefer to avoid unnecessary x-rays; I'd rather take a 'wait and see' approach. But at this camp, I'll send a stubbed toe for an x-ray, otherwise parents have been known to come up here and take the kid to the hospital themselves. At times, I practise defensive medicine. I may order things that aren't necessary because I know the parents will demand it."

I wondered what the local hospital staff thought about our sending campers for x-rays for every fall, twist, or turn of a joint or limb. I found out later when I'd gone to that small (only thirty beds) but busy hospital and heard one of the nurses grumbling. "You're giving us lots of work," she said, and muttered under her breath, "Bunch of clumsy oafs and hypochondriacs at that fancy camp."

Limb injuries could be complicated. Kitch brought me in on interesting cases.

"Watch this," he said when a boy came in after an injury on the soccer field. His arm hung at his side at an odd angle. Before the child even knew what was happening, Kitch deftly popped the dislocated shoulder back into place. The boy looked shocked, then pleased to have his arm back where it belonged.

"Show us your wrist," he told a ten-year-old boy who was brought in after an accident on the baseball field.

The child winced as he placed his right hand on the table. I examined his hand gently but thoroughly, poking and prodding it and putting it through its complete range of motions. The boy held himself rigidly, his face twisted in pain. I looked carefully at his hand and arm, palpated them all over, but could find nothing abnormal.

Kitch whispered a clue. "Always examine both sides."

The boy had kept his left wrist on his lap, hidden under the table. When I took it out to examine it, he yelped in pain. He had been too scared to show me the arm that was causing him pain. However, with one look anyone could see it was fractured. It was folded back on itself with the bone poking up through the skin.

Kitch asked the boy to tell us exactly what happened. He had told me how important it was to always get a detailed account of the "mechanism of injury" – meaning, what happened. That account would always provide clues to the diagnosis. The boy said he'd landed on the palm of his hand when he fell, running for a catch in the outfield.

"Just as I thought," said Kitch. "It's a FOOSH – a Fall On Out-Stretched Hand." He pointed out the bend in the wrist. "That's a 'silver fork deformity.'" He reminded me to check the radial pulse and showed me how to make a splint that effectively immobilized the limb, snug enough to provide support, but with enough give to allow the inevitable inflammation that would soon follow and not to restrict circulation. Together we tied a sling that would comfortably bear the weight of his arm.

"But did you make the catch?" Kitch asked the boy.

"Yup," he said proudly.

"Way to go," Kitch said and high-fived him on his uninjured hand.

What a wake-up call for me! I'm quite sure I would have *eventually* discovered the obvious problem, but the incident showed me how easily one's thinking can be restricted to what the patient chooses to present. It was a reminder to stay open-minded, not limit my thinking, and be a detective, especially when examining children.

Kitch taught me how to "buddy-tape" sprained fingers together, how to make finger splints out of tongue depressors, and the differences between a sprain, a partially torn ligament, from a strain, which was a stretched ligament. "In both cases, it's the same treatment: RICE – Rest, Ice, Compression, and Elevation. After that, let pain be your guide. Pain will tell you what the child can and cannot do. The only thing is, at camp, it may be difficult to distinguish between pain and homesickness. Sometimes homesickness expresses itself as pain. We've seen them limp, moan, and groan their way in here, and after a little attention, they hop, skip, and jump out of here. For homesickness, the best thing is to keep them busy. Run them ragged all day so that they'll fall right to sleep at night."

Unfortunately, that plan wasn't working for Alexa Rose, who was busy and happy by day and homesick and unhappy by night. I was beginning to think that homesickness was a catch-all term for the process of learning to comfort oneself. At camp, far from home and parents, kids are challenged to soothe themselves. So many kids seem to have little ability to withstand discomfort, to push through the pain, or to be encouraged by the old, but oh-so-wise truism *This, too shall pass*. They thought there was a pill for everything, even transient sadness or temporary disappointment. And it would be easy to believe that was true, what with the availability of so many over-the-counter products. I was amazed how easily so many children could describe their symptoms and request specific products. They were fluent in the language of analgesics, antihistamines, decongestants, and anti-inflammatories. They scrutinized product labels and conversed knowledgeably about ingredients. Many knew the name of the drug they wanted, requested the tablet, capsule, or syrup formulation, and could even state the dosage they took. They expected a remedy that offered quick relief. And they didn't want the pain merely blunted or diminished; they wanted it gone. Nothing less would do. They looked at me reproachfully when I couldn't make their problem go away.

"I know," Kitch said with a sigh, agreeing with me. "My patients are always disappointed if they leave my office without a prescription."

I told him about a day in town when I'd dropped by the drugstore to pick up an order Wendy had put through. The pharmacist handed me a bag of antibiotics and painkillers. "There must be some gravely ill children at your camp," he had said.

"Actually, they're pretty healthy," I said. "They just don't realize it."

I kept my eye on Wayne, the reluctant swimmer who always kept his red bracelet prominently displayed. Often he sat on the dock, watching the others swim or paddle canoes or kayaks. I never once saw him get wet. The swim staff eventually gave up and ignored him. In addition to a fear of swimming, Wayne worried about germs and infection from toilet seats. He liked to use the bathroom in the MC, but only after wiping it down first. Kitch called him an FLK – a funny-looking kid – but I knew Kitch well enough by then to know he meant it as a term of endearment.

Wayne showed up one day looking worried. "I think I have beaver fever."

I tried to keep a straight face. "Lie down, young man, and I'll examine you."

"It's an infection from beaver pee in the lake." He felt his forehead. "I may die."

"Is it by any chance swimming period?" I asked, noticing his counsellor at the door, Wayne's swim trunks, goggles, and towel in hand.

"How did you know?"

On another occasion, Wayne took me aside to tell me he was itchy.

"Where?" I asked quietly.

"Back there. You know, in the *anal* area." He squirmed around as he spoke.

I nodded and asked him a few more questions, but he refused to be examined, so Kitch had to make a guess. "We could give him Vermox in case he has pinworms. It's harmless," Kitch reasoned.

This was another drug I was unfamiliar with. "Does it have any side effects?"

"Only one," he said, his eyes twinkling. "It may cause camp-wide hysteria."

Wayne came back on another day to show me a scratch on his leg. "Does this cut look infected?" He was wearing swim trunks and a towel around his neck.

"Are you supposed to be at swim class?"

"Yeah, but this cut is bad."

"Wayne, how's it going? Other than swimming, are you happy at camp?"

"Sort of. Sort of happy. Well, happy-ish."

I sat there, waiting.

"My parents sacrifice a lot for me to come to camp. Please don't call them."

"I wasn't planning to."

"Great. Can I use your bathroom?"

After learning so much from Kitch and as I got to know the children better, I grew confident in treating them. I knew who
needed a hug or a chat and who simply wanted to receive a comforting dose of some common over-the-counter product they
were familiar with from home.

But Caitlin had a better connection than I did with many
campers, especially the teenagers, who gravitated to her. They saw
her as a friend, whereas I was more like a mother. With her
banana-split-flavoured lip gloss, adorable figure, stylish clothes,
and natural way of conversing in their language (casually using
"phat" when it didn't mean overweight and "way cool" as a complete sentence). They identified with her. I was coming to realize
that I no longer spoke the language of the people around me. They
understood *my* dialect, but it was an effort for me to grasp *theirs*.

For the most part, anyone could treat the minor, everyday
things the kids came to see us about. By and large, the problems
they arrived with on our doorstep were all the things parents
treat their own kids for on a daily basis. And when they prof-
fered their sore finger or cut knee, what they really wanted, more
than anything, was attention. Once, when a girl came to me for
something I considered trivial, I asked in annoyance, "If you
were home, would you go to the doctor for this?"

"No, but I would go to my mother," she answered, pouting.

Touché. Okay, I got it. At camp I was everyone's mom – except
for my own kids, from whom I was expected to keep my distance.
When it came to Max and Harry, I could look, but not touch. I
threatened to start them on a four-times-a-day regimen of pills,
just so they'd have to come for pill call and I'd get a chance to
connect with them!

Happy campers came and went, but one camper who proved to have a persistent case of unhappiness was Alexa Rose. I kept an eye out for her around camp, and she seemed always to be with friends and enjoying her popularity. The other girls clearly admired her outfits, such as a pink Juicy Couture sweatshirt with camouflage cargo shorts, and designer sunglasses. But she continued to come to us every evening right before bed, asking for a few drops of Rescue Remedy. When I tried one night to get to the bottom of what was bothering her, the tears welled up instantly.

"I am soooo unhappy," she said. "This is so not a fun camp. It's more like boot camp."

"But you seem to be having fun," I countered, "at least during the day."

"There are so many rules and I miss my parents. Camp is supposed to be a vacation from your parents, but I like my parents, my mom, especially."

"What would your mom do if she were here?"

"She'd let me do whatever I want. She never makes me do anything I don't want to do."

"Anything else?"

"She'd make me feel better. She'd hug me." Her counsellor was at her side, trying to do that very thing, but Alexa Rose pushed her away. "It's not the same."

"No, it's not," I admitted, "but your counsellor can help you while you're here."

She shook her head. "No, nothing will help me."

Her counsellor, who'd been giving her lots of extra attention, was getting frustrated. "I don't know what to do. I've tried everything," she told me when we went aside to talk.

"You're doing a great job," I said. "It's not easy."

"I didn't know it would be so hard to be a counsellor," she whispered to me. "I can't wait for my day off."

We returned to Alexa Rose, who articulated her complaints only too well.

"I hate how they make us do activities all day. Why can't we relax? It's supposed to be our vacation."

"Did you want to come to camp?"

"I thought so, but not any more. Every minute here feels like an hour. I want it to go by like that!" She snapped her fingers to show just how fast. "At first, I thought the tuck shop would be good, but it's a joke. It's a hut with a few candy bars and potato chips – what is that? Like, hello! There's nothing to buy. At my other camp, there was a vending machine. And there's only three sinks for twelve girls and four counsellors. Don't you agree something's wrong with that? If I don't get there first, do you know how long it takes? Oh, how am I going to get through the next twenty-two days? I want to be in my own bed, in my clean house."

I gave up. Talking to me only gave her more opportunity to dwell on her problems.

One day I received a message from her mother.

"How's my baby doing?" she gushed into the answering machine. "I'm so worried! Alexa Rose is very sensitive and it's been so hard for me, too, because, well, we're best friends. She and I, we're practically attached at the hip, and I miss her so much, but I do think it's good for her to stay at camp. Of course, both my kids are *numero uno* in my life, but Alexa Rose is . . . she's special. I just want her to feel good about herself, but her letters are breaking my heart."

"Did you speak to my mom?" Alexa Rose asked the next time I saw her. "Did she say I can come home?"

"She said she wants you to stay and that . . . you're . . . *special*."

"My mom always says I'm special, but at camp, I don't feel special. Here, I feel just like everyone else." She looked dejected but ran off to join her friends.

Just like at Camp Na-Gee-La, it was not only campers who needed attention. The counsellors also got colds, sore throats, and headaches, and could be just as miserable and needy. Sometimes, the counsellors needed counselling, like the girl who returned from a day off sporting a new tattoo, a black and white Chinese yin and yang symbol, on her backside. It was inflamed and swollen, and she had a low-grade fever.

"Does it hurt?" I asked, touching it gently. "It looks sore."

"No, I don't feel a thing," she said with an odd giggle.

"Is your hepatitis vaccine up to date?" Kitch asked her.

"I don't know. Can you call my mother and find out?"

"Did you get this tattoo in a reputable place? Was it clean?" Kitch inquired, ever so sharply.

"I think so . . . The guy seemed to know what he was doing. My friend got hers there." She hiccuped loudly.

"Do your parents know about it?" Kitch asked.

"I *am* seventeen," she said, "but yeah, they know and they're cool with it, anyway. Hey, your questions are majorly freaking me out."

Kitch and I went into his office to talk privately. He told me that a tattoo in that place was called a tramp stamp, and that it was a dangerous practice. "If these girls ever require an epidural anaesthetic, during childbirth, for example, the ink can track right up the spinal column and cause serious complications. But they won't listen to reason about these things and besides, legally, they don't require parental consent. I just know that if she were my daughter, I wouldn't be too pleased."

The counsellor agreed to let me take a blood sample to send off to test for HIV and a hepatitis screen. Afterward, as I applied antibiotic ointment to the reddened area, I asked her why she got a tattoo back there where she can't see it.

"I can't, but my boyfriend can." She grinned. "He thinks it's a real turn-on."

As she got off the examining table, she stumbled, and as I reached over to steady her, I caught a whiff of alcohol on her breath. She looked at me sheepishly. She was drunk and she knew I knew it. I had to tell Coach Carson and he fired her later that day. She packed up and stormed out of camp, upset only about losing the six-hundred-dollar bonus Coach Carson gave every counsellor who completed the summer.

I would rarely treat a counsellor before a camper, but I made an exception one evening for a young woman in genuine distress. It was just after pill call and suddenly the waiting room inexplicably filled up with campers, all with minor complaints. In the midst of that, the female counsellor arrived, clearly upset and fighting back tears. I went to her right away; however, it wasn't me she wanted.

"Is Caitlin here?" She looked around.

"No, it's her day off. She'll be back tomorrow."

Face it, Caitlin is younger, prettier. Who wants the wise and witty nurse when they can get the cool and phat one?

"That sucks . . . but I can't wait."

"What's the problem?" I was all business, pen poised over the clipboard.

"Can I talk to you? Privately?"

"Of course." I invited her into the examining room and closed the door.

She faced me down. "You *have* to keep this one-hundred-percent under your hat. Not a word! If Coach Carson finds out, I'll be fired. You know the rule, no sex at camp."

"Yes," I nodded, "it'll stay confidential unless it involves health or safety."

She didn't look too pleased with that proviso but continued. "My boyfriend . . ." She twisted her hands in her lap. "He pulled out . . . too late. We were in the middle of it, you know . . . and he'd told me he was an expert in withdrawal. He said he knew what he was doing . . . so then I stood up right away, but . . ."

Together, we figured out where she was in her cycle and I convinced her to talk to Kitch, which she did, but only after swearing him to secrecy, too. He promised to obtain the morning-after pill for her, but only on condition that she and her boyfriend would come in for counselling on birth control and safe sex. "This is a one-time rescue," he warned her. "You have to make a contraceptive choice."

"No worries," she said. "We've broken up. I dumped him."

Most afternoons, Kitch took a break. "Don't hesitate to call," he always said. I didn't want to interrupt his rest, but that wasn't the only reason I didn't like to call. I had worked with doctors in hospitals for many years and was all too familiar with the nurse-doctor game. For a nurse, there's always a certain pride in figuring things out by yourself and using your own judgment. However, doctors varied hugely in the way they regarded the nurse's role. Some freely collaborated with nurses and relied upon their judgment and initiative, especially at night or during their off-hours when a capable nurse could keep them from being disturbed. Others wanted complete control and expected to be woken up for every little thing. But in many cases a nurse's hands are tied: we know what the patient needs – sometimes it may be something very basic, like a laxative – but we can't give it without a doctor's order. If I were to call the doctor in such a situation, the doctor might get annoyed with what he saw as my lack of initiative or judgment. Nurses have to be able to accurately read the doctors they are dealing with and know the degree of mutual trust and respect. They have to be confident, have excellent assessment skills, and know their own abilities and limitations. All of these are factors that go into a decision to call the doctor.

One afternoon, there was a true emergency – though it didn't appear to be one at first – for which I had to take independent, immediate action *and* call the doctor. In order to give the best care to this serious situation, we had to work together. An effective response required teamwork between Kitch and me, and luckily, by then, I had won his respect enough that we could collaborate as equals, with our separate, but interdependent roles.

It all started very quietly. I'd been sitting in the MC enjoying the air-conditioning when Jared, the water ski instructor, showed up at the door. He stood there, dazed and disoriented. He told me only a few details about what had happened.

"I was doing tricks . . . skiing for . . . to show the kids," Jared had said slowly, haltingly. "A back flip . . . and a tantrum, I think that's what . . . and went down. I wiped out and hit the water hard."

I knew immediately that this was a serious situation. I called for Kitch and then got straight to work.

"What hit the water, Jared?"

"My head." He rubbed his neck. "My back, too."

As I ran to get the spinal board from the examining room, I heard him mumble that his arms were tingling. He lifted his chin slowly. "My neck is sore."

I laid the board down on the floor and strapped him in, careful to stabilize his head and neck with the collar. Then Kitch was there and I told him what had happened and what I'd done so far. We were both thinking the same thing: spinal cord injury and possibly head injury, too.

Kitch examined Jared while I called for an ambulance. Kitch said Jared would need an emergency neurosurgical consult and a CT scan of his head and spine to rule out spinal cord compression, bruising, or even a rupture. Kitch was worried, but angry, too. "Jared, you should have known better! We've gone over emergency procedures with a waterfront injury. Would you have let a kid get up and walk after an accident like this? Don't you realize how serious this could be?"

Jared closed his eyes, wearily. He had no explanation for why he hadn't taken the proper action. Maybe he'd been stunned by the blow to his head. However, even if he'd had his wits about him, when it comes to treating ourselves, most of us lack the clinical objectivity needed to make rational decisions.

I took his vital signs frequently, including neurological checks that involved assessing the reaction of his pupils to light and the strength of his hand grips. I knew that he was at risk for "spine shock," a rapid worsening of his situation that could be fatal. It would start with a sudden drop in heart rate and other vital sign disturbances. It can lead to cardiac arrest. I stayed near and observed him closely. He remained in stable condition. Soon, the ambulance arrived and Jared was taken to the local hospital and then air-lifted from there by helicopter to a Toronto trauma centre, a hospital that specialized in treating accident victims with head and spinal cord injuries.

Later, Kitch called for the report. Jared had suffered a significant spinal cord injury. He didn't return to camp that summer, but I did hear through the grapevine that he made a full recovery, both to health and to waterskiing.

As I assessed the patient and worked to stabilize him, Kitch had backed me up by taking in the bigger picture and making the decision and arrangements to transfer him out of camp to a medical centre for treatment. It all went so well – and had a positive outcome for the patient – because we worked as partners.

Most afternoons were quiet and uneventful and I went either to my hip hop class, down to the lake for a swim, or succumbed to the lure of a blissful nap on my bed with the wind whistling through the pine trees outside my window.

Caitlin and I took turns being on call and carrying the walkie-talkie. It crackled noisily throughout the day, and occasionally at night, with general camp chatter, most of which I ignored. But one afternoon I heard, "Is there a nurse on the walkie?" I reached for it on my hip and pressed the talk button.

"It's Tilda. I'm here."

"There's a problem at the waterfront. Can you come, like, now?"

I grabbed the spinal board, though there was one there too, plus a first-aid kit. I'd need a lot more than what was in this box if it was a true emergency. The potential for danger at the waterfront was immense. When I got there, a crowd had gathered around a tall girl stretched out on the dock. It was Samantha, the girl I'd seen sitting under a tree during the swim test. She was shivering in wet clothes, trying to sit up, with two counsellors on either side helping her.

Her swim instructor and I stepped aside to talk. "It's been a week and she wasn't going in," she said. "Everyday, it was a different excuse. She had her period, a cold, a stomach ache, a headache. She couldn't find her bathing suit. I don't know what her problem is, because she's an excellent swimmer. So, I gave her a little nudge, to get her in, and she panicked. It looked like she was going down, so I jumped in and pulled her out. She used her puffer because she says it's an asthma attack."

I kneeled down to examine Samantha. Her breathing was rapid. I pulled out my stethoscope and listened to her chest. It was clear of wheezes but her heart rate was only forty-five beats a minute. She was too weak to walk, so we carried her to the Medical Centre. I put her in bed and covered her with blankets. On her health form, Samantha's mother had described her as a picky eater who had been recently hospitalized for "extreme weight loss." No baseline weight was recorded, but it didn't seem appropriate to weigh her now in this fragile state. In a weak voice, she told me she didn't like camp food – "too many carbs." When I rolled up her sleeve to take her blood pressure, I saw that her arms were thin sticks, covered in goose bumps. I helped her into the dry clothes her counsellor had brought for her. Samantha sat listlessly as I lifted her top. I gasped in shock at what I saw. Running across her abdomen and upper arms was a crisscross of horizontal slashes. Some were fresh, others older. It looked like she had been violently attacked. It took me a few long moments to register the fact that Samantha had deliberately done this to herself. "Why?" I had to ask.

"I have to. It makes me feel better." Her voice was barely audible and her teeth were chattering. "It expresses how I feel inside." She looked away a moment, then directed a saddened gaze back at me. "Please don't tell anyone," she begged, and when I couldn't promise her that, she looked so disappointed. "Well, then, I guess I can't trust you. It doesn't matter; I can't trust anybody."

"Do your parents know about this?"

"There's only my mom and I can't tell her because she makes me feel worse. Grandma and Grandpa don't need to know. Mom doesn't want them upset because, you know, they're not getting any younger."

Samantha didn't want Kitch to examine her. "He's nice, but it's embarrassing."

"I understand," I said, but I didn't really understand a thing except that Samantha was not well enough to be at camp. "Do you want to be at camp?"

"If I go home my mother will make me go back to the hospital. It's better if I stay here."

I spoke with Kitch. He explained that some troubled young people use this self-abusive behaviour to substitute one pain for another and to make their distress visible. He felt that camp was a haven for Samantha, a better place for her than in her unhappy home life with an abusive father, who was now out of the picture, and a self-absorbed mother, who was in total denial about her daughter's distress. "I know the mother," Kitch said. "She travels a lot and won't be agreeable to taking her home."

That was it. Samantha was staying at camp, but I didn't believe it was the right decision.

Camp Carson had an on-site professional photographer and a videographer. They strolled around camp with digital cameras and video cameras, taking still shots and video clips of campers involved in activities. At the end of each day, they uploaded the images onto the camp Web site for parents to view at home. I started receiving calls from parents once they'd had a peek into their kids' world.

My son looks sad. Can you find out if he is homesick? Please get back to me.

Who do you have to pay off to get your kid's photo on the Web site? It's been three days now and there've been no pics of my kid.

In every shot my daughter is wearing the same yellow shirt. Were these all taken on the same day or is she not changing her clothes?

In the July 10th photograph, I don't recognize the girl my daughter is with. Could you please find out who she is?

And the photos were not the only things drawing responses from the parents. I knew the letters from the campers had arrived at home when the phone started ringing off the hook and my answering machine filled up. One mother called to complain that her child wrote only one line in her letter home: "Camp sucks." "Can you find out what's going on and get back to me?"

Another mother had a worse problem. "My son hasn't sent me a letter, not even one!"

"That's a good sign," I tried to soothe her, "they *always* write when they're unhappy."

In a recorded message, an irate father informed us that his daughter must have snuck her cellphone into camp (she'd handed over one before boarding the bus but kept a spare one hidden) and racked up a bill of over three hundred dollars of text messages to her boyfriend in the city. "Take her phone away," was the terse message.

"The parents don't seem to realize how well their kids are doing," I said to Coach Carson. *Well, most of them,* I thought.

"They'll soon get a chance to see for themselves. Visitor's Day is only two weeks away," he said, but he didn't look too happy about it.

7

HEY, NURSE!

The photographers roved around, snapping shots of happy children playing on the beach, sailing on the lake, making clay pots, and – the best photo op of all – sitting around the campfire. Needless to say, no pictures of Wayne's fearful swim test, Alexa Rose's tearful misery, Wesley's oozing impetigo sores, nor Samantha's self-mutilation made an appearance on the Web site photo gallery. The unhappy few were not represented. The vast majority of the campers were having a fabulous time. Everywhere I looked I saw smiling faces. Everywhere I went I heard the sounds of joyful laughter, the light-hearted banter of voices, and enthusiastic singing – even a group of kids bellowing "Stairway to Heaven" as if it were a sporting cheer. (This song was going to be ruined for me if I kept coming to camp!) When they were physically active or creating something with paint, clay, or string, the kids were content.

But if you spent each day as I did, attending to the handful of children with minor complaints, who were therefore temporarily miserable, or the even fewer individuals who were desperately unhappy (possibly at home, too?), you might forget that most kids loved camp. As a nurse, my radar zoomed in on the unhappy ones, such as Alexa Rose who now cried throughout the day (no longer just at night) and begged to go home. Wayne didn't say as much, but his sad face told the same story. Max said the other kids picked on Wayne and that he cried himself to sleep at night. There was also Hailey, a fourteen-year-old whom I hadn't yet spoken to but had certainly noticed around camp in her black clothes and dark, heavy makeup, a look that was in stark contrast to the other girls' bright, candy colours. Her counsellors told me she hated camp and was threatening to run away.

But unhappy didn't always mean homesick. Samantha, for example, had problems that went way beyond homesickness. Kitch, Coach Carson, and Wendy agreed she wasn't well but weren't as concerned as I was.

"We've been through this nonsense with Samantha before," Wendy said. "It's pure attention-getting behaviour. Princess Diana was a cutter, too. She used a lemon peeler."

She was so matter-of-fact that I couldn't tell if she was joking or not. How could they be so casual about it? The only thing that put my mind at ease somewhat was that Samantha had a tight bond with her counsellor, who promised me she'd keep a close watch on her. That was reassuring, but I saw that Samantha was too weak to participate in most activities. She stayed on the sidelines and hardly spoke. When she did, it was in a whisper and with downcast eyes. I tried to connect with her but she offered barely audible responses to my attempts at conversation.

Meanwhile, the daily routine continued. Pill Patrol still delayed the morning clinic and put us behind in paperwork, charting, and answering the growing number of phone and e-mail messages from parents. Coach Carson tried to help out by driving me around in his golf cart in hot pursuit of kids who missed their breakfast meds. He was like the merry host of a big summer party out on a "meet and greet." He loved this opportunity to ensure everyone was having fun, and loving camp. He knew most of his "guests" by name, including their nicknames. He knew who had portaged or soloed a canoe in Algonquin Park and who had gotten up on water skis for the first time. He knew all about the CIT boys' recent late-night raid on the CIT girls' cabin.

"Don't be pulling any pranks tonight," he warned them in mock sternness as we passed by. "Tonight I'm on patrol duty and I'm not going to let you off easy. I'll make you do a hundred push-ups if I catch you out of your cabins after lights-out."

As we drove along on the bumpy ride in the golf cart, he shouted out greetings to children he saw along the way, especially, it seemed to me, the ones he deemed exceptional campers, such as the athletic, popular, talented ones, or simply the happy-go-lucky, non-complaining, content ones.

"How's it going, Blake?" he called out to one boy as we drove past and waved.

"Camp's a blast, Coach Carson!" Blake grinned and waved back.

"I love that kid! He's so *easy*." Coach Carson shook his head in admiration of a successful camper like Blake who confirmed all he believed about camp's ability to bring out the best in children.

I admired the happy campers, too. By then, I had a pretty good idea of my own what made a happy camper. Happy campers felt they belonged; they didn't question their membership in the group. They never held themselves back or apart and moved with the pack. They loved to be silly and revelled in (and often contributed to) the cacophonous noise. These extroverts adored (and wholly participated in) the relentless activity from morning to night, and didn't mind one bit the lack of personal space, privacy, or downtime. The happy campers never yearned to be elsewhere or to be doing anything other than exactly what they were doing. They knew how to find their place and fit in.

As part of my ongoing field study of the happy camper, I asked a group of boys from Harry's cabin what they liked about camp.

"I don't like camp," said one boy with an uncharacteristically grave expression. He was the joker who had kidded me about my "wenis." Then his face broke into an enormous grin. "I love, love, *love* camp! I *live* for camp!"

"Camp has made me who I am," a boy, all of ten years old, solemnly told me.

"Camp's, like, the only place where I can be myself," another boy said. "Oh, sure, there are rules and stuff, but it's nothing like at my parents' *gulag*."

Around about the middle of the second week of camp, as I was jostling alongside Coach Carson in the golf cart on Pill Patrol, I decided to ask him about *unhappy* campers, such as Alexa and Wayne. "Aren't there some kids who aren't cut out to be campers?"

"I consider it a personal triumph to win over a camper," he said with missionary zeal. He waved to someone and gave him a thumbs-up about something.

"Do you think every child can become a happy camper?"

"Every child can be turned around."

"I'm beginning to think there are a few kids here who shouldn't be here," I persisted.

"Nonsense! What's not to love about camp?" He seemed uncomprehending. Either he wasn't seeing what I saw or just didn't want to acknowledge the downside of camp.

"But what's the benefit of making a miserable kid stay? Who wins?"

"It teaches a child the value of never quitting, of never giving up." He stopped to high-five a camper – "Hey there, D-Bomb!" – then turned back to me. "Think of the words of Winston Churchill: 'Never, *never*, NEVER give up.' Every child can succeed at camp."

"There are a few *really* unhappy kids here and I still can't see the purpose –"

"Well, their parents see a purpose," he snapped, beginning to get irritated. "A child who goes home will always regret it and look upon it as a failure. If children leave, it is *very bad* for their self-esteem."

Coach Carson had a vested interest in keeping every kid at camp. As for the parents, there was no question that the vast majority wanted their kids to stay: that was the plan, and it was what they'd paid for. Summer vacation was long, and many, if not most, parents worked and needed to keep their children safely occupied. Parents also needed time to themselves in the summer, to recharge their batteries.

After a few quiet minutes' riding together, Coach Carson reprised his beliefs about the virtues of camp, where new skills are learned, lifelong friendships made, and beautiful memories created. "Camp lays down the foundation for success in life. Camp parents understand this because many were once Carson campers themselves." He paused for a breath. "Winston Churchill also said . . ."

Here we go again.

". . . 'Success is not final, failure is not fatal; it is the courage to continue that counts.'"

He told me about his plans for improvement, such as a Camp Carson radio station and the purchase of more motorboats for the water-skiing area. His son Eric, who'd now completed university and was too old to be a counsellor any more, would be leading some of these new projects. "We've supported this theatre hobby of his for years, but starting next summer, he's going to transition into Camp Director. It's always been his dream to run the camp."

When Coach Carson had other business to attend to, and Eric wasn't too busy with play rehearsals (he was directing the camp production of the Broadway musical *Wicked*), Eric would give me a ride on his ATV to do Pill Patrol. The kids all called him

"Shakespeare" because of his love of theatre. As we flew around camp, me giving out pills from the basket looped over my arm, Eric would fill me in on the social scene. Because of his wide-spread popularity Eric connected me to counsellors and kids who weren't the MC regulars. With Eric by my side, I didn't trigger the "incoming mom, grown-up approaching" alarms that usually sounded whenever I showed up. Eric was very good-looking, with dreamy, expressive eyes. He often dropped by the MC to ask if we needed anything or sometimes just to visit. Caitlin had developed a crush on him. I agreed with her that he was very attractive, but to me, what was most appealing about Eric was his kindness.

From Eric, I got the inside scoop on camp gossip. He gave me the skinny about all the crushes, hook-ups, break-ups and make-ups going on around camp. He pointed out the "Sex Tree" I'd heard a lot about. It was the destination spot for heavy-duty making out. He told me who'd gotten into the university of their choice and who'd been turned down by medical school. In my role as camp nurse, it wasn't at all necessary to know any of this, but hey, I'm nosy.

One day, Eric introduced me to his buddy, Wallace, whose nickname was Einstein. He was a counsellor and also the camp tutor. Einstein wore a T-shirt with "I love π" on it and the number 3.14159265358 . . . that wrapped around his chest. "Hey, did you know Tilde is a scientific symbol?" he said when he heard my name. "It means a similar or approximate value."

"Wallace is a major brainiac," Eric said with admiration.

When I had to track down kids in their cabins, Eric waited patiently outside for me. The boys' cabins were messy and smelly, with dirty clothes strewn about, bottles of insect repellant and sun screen scattered on the floor, and heaps of discarded sports equipment and damp towels. One boy, whose clothes had been sent to camp organized into separate outfits, each in a clearly labelled bag, had dumped them all out onto the floor in a tangled pile. The girls' cabins were more orderly than the boys' but crammed with considerably more stuff. Beside each girl's bed was a brightly coloured canvas director's chair – turquoise, purple, lime green – with her name spelled out in glitter on the back. Since I didn't have daughters, I found it thrilling to examine their paraphernalia – personalized stationery sets, pre-addressed and stamped; piles of teen fashion mags; tubes and bottles of makeup and hair products (was bubblegum shampoo with cotton-candy conditioner for eating or working into the scalp?); fluffy cushions (some in zebra or leopard patterns) and a rainbow of quilts and coverlets; stuffed animals; folding plastic fans in pink or orange; plush slippers; hair dryers and curling irons. In addition to their designer clothes, assorted sports equipment, and iPods and MP3 players, there was an array of decorative trinkets, motorized mini gizmos, and gewgaws, such as pens with feather tops and glow-in-the-dark shoelaces.

I would never go into anyone's private things, or read a diary or a letter, but I had no compunction about reading a note left out in the open, such as the following "questionnaire" fluttering around outside a Wildflower Girls cabin.

Do you like me?
Yes   ☐
No   ☐
Not sure   ☐

Love, Me

One day I visited Alexa Rose's cabin to find out why it was so hot. "There's no AC! It's boiling in there! I can't sleep," she'd been telling me. The windows were all closed, so I opened them up, and while I was there, I picked up a few pairs of Lululemon yoga pants from the floor and put Alexa Rose's designer sunglasses that she'd left on the bed back into their case on her shelf. She was always losing her flashlight or her sunglasses, and had already lost one of her flip-flops. When I'd found Wayne's plastic water bottle and raincoat left on the porch of the dining hall in the rain, it made me wonder if perhaps it was the kids who could take care of themselves and their stuff who enjoyed camp more.

A few times, I had occasion to go into my own kids' cabins and got to peek at their stuff. I don't know many mothers who could resist that glimpse into their child's private world. As I predicted, Harry's belongings were orderly. More surprising was to see Max's clothes neatly folded on the shelf, his bed nicely made. This wasn't my kid, nor the kid his teachers knew, the one who was "all over the map." How did he suddenly manage to organize himself here at camp?

Both kids were having a great time discovering new interests. Harry was getting into breakdancing and playing the guitar, adding to his hockey and snake interests. Max was enthusiastic about everything. The way they both dived in and tried everything inspired me to try new activities myself. I took a sailing lesson and learned about the mast, mainsail, and swinging boom (discovering that the hard way). At the ropes course and climbing wall, I watched how one cabin worked together as a team to get each person across. For a moment I considered trying it out, but Harry happened to be there and looked worried.[*] "Please don't, Mom," he begged me. "Don't even think about it." I gave it a pass. In the Eco Zone, I made bubble bath and lip gloss from baking soda, glycerine, and rose petals and learned to identify

---

[*] He has worried about me ever since I attended a circus-themed birthday party for his friend Rachel when they were both six. That was when I decided to give the child-sized tightrope, four feet off the ground, a try. I executed the stunt gracefully, but upon my dismount I toppled over and broke my ankle.

poison ivy, poison oak, and sumac – "leaves of three, let it be."

"Look at you!" Eric said when he saw me taking a mountain bike from the shed. He gave me a big grin and a flash of those gorgeous eyes of his. "It's great to see you livin' in the moment. My dad'll be pleased with you. He swears he'll make a camper out of you yet."

On hot afternoons, I often went for a swim in the lake, sometimes quite far out. I always felt like I could swim forever without tiring.

At "A and C" I sat alongside the kids and made friendship bracelets out of plastic, colourful string called boondoggle or gimp. They taught me the flat stitch, zipper, and spiral. One day, I noticed a girl in dark clothes sitting by herself, away from her cabin mates, dabbling with paint and brushes. I suspected it might be Hailey, the gloomy girl I'd been hearing about. I asked her counsellor about her.

"Yup, that's Hailey. She's gone Goth. She doesn't fit in, doesn't even want to."

"Is that what she says?"

"She's, like, always saying how much she hates camp. She used to be really sweet, but this year, she's got an edge. She's managed to turn all the other girls against her."

Hailey heard us talking about her and got up and flounced away. I wanted to see what she'd painted. In dripping red was one word: *DIE*. I went outside to where she was sitting on the porch steps.

"Hailey, you look upset. What's going on? Do you want to talk?"

"Talk to you? Why should I talk to *you*? What have you done for me lately?" She said she had nothing to say to me, would never talk to me, and that I should go far away and stay away. I sat with her for a few moments, then told her I was around if she ever did want to talk.

But I wasn't going to give up that easy. Later, that night, I went to find her in her cabin. Her bunk mates were out. She was in the corner upper bunk, pretending to be asleep when I walked in. I knew she was faking it because it was still early and it would have been impossible to doze off with the commotion outside from that night's "Camp Survivor."

"Hailey." I rubbed her shoulder. "Please sit up. I want to talk to you."

She turned her back to me. I let her be for now. But the next day, right after lunch, I cornered her outside the dining hall and wouldn't let her get away.

"Hailey, can we talk?"

"About what?"

I wasn't sure myself, but she walked with me along the path away from the dining hall, then she dropped back, keeping a few steps behind me. I kept on going, hoping that by staying in motion, she'd open up to me. It never seems to fail.

"Is this a good time to talk?" I prodded gently.

"What about never? Is never soon enough for you?" She turned away from me. "I told you. I have nothing to say."

"It may help to talk. You seem really unhappy."

"Well, *d'oh*! You're just like my mother. She says I have a 'bad attitude,'" she said with air quotes. "'Change your 'tude, dude,'" she said in mock imitation. Her black-rimmed eyes were angry. "It'll probably improve *her* attitude to have me away all summer." She narrowed her eyes. "Hey, maybe you can help me. Tell me, what do I have to do to get sent home?"

"Are you homesick?"

"No, but I hate camp. My mother thinks she's doing me this huge favour by sending me here, but it's just to get me out of the picture so she can screw her asshole boyfriend all summer. They're always making out. It's *sooo* gross. I even saw them drunk one night."

"What would you do for the rest of the summer if you went home?"

"The only place I feel good is in my bedroom alone, with the door closed."

"If that's the case, it must be very hard for you at camp."

"I hate every minute here." Her voice was full of bitterness and her body was tense with rage. Even her clothes were angry. She wore a plaid grey-and-black mini-skirt that was held together with a large safety pin, and a black T-shirt with a skull and crossbones on it. She had a purple streak in her hair that hadn't been there yesterday. "There's no point trying to convince me. I won't stay. Nothing you say will change that."

"So, you've made up your mind not to enjoy camp."

"That's right and I'm warning you, I'm relentless. I will not give up until they let me go home. I am so not staying at camp. Staying here is not an option." She glared at me. "I'll hurt myself if I have to."

I switched tactics. "What music are you into?"

She looked surprised at the change of topic but I knew how that question could open doors.

"Metallica. Alice in Chains. Indie bands like Burn Planetarium and The Harold Wartooth. But I can't listen to any of that music here."

"No, probably not."

"The music they play here is so *yesterday*. These people are all cheerleaders or jocks. Well, let's just say, Avril Lavigne is the extent of their angst."

How well I knew what it felt like to be on the outside. I had also been a morose, sullen kid at Hailey's age. Like her, I didn't fit in, felt angry at the world, and expressed my barely contained rage by putting myself in dangerous situations, being rude, and acting out toward authority figures. I too had been just as desperate to run away from my problems and reject everything and everyone. Perhaps Hailey sensed my empathy for her because she began to open up. Without any prompting, she told me about her biker boyfriend who was in his twenties and came from a really messed-up home and how she believed she could help him get off drugs. "Sending me to camp is my parents' twisted way of keeping me away from him," she said, "but it's not going to work. I'll run away if I have to."

"Will you promise me something, Hailey?"

"No way!" She folded her arms across her chest. The door slammed shut again.

"Please, I just want you to promise to keep talking to me, okay? Please."

That was it. We'd reached Hailey's cabin and parted ways for now.

I added Hailey to my list of kids I worried about. That list remained short compared to the number of happy campers. However, the ratio of happy to unhappy was reversed with the parents: more were displeased than satisfied. Or perhaps it just seemed that way because the dissatisfied parents were the ones I heard from the most. There were days when I spent more time on the phone with parents than I spent with their children at camp. In some cases, the child was perfectly content, but the parents were not. I remember one teenage girl who happily bounced in to phone her parents who had insisted on having her call them, and when she emerged from the private office after talking to them, her eyes were red and puffy from crying. "They said how much they missed me and now I'm worried about them," she said, wiping her face with her sleeves. "I wasn't homesick before, but I am now." It took her awhile to collect herself enough to run off and be with her cabin again.

Sometimes we called parents. It was camp policy to call parents when a child was started on a medication or stayed overnight in the MC, even if the child was already feeling better.

I was always able to reach a parent quickly, even if he or she was a busy surgeon or a lawyer. No matter what operation she was in the midst of, or what cross-examination he was involved in, I was put straight through. A call from camp took top priority! Of course, there were some parents who weren't satisfied with the nurse's report; they were reassured only after speaking to the doctor. After so many years working in the ICU, informing and counselling families about the highly technical and complex medical conditions of their loved ones, it was frustrating to hand over the phone to the doctor for him to repeat what I had just told mom and dad about their child's headache or sore throat, but that was what they expected.

Some parents called with very specific questions about their child's moods, behaviours, and interactions with others. Based on my observations of their son or daughter, they tweaked the child's medication regimens accordingly.

There were times when what seemed like a straightforward call would become more complicated. For example, once I called a mother about her child's ear infection.

"What about his leg?" she asked.

"I'm calling you about his ear. Tyler has an ear infection."

"But he had a sore on his leg when he left for camp. Has it healed? And now, he has an ear infection? How did that happen? Do you think it could be MRSA?* Did you check for that?"

"It's not something we normally check for, here at camp."

"I saw a TV special about an athlete who had MRSA in a wound and he died within twenty-four hours," she said. "I need to speak to the doctor."

Parents were hungry for any information, medical or other-wise, that I could provide about their kids. They were grateful

---

* Methicillin-resistant staphylococcus aureus, a bacterium that is a difficult infec-tion to treat. One of the new super bugs.

for even the smallest detail, such as having seen their child eat a slice of pizza at lunch. I was sympathetic to their feeling of being cut off, because even right there at camp I felt frustrated, knowing so little about my own kids! But then I might be asked to do favours like arrange for a change in their child's bed position in the cabin or a switch to another cabin altogether. "Meaghan won't speak up for herself, so we have to do it for her," one parent explained. I was reluctant to follow through with these demands, because if there was one thing I had learned by then, it was that there were benefits in allowing kids to solve some of these problems by themselves.

Then there was Wayne, who I saw bravely, dutifully, going through all the motions required of him, and still looking miserable. His counsellor pulled me aside. "That kid reeks," he told me. "He stinks, and it's way worse in the cabin." I went to the cabin and followed my nose to Wayne's bed. Stuffed under his mattress were rolled-up soiled pairs of underwear.

"It's disgusting!" the counsellor said. "He's doing it to get sent home."

Now I understood the pinched noses and the nasty jokes I'd heard from time to time around camp:

"Hey, Wayne, have you read the bestseller *The Brown Spot on the Wall*? It's written by the Chinese author Hu Flung Poo!"

"Pee yuuuu . . . Hey Wayne! Haven't you heard of soap and water?" someone said.

A few kids were in the cabin and I heard them snickering as I talked to the counsellor. One kid muttered something about running the dirty underwear up the flagpole. That did it! I became incensed.

"This bullying will stop immediately!" I shouted at them. "There will be no more teasing. That goes for everyone." I glared at the counsellor and the kids and made everyone feel ashamed and guilty – I hoped! I ran to another cabin where girls had stuffed their T-shirts to mimic a girl who had large breasts, and I came down hard on them, too. Next on my crusade was a cabin known for short-sheeting the bunks, and for dipping the fingers of sleeping campers in warm water to make them pee in the bed. So far, it hadn't worked, but I let them have it, too, just for trying. All around camp, I heard their astonished reaction to my rampage.

"The nurse is going ape!"

"She's losing it!"

"She's so random!"

At the time I didn't care what they said, but, in retrospect, it probably wasn't the best way to address the problem. At least I'd had my say. I've heard some people call bullying harmless teasing; they say it's one of the rites of passage, just kids being kids. However, I suspect that it's only those who did these things themselves as kids who believe that, it's never the ones who were on the receiving end. Yeah, camp is a great place, I wanted to tell Coach Carson, unless you don't fit in. Then, camp can be torture. I've always felt an affinity for the extremely uncool.

Wayne's mother didn't seem surprised when I told her about his hygiene problem. "I feel sorry for him," she said. "We thought it would be good for him to go to camp, that it would help him with his shyness. He has no friends."

"He's in my son's cabin. He and Max are friends."

"Well, that's nice. We promised him a new computer if he stays at camp the whole summer. I've already bought it and had it set up in his room."

The next day, I took Wayne for a walk and told him I had spoken to his mother.

"Did she say I could come home?"

"No," I said gently.

"I figured they'd want me to stay," he said, despondently, as if he could see their point of view and even commiserated with

them. "I just have to deal," he said to himself more than to me.
He told me how he hated swimming, of course, and the bathroom stalls, because they were dirty and there was no privacy.
He couldn't do *that* with other people around. I said he could use
the MC bathroom whenever he wanted and could come to me at
any time, even during the night. Then, impulsively – despite his
mother's note that Wayne needed a "warning" before being
touched – I reached over and gave him a hug. Then – what a gift –
he hugged me back!

Every day after lunch, I spent the afternoon calling parents. I
usually made my calls in the MC where it was quiet. The MC was
officially closed, but one afternoon I forgot to lock it and a group
of girls gathered in the waiting room, chatting and checking themselves out in the full-length mirror. Shamelessly, I eavesdropped.

". . . we'll tell the nurse they're spider bites so she'll give us
Benadryl and then we can sleep in the cabins all afternoon,"
one said.

"I have such a crush on Eric. He's sooo hot!"

"Don't you just want to fall into his eyes?"

(Swooning sounds and muffled sounds of surrender.)

"My counsellor and her boyfriend were doing the dirty in my
cabin. I came back to get my towel for swimming. I thought she
was on her day off . . ."

"I'm so thirsty but I can't stand camp water. We only drink
Fiji water at home."

"My nanny is so clueless – she put water bottles in the freezer
and then expected us to drink them. Doesn't she know they get
all toxic and yucky when they're frozen?"

"I hate camp water, too. They never give us ice cubes!"

"Omigod! I hate this mirror. Look at my thighs! They're huge.
I'm such a cow!"

"Get out! What are you talking about? You look great."

"I figured I'd lose weight at camp, but I've been sneaking in here, weighing myself every day, and I haven't lost a pound. I'm going on a starvation diet!"

(I wanted to smash that damn mirror. It was almost as if they were obligated to express dissatisfaction with whatever they saw in it.)

"Have you seen Samantha's legs? They're soooo thin!"

"Yeah, and she's got those leg diamonds happening, you know, that space in between her legs at the top where you can see to the other side 'cause she's so skinny."

"What about her baggy clothes? They are sooo disgusting."

"You know, she should change her name to Anna."

"Why's that?"

"You know, Anna Rexic! I think I heard her throwing up once after lunch."

"I heard she was in the hospital for it. I wish I could be anorexic, too."

"She freaks me out, but it's better than being fat. I couldn't be friends with someone who was fat, could you?"

"Which nurse is on duty?"

"I hope it's the young one."

"The old one is kind of grouchy. What's her name, anyway?"

"I dunno. They call her 'Nursezilla.' I just say 'hey, nurse' if I need something."

I opened the door. There were only three fourteen-year-old girls – all slim and pretty – but it had sounded like ten of them.

I put on my sweetest smile, stuck my hands in my pockets. "Yo, girlfriends! How're ya doin'? Just chillin'?"

The party screeched to a halt. Their horrified expressions, fired at me faster than a high-speed instant text message, made me immediately shift back to behaviour more befitting my age and status. "How may I help you young ladies today?"

"We need to talk to you. Privately."

"All three of you? Together?"

"Yes. We have the same problem."

"That's quite a coincidence," I said dryly. I took up a seat facing them.

"We have constipation," they said, practically in unison, giggling madly.

After the hilarity settled down, I asked a few questions about their condition. It turned out that what they were really doing was trolling for laxatives.

"Why not try eating more fibre?" I suggested.

"I hate fibre," said one girl.

"What *is* fibre, anyway?" asked another.

The third girl slumped into the couch, examining her split ends. "Why can't we just have the pills?"

"You don't need them and they can disrupt your system." By then they had tuned me out, so I sent them packing, each with a plastic bag of dried prunes for medicinal purposes. I wanted to tell these popular, cool girls to go easy on the others who weren't like them, but I held back from lecturing. I locked up the Medical Centre. Caitlin would be taking over and I had the rest of the day to myself. Just as I was leaving, I caught sight of myself in that mirror and stood there for a moment. I looked so *parental*. I saw what they saw: a *mother*, a ranting, raving mother.

I went to my room, put on my swimsuit, and walked down to the lake and dove in. I swam far out as if to get a distance from my disquieting feelings. Usually when I swam, campers would stand on the shore and call me back for something, but that afternoon, no one disturbed me. I knew I probably shouldn't go this far alone, but I was a strong swimmer. It's the one brave (okay, reckless) thing I do.

I swam until I reached a small island in the middle of the lake and climbed up onto the rocky shoals to sit there for a while.

Looking back, Camp Carson was so very tiny. All around me was the lake and the sky. The beautiful view buoyed my spirits. I lay back on the rock and closed my eyes.

Within minutes, a motorboat roared up. It was the camp's crash boat zooming at me like the Coast Guard in hot pursuit of a high seas pirate. The boat made a wide arc and pulled up in front of me. "Hasn't anyone ever told you not to swim alone?" the swim counsellor scolded me from the boat.

I nodded guiltily.

"You should never swim without a buddy," he continued.

"You're right." I got into the boat. By the time we returned to camp, I had a plan.

I got dressed and drove to the nearby town. First, I treated myself to a nice dinner and a glass of wine at the local diner. Then I went on a shopping spree at the Giant Tiger – "Your All Canadian Family Discount Store" – and spent over one hundred dollars on skinny jeans (for my not-so-skinny body), a halter top, a fleece hoodie with "City Grrrl" on it, sparkly eye makeup, and a bottle of Britney Spears's perfume, Curious. (Like her, I'd probably be asking myself one day, *What was I thinking?*)

Back at camp, my new look made an instant impression. Counsellors and campers alike flashed me appreciative nods. Caitlin, anxiously waiting for me, also noticed. "Hey, girl, you look freakin' fabulous!" she said, hastily applying a layer of cherry lip gloss. "I have to talk to you, like, asap!" She hustled me in and launched straight into her news.

"Samantha fainted! Eric had to carry her in. She had new cuts on her arms and legs and when I went back to her cabin to get her stuff, I saw blood all over her sheets."

"Did you tell Kitch? What about Wendy and Coach Carson?"

"I promised Samantha I wouldn't tell anyone."

"You shouldn't have done that. You have a duty to tell them."

"She'll have to go home, won't she?"

"I don't see how she can stay here. She's not well."

I went to talk with Kitch and Coach Carson about the situation.

Again, Kitch dismissed my concern that Samantha was not well enough to be at camp. "We've been down this road with Samantha and her mother before."

"She feels secure at camp," agreed Coach Carson. "We'll keep an eye on her."

Wendy, the ever-cautious risk manager, suggested the cabin be checked for scissors or razors. Carson agreed with that, but Wendy went further. "I'm thinking we should remove the plastic knives from the dining hall."

"Is that necessary, dear?" he asked.

"It's a liability issue. We need to take all precautions to protect her and the others, as well."

We were way out of our depth with Samantha. I didn't have the skills or knowledge to help her, nor did anyone else there. I was uneasy with their decision to allow her to stay.

Hailey was another ongoing worry. Just that morning, Dana, her counsellor, had told me of a disturbing development. "Hailey's been scaring the other girls with these freaky notes with fake blood drops all over them," she said, handing them to me.

Things I Hate About Camp.

1. Everything
2. Everyone

This camp is history!
I'm out of here!
Who do I have to hurt to escape from this prison?

"She's getting worse," Dana said. "This morning she flew into a rage and was swearing at me for absolutely no reason. I just hope she doesn't try something stupid."

I didn't think Hailey would harm herself or others. That was my gut instinct, but I couldn't take that chance. What if I was reading her wrong? How could I know for sure?

It was Caitlin's turn to give out the evening pills, so I had time to myself. I called home. Ivan asked about the kids, but I didn't have much to tell him. Hearing his voice made me miss him. I signed off quickly and went to join the nightly campfire. I took up a place outside the circle's edge, careful not to encroach on their space. The campfire was such a unifying place – the campers were equals here, whereas in the cabins lines of loyalty and power were often drawn. It was their "nursing station," the place where they shared their stories and felt a sense of togetherness. The kids roasted hot dogs and went off in search of sticks and branches to toast marshmallows for s'mores. I stayed by the fire. I was beginning to appreciate their need to just chill. Their lives at home the rest of the year were so jam-packed and stressful. Camp was a break from all of that. I watched their noisy delight in the novelty of preparing their own food with something as primitive as fire. We were all novices with fire, coming from our fossil-fuelled homes filled with electrical appliances. None of us were used to seeing fire, much less using it.

The songleader tuned his guitar and led the campers in dances like the Cha Cha Slide or the Macarena and in singing TV theme songs from shows such as "Friends" and "Family Guy." When the youngest campers went off to bed, I got up to leave, too. I was tired but enjoyed the sensation of well-earned fatigue at the end of each active day. As we strolled away from the campfire, one girl complained to her friend.

"Tonight's E.P.* was just a campfire? How lame is that? At my other camp I got to sing 'Party Like a Rock Star' in front of everyone at talent night."

"At least a campfire is way funner than an E.T.B.,†" her friend answered.

"But still, it's the same old, same old."

Yeah, right. Another borrring day.

---

* Evening Program
† Early To Bed

8

LOST AND FOUND

"Woohoo! Lookin' fly, Nurse Tilda!"

"Check it out, fellas! Smokin' nurse headin' our way!"

"Hey, guys, who knew our nurse was such a babe?"

That was how the trippers greeted me when I visited them in their cabin one evening. It was the day after my big fashion intervention at Giant Tiger and I guess my new look was still making a hit! Perhaps they now saw me differently, or maybe, for the first time, at all. I wouldn't normally venture into tripper territory, but I needed to bring them the first-aid kits and camper medications they'd forgotten to pick up before leaving early the next morning on a six-day canoe trip.

I hesitated before knocking on the door, nervous to enter their all-male domain where, rumour had it, there were wild, late-night goings-on. Jordan, the head tripper, tall and strapping, welcomed me, along with six (or seven or eight – I couldn't count due to sudden light-headedness) trippers that crowded around me. They were wearing shorts, plus or minus muscle shirts – some in the midst of hastily pulling on those very items, as I walked in. Well, what can I say, but I was getting flustered, rather *verklempt*,* and highly *hormotional*!†

---

* A Yiddish expression meaning a crazy-making mixture of excitement and emotions.

† A more recent coinage, meaning a crazy-making mixture of hormones and emotions.

Get a grip, I told myself. *What's wrong with you? They're eighteen- and nineteen-year-old boys and you're a grown woman! Act your age!*

"What can we do you for, Nurse Tilda?" Jordan turned down the volume of the pumped-up, throbbing music playing on his boom box.

I came to my senses. "You were supposed to pick up these first-aid kits. Were you planning to wake me up at five in the morning before leaving?"

"Geez, sorry." He hit his forehead and flashed me an endearing grin. I melted.

"We also have safety information and camper medications to review."

"I know all that stuff, but you run it by the noobs here who haven't taken out a trip, yet." Jordan offered me a seat atop one of their massive knapsacks, packed for the trip. The other trippers gathered around, taking up positions at my feet, or on the edge of their bunks. They gave me their respectful attention. *Okay, this is good!*

"What about him?" I pointed at someone sprawled on his cot, softly snoring.

"Oh, the Frog Man? We went out last night and he got . . . *sick*."

"Is he well enough to take kids out on a trip?"

"Oh, he'll be okay," Jordan said with another grin.

I get it, I get it. He's hungover.

We started with a review of basic first aid. I tested them on splinting a fractured limb and treating sunstroke. I watched them demonstrate taping a sprained ankle. I questioned them on bee stings, deep wounds, and blackfly bites. I put them through their paces for emergency procedures, quizzing them on the signs of anaphylactic shock and making them enact a mock CPR drill while I observed closely. I told them to double-check that they'd packed enough epinephrine and syringes. They were impressively knowledgeable and confident. They were also skilled in wilderness survival techniques, making shelters, tying ropes and knots, and predicting the weather. They knew what to do in the event of earthquakes, quicksand, electrical storms, and hurricanes.

However, when we started reviewing the camper medications, I began to lose them. Their interest waned with the move to this more prosaic topic. It's always like that: everyone prefers heroic rescues, life-saving, fixing, and curing. Nursing care, with its daily tending, monitoring, and paying close attention, takes more stamina and patience – and has no status. The guys were getting restless as I spoke about medications that could be given on an "as needed basis." One guy started juggling oranges. Others stretched out and lazed around the room. Someone turned the volume back up on the music, obviously a cue to me to cut to the chase. I continued on, all the while trying not to notice their muscular arms and legs, their strong backs and rippling chests . . .

What hot bodies, Caitlin would have whispered to me if she had been there. *Gorging on the eye candy, are you, girlfriend?*

As I spoke about the properties of acetaminophen versus those of ibuprofen, I was envisioning them hauling canoes out of the water and hoisting them onto their backs, getting hot and sweaty as they led the way through the wilderness. I had heard about their legendary end-of-summer trip. I knew that after the campers all went home, the trippers went out on a two-week survival trip, deep in the wild bush. *Maybe I'll join them, go off and tough it out in the wilderness . . . me and the trippers.*

I jumped up to clear my head and fell over one of the heavy backpacks. Jordan helped me to my feet and was kind enough not to snicker.

"Okay! Any questions about the medications?" I asked.

"Which is the drug that knocks them out?" one guy asked. "Is it this one?" He picked up a bottle of Gravol, also known as dimenhydrinate, used to prevent vomiting, and then a bottle of Benadryl, diphenhydramine, which is an antihistamine that helps to relieve itchiness or nasal congestion due to allergies. He was clearly mixing them up. It was an easy thing to do because of the similarity of their generic names and also because both drugs can cause drowsiness. However, neither is to be used for that purpose.

"Are these painkillers?" another guy asked, picking up another bottle of pills. "I'm not giving any painkillers to the wimps!" he said. "They'll have to tough it out."

They were getting me worried. I hastened to correct their misunderstanding of these drugs. Jordan asked me about a boy who was well-known for his hyperactivity and hijinks. "Where's Ryan's ADD meds?" He searched though the bags.

"Ryan isn't on any meds."

"Well, last summer he was, and man, he still needs them! That kid is majorly high maintenance." He glanced at me, trying to gauge how far he could go with this. "I think I liked him better when he was a zombie."

That cracked them right up. These guys hadn't earned the right to make these kinds of jokes. Given their cavalier attitude, these jokes were wrong, possibly dangerous. These kids were scaring me.

"You guys aren't getting it," I said. "This is a serious matter."

So many things can go wrong.

"We'll look after the kids, don't worry," Jordan said. "They love us! We won't leave them out for the wolves!"

"Listen carefully. Each of these drugs has the potential to harm a child if it is used improperly. You can *kill* someone by giving the wrong drug to the wrong person or in the wrong dose, or at the wrong time, or in the wrong way."

Now, I had their attention once again.

"You guys have the most important job at camp. Being a tripper is the job with the greatest responsibility. You take the children out of camp, into the wilderness, far from any help. If something goes wrong, you will have to handle it alone. These kids' lives are completely in your hands. It is up to you to keep them healthy and return them safely."

That did it. The room fell quiet.

I wanted to end on a positive note. So I told them about what I'd observed when a cabin of kids had returned to camp after the last canoe trip. I had stood aside, watching them bound off the bus. They looked pleased and proud of what they'd accomplished out there, roughing it in the wilderness. Overcoming the challenges they'd faced together had forged strong bonds between them. Even with their bug-bitten legs, complaints about getting rained out, and the burnt food, they were triumphant. In particular, I noticed the kids who'd been scared to go on the trip but who had gone anyway. I could see on their faces the new confidence and self-esteem they'd earned by conquering their fears.

"You taught those kids how to survive in nature and it made them stronger," I told the trippers. They listened and nodded. I was pretty sure they got my message.

It was almost midnight and time for me to go. Just then, a knock came at the door. Jordan greeted a group of swim and drama counsellors who'd shown up for a late-night rendezvous, eager for some tripper-style fun and games.

"Hey, sluts," he called out to them. "Quiet down. We gotta finish going over some stuff with the nurse. Come back in a few minutes and we'll have a cuddle party."

"We can't wait that long, you sexy beasts!" someone called back.

Involuntarily, I cringed. It was offensive to me the way they talked to each other. I don't think they even realized just how crude those words were. I'd heard this language before at camp, many times. At least they refrained from using it when campers were around. Once, I'd asked a female counsellor about it. "It doesn't mean anything. They're just words. Things we say. It's no biggie," she'd told me, but I remained unconvinced.

Jordan cranked up the music.

"Well, I see my work here is done." I got up to go.

Jordan dropped down to one knee, grabbed my hand, and placed a soda pop ring on my finger. "Hey, Nurse Tilda, will you marry me?"

"You guys really should have an early night." I tried to sound stern.

"You're absolutely right, but the thing is, there's this little party happening, like, right now," Jordan flashed me that grin again as he walked me to the door. "But thanks for coming, it was a slice!"

One tripper gave me a lazy high-five. "You da bomb, Nurse Tilda!"

"Stay real, Nurse Tilda," another called out.

I was hardly down the path from their cabin when Jordan flung open the door to bring on the girls and let the cuddle-fest begin.

The trippers left bright and early the next morning, taking two cabins of thirteen-year-old boys deep into the remote wilderness of Algonquin Park. They would be paddling canoes on its pristine lakes by day and pitching tents and setting up a campsite each night. Whenever a trip went out, Coach Carson became preoccupied and tense. He kept in touch with the trippers by satellite phone on a daily basis, but still, his campers were out of his reach. He wouldn't be able to relax until they were all back, safe and sound.

A few days later I was working in the MC. I was bent over a child's foot, soaking it in warm salt water to soften up an inflamed ingrown toenail. The walkie on the countertop crackled and a female voice came over the air. "Has anyone seen Max?"

Voices from various locations around camp volleyed back and forth: "Max who?" asked someone at A and C.

"You know, the nurse's son."

"Nope, haven't seen him."

"I think I saw down him at the waterfront . . . that was earlier this morning."

"Where's he supposed to be?"

"His cabin is at the ski docks."

"Hey, it's Sandy here on ski. There's no Max here."

"Shit!" someone muttered. "The kid's gone AWOL!"

Something purely primal, a deep animal instinct inside me, kicked in. I dropped the camper's foot into the basin of water, nodded at Caitlin and Kitch, and took off for the water-ski area, just south of the main swim docks.

Don't wander off! I'd told Max so many times. *Stay with the group! Follow the rules! Sit still! Listen! Pay attention!* I yelled at him in my head as I'd done many times, for real. But Camp Carson was so vast and sprawling, a child could easily go missing, and Max was someone who didn't always follow the crowd . . .

He wasn't at the canoes or kayaks, nor in his cabin. Others joined in the search. I knew that any minute Wendy would sound the emergency alarm and there'd be an all-out missing-person alert. Suddenly, I came to a halt and stood there, forcing myself to slow down and consider the situation rationally. I knew my kid. He was an explorer, a dreamer, and an inventor. He was full of mischief and highly distractible but neither reckless nor foolish. Max knew how to look after himself. He wasn't lost. Of course, *we* didn't know where he was, but *he* did. That's how he would see it. He'd show up, I told myself, and that calmed me down.

Less than an hour later, Max was found, sitting in Harry's cabin, surrounded by a stack of Archie comics, engrossed in reading and digging into his brother's stash of candy (his own long ago devoured). He said he'd gone off by himself to test out an idea he'd come up with for "forest hockey" using branches for sticks and pine cones for pucks. Then, he thought he'd poke around in Harry's cabin. Luckily, he was found before Wendy had a chance to enact the disaster plan, which included dragging the water, fanning the forest in a human chain, and calling the RCMP.

We barely had time to relax when, only a few hours later, there was a real emergency.

Coach Carson received a frantic call from the trippers: two boys were missing. It had been a long day of paddling and portages. When they got to the campsite, Jordan had told the kids to go off to gather wood for a fire. Two boys did not come back. They'd been missing now for three hours and night was falling. They had no flashlight, food, or water. Neither was a strong swimmer and, worst of all, a canoe was missing.

A meeting in the office was held. Kitch and I came, too. Coach Carson called the provincial police and park officials. A helicopter with searchlights and heat sensors had already been deployed and would work into the night. Then, Coach Carson had to call the parents of each of the missing boys.

"Everything is being done," he told them calmly, "we will find them."

Both sets of parents got into their cars to head up to camp immediately. They couldn't sit at home, worrying and waiting for word from the camp. "Let us know the minute you hear something," one father said. The speakerphone was on and I heard the terror in his voice.

"This can't end well!" Wendy wrung her hands.

She was losing it, but Coach Carson kept his cool. Kitch looked grim. Quietly, he and I discussed the possibilities: disorientation, shock, hypothermia, exposure, bear attack, drowning, or the worst of all, no rescue at all, only the retrieval of remains.

A few hours later, long past midnight, bolstered by cups of black coffee, we were still sitting there when one set of distraught parents burst into the office.

"We were driving so fast, I was afraid the kids would be found, only to be orphans!" one father said, nervously joking.

"I want to reassure you," Coach Carson said, "our trippers are very experienced and responsible young men. They will find your children."

A short while later, the other set of parents arrived. The parents were anxious and, understandably, inconsolable. We offered them a cabin, beds, and blankets, but all four went to a hotel in the nearby town to rest.

The light in the Carsons' bedroom burned all night.

By morning, the boys were still missing.

To avoid hysteria, no one else at camp was told about the crisis. Camp continued as usual. The few of us who knew did our best to contain our worry.

At the same time this crisis was happening, the counsellors were busy with their own secret. For the past few days, they had been staying up later than usual, preparing something big, but no one would tell me what it was. In their free time, groups of them gathered in excited huddles, busy with piles of art supplies. They were painting huge signs, drawing charts and maps, choosing captains and mascots, making costumes, writing songs, and practising special cheers.

"What's going on?" I asked one counsellor.

"I can't tell you."

"As the nurse, I *need* to know." I didn't, really, but I was curious.

She shook her head and pretended to lock her lips, throw away the key.

I glared back at her and stood my ground.

"Well, okay, I'll tell you, but you can't tell any kids. It's Colour Wars."

"What's that?"

"Get out!" she gasped. "I don't believe you."

Now, I have heard it said that many young people these days are unable to name their nation's capital city or leader and I guess I find that as appalling as this counsellor found my ignorance of her world. However, after recovering from her shock, she explained to me that Colour Wars was a huge deal, the highlight of the summer. The camp would be divided into four teams to play all-day games. If you were on the winning team, well, it totally rocked, she said in summary.

"What's the prize for the winning team?"

"Candy and a sleep-in!"

"When is this event taking place?"

"I definitely can't tell you that. It's top secret."

This girl had potential as an intelligence operative, but she'd met her match: I was a counter-intelligence agent. I gave her a menacing look.

She caved and threw me a bone. "All you need to know is when the obstacle course race happens. That's when everyone gets injured."

Thanks for the heads-up.

As I walked away, her friend went over. "You didn't tell her, did you?"

"Yeah, she made me."

"We're going to have to kill her now."

Almost a full two days after the boys had gone missing, the police called with good news. They'd been found! Sunburned, covered in insect bites, scared to death, hungry, thirsty, and in shock, but alive! After a check-up at the local hospital, they'd been discharged. They had suffered no injury from exposure. They said they had gone to gather firewood and decided to take out a canoe on their own, but on their way back they couldn't find the campsite.

Coach Carson approached one pair of now-relieved parents. "I want you to know that at no time was your son in any danger whatsoever."

"Don't bullshit us, Carson!" the father snapped. "What kind of training do these trippers have? How could they lose our child?"

"I'm sorry, what I mean is that *your* son wasn't lost. The trippers mixed up the names. It was another boy also named Brandon, not *your* Brandon."

They were stunned, unsure how to react. They hung between relief and anger. I thought about the parents whose son had been lost, who were still at home, blissfully oblivious to their possible tragedy.

After ensuring their children were all right, both groups of parents left to return home, but not before Coach Carson offered to waive all camp fees for their kids for the following summer to compensate for their emotional distress.

"I've lost ten years off my life." Coach Carson dropped down onto the couch in his office, utterly exhausted.

Wendy sighed. "At least it all ended well," she said.

Camp had been in swing for three weeks. Tomorrow was Visitor's Day, and a few days after that, my kids and I would be leaving. My days were pleasant and I was enjoying myself immensely, confidently and competently treating the daily flow of blisters, splinters, sore throats, headaches, and stomach aches.

The counsellors were still busy with their surreptitious late-night activities, but meanwhile, a daytime flurry of hustle and bustle had kicked up around camp, this one in preparation for Visitor's Day. Extra gardeners were brought in to pick up litter, mow lawns, and clip hedges. Maintenance crews spruced up the outside of the buildings. Campers and counsellors did a massive clean-up inside their cabins, followed by inspection by the unit heads. The kitchen staff was getting ready for the special lunch for the parents, and as a result breakfast was even more rushed than usual. Amid all of these distractions, Caitlin and I suddenly became aware that the picnic basket of meds, always kept on the bench with one of us, was missing. That basket held amphetamines, antidepressants, sedatives, and antibiotics. Wendy was furious at us and told us what we already knew.

"If a child gets into those meds it could be disastrous! This can't end well."

She called a camp-wide roll call and gave a stern warning to whoever had pulled this dangerous prank to come forward immediately. I noticed Hailey was missing. I ran off with a good hunch where she might be.

I had been spending a lot of time with Hailey. Almost every day, she would duck and dive when she saw me, but end up agreeing to take a walk with me. We went on the path I hiked with Caitlin in the mornings. The trail led into the woods and then out onto a quiet country road that ran alongside camp. During those walks, I gave Hailey full rein to express her unhappiness. She was still angry and defiant, more determined than ever to leave on Visitor's Day when her parents arrived. She even had her bags packed. Yet her parents had signed her up for the entire summer. I wondered who would win.

"If she comes home, she wins," her mother had explained to me on the phone.

"That girl is not coming home," her father told me in a separate conversation. "We paid for this camp. She's staying. End of discussion."

"I'm at war with my parents," Hailey said, looking resolute.

I knew I couldn't fix anything, but I also knew, from so many years of being a nurse, the value in simply listening and being open to another person's pain. Hailey had to go through it alone, but if it helped knowing there was a caring and understanding adult, I would be that.

I ran through the woods to the private spot where she and I usually sat. The moment I came upon her in the clearing, I could tell she was glad to be found, even though she scowled when she saw me. The picnic basket with the meds was at her side. I joined her on a slab of granite rock for a few minutes, talked quietly, and then we headed back to camp.

"You're the reason I've made it at camp this long. I hope you're not leaving," she said.

"Yes, after Visitor's Day. I have to get back to my job in the hospital."

"I'm going home, too. I'll do what it takes to get out of here. I warned you, I'm relentless."

After dinner that night, they held the long-standing tradition of the hilarious "Lost and Found Fashion Show," where counsellors paraded around the dining hall wearing items of unclaimed clothing and sports equipment, calling out the camper's name on the label. It was amusing to see the counsellors sporting the kids' clothes and acting silly, but there was also a sense of urgency to the game – Coach Carson and Wendy presided over it from the sidelines – of uniting those clothes and expensive items to the owners before the parents arrived the next day.

"V-Day" dawned bright and sunny. Camp Carson was abuzz with excitement. By mid morning, cars were lined up outside the gate. By noon, they were bumper to bumper in four converging rows, ready for the moment when Coach Carson opened the gate, which he did, precisely at noon. The trippers, now subdued and compliant after the disastrous trip, were very industrious. They had turned the soccer field and baseball diamond into parking lots and were directing traffic, acting as parking valets, and helping parents meet up with their children.

Caitlin ran over to tell me that a plane had landed and docked at the waterfront and someone's parents climbed out. "It's the coolest thing I've ever seen!"

Everywhere you turned, heartwarming greetings were ringing out across the Land of Camp!

"Mom!"

"Dad!"

Kids ran to their parents – and to step-parents, a slew of siblings and step-siblings, grandparents and step-grandparents. The parents looked refreshed and eager to see their kids. The time apart had been good for everyone, but how strange to see the place suddenly flooded with adults. Grown-ups were invading the kids' world!

The visitors came laden with provisions: picnic hampers and voluminous hockey bags stuffed with giant-sized bags of potato chips, boxes of party sandwiches, hamburgers (still warm from the local town's drive-thru), fried chicken, barbequed spare ribs, chocolate cakes, lemon meringue and apple pies, and cartons of lemonade and iced tea, cases of Coke, Styrofoam cups of dried noodle soups, huge slabs of chocolate, and party-sized bags of candy to replenish their tool boxes. They brought teen magazines, clothes, sports equipment, toys, games, and gadgets. Some of the things they brought the kids hadn't even been missing.

Other noteworthy visitors were the many family dogs, all well-behaved and on leashes. There were even a few purse pooches, their beribboned heads sticking out the top of their owners' handbags. I saw kids run with outstretched arms right past their parents to embrace their beloved pets. In some cases it was hard to tell if the children were happier to see their parents or their dogs, but in the end all were lavished with lots of affection.

I wondered how Alexa Rose was dealing with this canine onslaught, but Caitlin told me her parents had whisked her and T.C. out of camp for an afternoon of pampering in the local town. "She told me she was going to max out her parents' credit cards," Caitlin said. "It was the first time I've actually seen her smile."

Well, I couldn't hang around ogling and petting the beautiful dogs. I was expected to meet parents and answer any questions they had about their children's health. As I worked the crowd, I found the parents were as generous to staff as they were to their children. They tipped the counsellors – which was against camp policy but not actually enforced – and spoiled Caitlin and me with boxes of chocolates, bubble bath, gift certificates, even a voucher for a day at a spa.

The kids gave their parents the clay pots, vases, necklaces, and bracelets they'd made, showed them all around camp, and recounted their many achievements.

"I learned how to swallow pills!" said one girl as she saw me walk by. I'd obviously given her some sort of tablet. "The nurse taught me." I waved at them.

"They make us wake up at the crack of dawn," one boy said, but he didn't seem too upset about it. "We walk *outside* to check out the weather, 'cause there's no weather channel!" He told his parents about his canoe trip. "We didn't even take an alarm clock. We used the sun to wake us up!"

Another child was also excited about outdoor discoveries.

"Our cabin went stargazing! I saw a shooting star. It was way cool. Then we went out again and we saw the exact same stars in the sky. I thought every night would be different stars."

"Hey, Dad, listen to this," a kid yelled as he strummed a guitar. "I wrote a song!"

I noticed one girl who had no visitors, but it didn't seem to bother her. "At first, I thought my mom was coming and I was jiggy with that, but she nixed the idea when she thought for some reason that my dad was coming. But she should know he would never come here. His idea of nature is driving his convertible with the top down." She happily spent the day with a cabin mate and her parents.

Parents gathered around Coach Carson, bombarding him with their concerns, queries about their child's activities, requests to change cabins or counsellors, or to voice indignant complaints.

"My son had no pillowcase. Why didn't the counsellor see that?"

The counsellor probably didn't have one on his own pillow, I thought. I admired Carson's tactful restraint. He listened quietly even when a parent angrily cornered him. "There was a disgusting four-letter word on the wall of my kid's cabin. Is there no cleanup crew?"

Many parents also stopped by to tell Coach Carson and Wendy what a wonderful time their kid was having and what a great operation they were running. Perhaps it all evened out, complaints versus compliments.

"I love it when they're at camp," I overheard one mother say about her teenagers. "I don't have to worry about them. I know they're safe. My boys are telling me they don't want to come back next summer, but I told them I'd pay *them* – as well as the camp fees – if they'll just keep coming."

"I wish my son would do school as well as he does camp," a father said.

"Don't worry," Coach Carson said. "Camp is more important than school."

It was time for lunch. A sumptuous buffet was laid out. There were salads, sushi, and multigrain wraps filled with grilled veggies or smoked salmon and goat cheese. For dessert there were pastries and strawberries dipped in chocolate.

But outside the dining hall, on the front lawn, missing out on this feast, were Hailey and her parents, engaged in a furious stand-off. There were two separate combat zones: Hailey versus her mother on one side, and Hailey versus her father on the other. I went over to introduce myself, but Hailey was in the midst of arguing with her father, whom, when she addressed him at all, she called by his name, Douglas. Her mother, Eileen, whispered to me, "Hailey and I used to be so close, but she completely changed in the past few months. The boyfriend turned her against me. She's become cold and distant, like her father."

Douglas turned to me. "I don't know what she" – he pointed at Eileen – "has told you, but did Hailey tell you why we sent her to camp? I'm sure she didn't mention it was punishment for a certain house party when the police were called. We're still repairing the damage. Hailey is a liar. If I were you, I wouldn't believe a word she says, or her mother, either." He looked away in disgust. "This is a girl who has raised money for the starving children of Darfur and rescues abandoned cats, but treats her own parents like dirt." He pointed his finger at Hailey. "You are not coming home. You will stay here until the end of the summer. Case closed."

"Please stay, Hailey," Eileen begged. "Be good."

"Why don't you two just get a divorce? Get it over with." Hailey spat the words at them. "You hate each other, admit it."

No one would ever win this argument. I left them to duke it out themselves.

Toward the end of the day, Alexa Rose and her brother T.C. returned to camp with their parents. I immediately recognized their mother and her shrill voice. She was talking in an agitated way to Wendy. I went over to see if I could help.

"Someone stole my daughter's sunglasses!"

"We can't take responsibility for valuables brought to camp," Wendy countered.

"But they were stolen, here at camp. Alexa Rose told me the girls in her cabin have been touching her things. I'm expecting your insurance to reimburse us."

"Have you looked in your sunglass case?" I asked Alexa Rose. "Your glasses were left out on the bed and I put them in there last week so they wouldn't get broken or lost."

Wendy flashed me a grateful look.

Alexa Rose's mother and father were ready to take her home.

"Baby doll, shall we pack up your things?"

"I want to stay," she said, surprising us all. It was as if all she needed was that small dose of her parents. She must have decided that camp wasn't so bad after all.

Her mother put her arm around her daughter and hugged her close. "My girl – she's a keeper, all right!" Next, she hugged me. "Thank you for taking care of my children! It's so hard to say goodbye. I'm a Pisces and we have issues with separation." She gave herself a few drops of Rescue Remedy.

If this Visitor's Day goes on much longer, I'm going to need a swig of that Rescue Remedy myself.

Next, I went back to Hailey and her parents, who were now taking up their problem with Coach Carson.

"Hailey takes after her father," Eileen was saying. "She doesn't express her feelings, just keeps everything bottled up."

"She's been very expressive about her unhappiness at camp," I said.

"For so many years she loved this camp, and now she's completely changed. I hardly know her. What's happened, Hailey?" She turned to her daughter and looked into her pale face and dark eyes.

"Eileen, face it," Hailey spat out, "when are you going to come clean about the boyfriend? You're nothing more than a whore. Douglas is an alcoholic." She turned away from them.

"When you get back from camp, do you want to see the therapist again?" Eileen asked. "The nice one, the one you liked?"

Hailey pointed her chin at me. "Her. She's the only one I'll talk to. The nurse."

Coach Carson told Douglas and Eileen about the prank Hailey had pulled stealing the medications. He warned them that another stunt like that would get her kicked out of camp.

"Why are dangerous medications being left lying around?" Douglas demanded to know. "That's asking for trouble. Anyone could have taken them, not just Hailey. Why should we be held responsible for *your* negligence?"

Coach Carson was silent.

"Hailey, you're staying," her father said. He pointed his car key at her. "If you come home now, that would just be one more failure." He jangled the keys. "I paid for this camp for the full session. Case closed. Carson, you keep her here."

Coach Carson shrugged and offered his handshake as a pledge that he'd do just that.

"I hate you! I hate you both!" Hailey screamed and ran off, sobbing.

"She's been given everything," Eileen said to me quietly. "I stayed home, I didn't work. She's had trips, private school. I don't understand."

Later, Hailey came to find me. Her mascara and eyeliner were smudged and she looked so vulnerable, but she spoke more resolutely than ever.

"I'll hurt myself if I have to. I'll do whatever it takes. I want to see the doctor so I can ask him how I can kill myself. What if I stop eating and drinking? How long would it take to get dehydrated?"

"You will feel the symptoms within twenty-four hours. Sooner if it stays hot."

"Will that get me home?"

"No, it will get you admitted to the hospital. Hailey, I don't see any way out for you. If you think you might hurt yourself, I'm going to have to keep you on constant watch. You've got three more weeks here. Isn't there something – anything – you could do to get you through it? Isn't there anything here you enjoy that you could focus on?"

She had no intention of considering the possibility of enjoyment. Her focus was now on escape. She stared at me in disgust as if I had gone over to their side and betrayed her. "There is no way I will enjoy this place. I hate everything and everyone here. Believe me, everyone hates me, too."

"I like you," I smiled at her. By then, I really did.

"Yeah, right."

"I mean it."

"You wouldn't if you really knew me."

I had to laugh at that. "I admire you and I like your clothes. They must have a lot of meaning for you."

She nodded thanks and looked away.

"It takes a lot of courage to be true to yourself, especially here at camp, where everyone is supposed to fit in."

"You *do* understand! Then why won't you help me get out of here?"

What Hailey couldn't possibly know and wasn't appropriate to tell her, was that I knew exactly how she felt. Hailey and I had more in common than she realized: we were both on the fringes, each for our different reasons.

I met Samantha's mother, Veronica. She was absolutely stunning, model-thin in tight jeans, with manicured fingernails and wearing tasteful jewellery and makeup. She had difficulty manoeuvring around the grassy terrain of camp in her high-heeled slides, with her frail, skinny daughter hanging on to her. Of course she noticed Samantha's dramatic weight loss (it had been only ten pounds, but Samantha was already so thin that she couldn't afford to lose *any* weight), but her child's appearance seemed to embarrass her. She blamed the camp food. "She's a picky eater. Other than that, Samantha is a perfect child. She's a champion swimmer. An A-student. She's always been so easy. In fourteen years, I've hardly had to do anything for her. She says that something has been bothering her, but now she's feeling a lot better and wants to stay at camp."

I stayed quiet about my disagreement with that decision. Samantha's condition was precarious and she desperately needed psychiatric help. Camp simply wasn't the place for her right now, in this condition, but no one saw it as I did.

Wayne and his parents were easy to spot. The resemblance to their skinny, nearsighted son was uncanny, right down to the same stiff mop of hair. Despite so many difficulties he'd endured, camp had been good for him. He had withstood the bullying and survived. Did he realize how much he'd achieved, how strong he was? I wanted to go over and tell him but he was busy with his parents. They were very sweet and doting as they said their goodbyes, so I left them alone, especially when I saw Wayne holding back tears. Besides, if I'd gone over, I'd have started crying, too.

Visitor's Day was drawing to an anticlimactic, exhausting close when I came upon two brothers wandering around aimlessly. Somehow in the commotion, no one had noticed that their parents hadn't shown up all day.

"I told Jason, Mom probably won't be able to come," the older boy told me. "She's an artist – *enormously talented*, everyone says so – and probably had to go to Paris, but Dad should be here any minute." He kept scanning the path that led from the parking area at the entrance of camp.

I went to the office and called the father's cell number. He was in Los Angeles working on a film shoot. "Tell the boys I'll try to make it up this week sometime. That is, if Carson'll let me in after Visitor's Day," he added. "Their mother, the famous *artiste* – she's *enormously talented*, I'll give her that – must have forgotten to tell me. Please buy them something extra from the tuck shop and add it to our bill."

I went to tell the kids and they seemed okay with that.

The long day still wasn't over, but it had begun to wind down as kids slowly accompanied their parents to their cars. Then, even some of the happiest of campers started losing it. Some clung to their parents and said goodbye reluctantly, with tearful faces. Others ran off, sobbing.

"I love camp," one boy told me. "I do," he added, as if to remind himself as he waved goodbye to his parents and wiped away tears.

Another boy hung back, looking shell-shocked. He had expected to stay for the entire summer, but now his parents had packed his bags and were taking him home.

"His father's company went bankrupt and we can't afford it," his mother explained to me tearfully. They had sold the house and were moving into an apartment.

One boy stood in between his parents, crying. He had been perfectly happy at camp, but after seeing his parents he wanted to go home with them.

"You are working yourself up into a state," his mother said as she headed for the car. "You know you love camp." She rushed to catch up with her husband who was already starting up the car. He opened the window and the boy leaned in, sobbing. "I want to go home."

"You brought this on yourself, son," he said, shifting into drive. "You've talked yourself into it. Come on now, be brave."

The scene was breaking my heart. I watched as the boy wiped his eyes and stumbled back from the car as it pulled away. The parents waved goodbye out their windows. They weren't being cruel, and the boy wasn't acting up on purpose. They were trying to teach their son a lesson, and he, in turn, was trying to deal with the difficult situation. It was hard all around. I went over to him and put my arm around him, but he shrugged me off and walked away, preferring to collect himself on his own.

I also saw just as many other children who had gotten their fill of whatever they'd been missing from their parents and who were very pleased to return to their cabin and counsellor and to be at camp. Some were even asking to extend their stay.

"Sure, I miss my parents," one kid cheerfully told me after saying goodbye to his parents, "but I'm not homesick."

"What's the difference?"

"I've seen them. They can go. I'm good now."

By the end of the afternoon, Visitor's Day was officially over. It was just as well, as everyone was thoroughly overwrought, some laughing, some crying, some doing both. That night, dinner was quiet, and when the campers heard that there would be a dreaded E.T.B., they were too tired to raise their usual objections. Everyone was emotionally drained and down in the dumps. I wondered out loud if Visitor's Day was such a great idea, after all. "Do we really need it?"

"Didn't you see how proud the kids are of their camp, how they love to show off all they've learned?" Coach Carson said. "Besides, we have to have Visitor's Day so the parents can sign up to guarantee them a spot for next summer. We have a ninety-four-percent return rate!"

"But there's such a drop in everyone's mood. How're we going to pick them up?"

He smiled and patted my shoulder. "I wouldn't worry about it if I were you. It's been taken care of. Just wait and see."

9

COLOUR WARS REDUX

That night I was woken from a deep sleep by shouts and screams. I bolted upright in bed. There was banging and clanging and then, of all things, marching-band music! I jumped up and dressed quickly. What was going on? A parade? A carnival? *Armageddon?*

Counsellors ran past my window shouting, "Wake up! It's Midnight Madness!"

I ran to the flagpole. The children had been assembled, still in their pyjamas, dazed from sleep. The older ones were excited and seemed to know what was going on. We all looked up at a small propeller plane circling overhead. Suddenly, hundreds of leaflets were released and fluttered to the ground. Everyone raced around, grabbing at them, scrambling to collect them all. They were lists of all their names and teams! Clues and maps leading to buried treasure! Mysteries and puzzles to be solved! Prizes to be won! Coach Carson stood at the side beaming with pride. "We do Colour Wars right after Visitor's Day but the kids forget and are always taken by surprise."

The campers were led back to bed. A ferocious battle was about to be waged between all four factions – Orange, Red, Blue, and Green – and it would begin in the morning. Everyone was so pumped up I wondered how the counsellors were ever going to get them back to sleep.

Bright and early the next day, everyone was raring to go. The counsellors had transformed the dining hall into four colourful worlds: The Orange section was decorated in Looney Tunes, with Bugs Bunny, Tweety Bird, and Road Runner as the captains; Blue was covered in comic-book characters, caped crusaders like Superman, Batman, and Wonder Woman; Red was Disney, with Mickey Mouse, Donald Duck, and Winnie-the-Pooh; and Green was plastered with the Simpsons (Homer, Marge, and Bart). Breakfast was dispensed with faster than usual, including the Pill Patrol scramble, to allow the full-tilt, eighteen-hour day to get underway. The counsellors had planned every detail and activity and Colour Wars would be executed, right down to the second, like a military campaign.

Not surprisingly, no one showed up for the morning clinic. All discomforts were put on hold for such a thrilling day. Caitlin and I locked up, and I went out on my own to take in the action. Campers and counsellors alike were decked out in crazy costumes, waving scarves and banners in their team colours.

They started the day with the "cheer-off."

"Let's go gree-een, let's go!"

"Blue's the real deal! Yay, Blue!"

"Yo – Orange talks the walk, walks the talk!"

"Red has the power! Red rocks!"

After each cheer, the team punched at the air, whooped, and hollered.

For the first time, I saw all the ages mixed together on each team. It was sweet to see the little kids trying to keep up with the older ones and the older ones adjusting their pace to accommodate them as they took them on scavenger hunts, ran relays and races, played touch tag, tug-of-war, and water polo in the lake. Later, the plans included the camp's traditional buffalo stampede, treasure hunt, and Capture the Flag.

"Colour Wars is insane this year!" a kid yelled out as he ran past me.

"Yeah, it's right off the hook," his friend said.

A boy staggered along, huffing and puffing and clutching at his chest, pretending he couldn't make it, though I could plainly see he could. "I'm gonna crash and burn."

I was dreading the commotion in the dining hall that I assumed would be even more over-the-top that day. When it was time for lunch I popped a few pills myself to stave off a headache and headed over. Unexpectedly, I entered an oasis of peace and quiet. The Silent Lunch was a hallowed Colour Wars custom. However, I braced myself when I read on the schedule that after lunch was the infamous obstacle race (the one where "everyone gets hurt"). I knew where I'd be stationed the rest of the day.

That afternoon, Kitch and I worked together in the Medical Centre while Caitlin roved around camp with a walkie and a fanny pack chock full of disinfectant, bandages, and gauze so she could attend to minor injuries along the way. It was a steamy, hot day, so I was happy to stay in the air-conditioned comfort of the MC while I treated the steady stream of bumps, cuts and scrapes, twisted fingers and ankles. As the day wore on, kids with headaches and heat exhaustion started rolling in. By mid after-noon, the kids were lined up on the couch and the beds were full while I rested, iced, compressed (taped), and elevated arms and legs, and medicated the children attached to those sore limbs.

A boy lay on a bed, groaning after throwing up from the lemon-eating contest.

A counsellor was beside herself with disappointment because she'd lost her voice from screaming on the chant-a-thon and wouldn't be able to lead her team.

A thirteen-year-old girl was in severe pain. Her likely frac-tured arm had been splinted and she was waiting to be driven to the hospital for an x-ray and probably a cast. She was moaning in pain because she couldn't swallow painkiller pills and was slowly sipping a yucky liquid substitute, trying to get it down without gagging.

A CIT boy had a possible concussion from a whack over the head during a mud-wrestling contest (he couldn't remember the injury, which was worrisome). He stayed under my close watch so I could check his vital signs and neurological status every hour.

Another camper lay on a stretcher recovering from the effects of unnecessarily injecting himself with his epinephrine syringe. What he had thought was anaphylactic shock was only extreme excitement during Human Battleship on the sports field. He'd panicked and given himself a shot in his thigh. His heart was racing and his blood pressure elevated, so I kept him for observation.

In the midst of all of this, a pack of sweaty kids barged in and rushed at me, begging for tongue depressors. I didn't have a chance to ask what they wanted them for or why they all had miniature corncobs stuffed up their nostrils, making them look like charging bulls. As I handed over the booty, an ominous call came on the walkie.

"I need help! Someone, help!"

It was Trish, the kitchen supervisor. Her voice was trembling.

"Hi, Trish, it's Tilda. What's wrong?"

"Come quick . . . now!"

"Can you switch to medical and tell me what the problem is?" (That was the channel we used for confidential information or to avoid camp-wide hysteria.)

"Please, just get here! Now!"

Gotcha! I grabbed the "crash box" – not the everyday first-aid kit. I had a feeling I'd need it. I'd put this box together shortly after my arrival at camp so it would be ready in an emergency. It contained plastic airways to deliver breaths in the event of an obstruction or respiratory arrest, and face masks and tubing to administer oxygen. There were lots of syringes and resuscitation drugs such as epinephrine, intravenous equipment with large-bore needles to run large amounts of fluid quickly into big veins, bags of glucose and saline, and large, thick bandages.

Kitch was out somewhere examining a child so I was on my own. "I'm coming," I yelled into the walkie. Just then, Eric dashed in and grabbed me. "Let's go!" he shouted. I jumped onto his ATV waiting outside the door and we barrelled off to the dining hall.

In the kitchen, I walked into what looked like a murder scene. Blood was everywhere: splashed against the tiled white walls, splattered on the floor, sprayed on the white aprons of the kitchen staff and head chef like some abstract paint job. They were standing around, speechless, paralyzed with fear and shock, as a young man lay on the floor writhing in a pool of blood that streamed out from his hand – what was left of his hand – hanging off the end of his arm. He was a fifteen-year-old kitchen worker who had been cleaning the meat slicer when it accidentally got turned on.

For one infinitesimal second, I paused, playing a mind game. Even after all of these years of dealing with emergencies, I sometimes need to calm myself down and I have a little technique that's very effective.

This is only a pitcher of cherry bug-juice spilled onto the floor, I told myself. *It's some joke, a Colour Wars prank from the Red team. These crazy kids are playing tricks on me!*

That second was all it took for me to come to my senses and take charge of the situation. I pulled on two pairs of vinyl gloves and rushed to the boy, careful not to slip on the slicks of blood. By the bright colour I knew that arteries had been severed. Parts of each of his fingers were missing, but the thumb hung on tenuously by a piece of fibrous tissue. Chunks of fingers were strewn across the floor. I grabbed a dishtowel and made a tourniquet on his arm. I grabbed a roll of paper towel and slapped that on the wound. Crouching beside him on the floor, I held his arm up, above the level of his heart to divert blood as much as possible from pumping out. All the while I shouted out orders, one after another, to the crowd gathered there.

"Someone, bring more towels!

"Buckets of ice, too!

"Call Kitch! Call 911 for an ambulance!

"Get the oxygen tank from the MC!"

I pointed at a gawker. "You! Gather up whatever parts of fingers you can find and put them on ice." He looked horrified but did as I told him.

The boy was now cold and clammy and had begun shivering. "Bring blankets!" I called out. The roll of paper towel was drenched in blood. Quickly, I replaced it with a new one.

"Am I going to die?" the boy mumbled.

"No!" I told him firmly. "You're going to be just fine. We're taking care of you."

I kept his hand raised high and maintained pressure on the wound, not even releasing it to check it. I kept talking to him, asking if he could feel what was left of his fingers. He couldn't. He had no movement or sensation in his arm. His pulse was fast, weak and thready, getting more difficult to palpate: I got someone to take over applying pressure, while I started an IV in his other arm and then opened the clamp to let the fluid pour in to stave off hypovolemic shock caused by such massive blood loss. Kitch arrived and nodded that I was doing everything right. Soon, the ambulance came and then the paramedics took over. By this point, the boy had lost consciousness and I realized I didn't even know his name. Trish told me it was Tom Adams. I looked at him lying on the stretcher, alone and without family or friends. I felt like a critical care nurse again, and all I knew was that I had to be with my patient and see him through to safety. I was tempted to jump into the back of the ambulance with him but decided I'd better drive my car there so that I'd have a way to get back to camp later.

In the emergency department the doctors and nurses transfused him with three units of blood. They prepared to take him into surgery to get the bleeding under control, but were also making arrangements for him to be transferred to Toronto for highly specialized surgery to re-attach his fingers by a top expert. I could hear the whirring of a helicopter on the hospital landing-pad, waiting to fly him there.

"I'll call your parents," I told Tom, who was now more alert after the transfusions and the fluid resuscitation but still groggy from painkillers.

"Don't got no parents," he mumbled. "Mom's dead and Dad's in jail."

"Who should we contact to let them know what happened?"

"I've an uncle but he don't like to be disturbed."

"What's his number?" I pulled out a piece of paper and a pen.

"He don't have no phone or nothin' like that."

"Well, give me his address and I'll go and tell him."

Instead of an address Tom gave me directions that involved a country road, a turnoff that was a "fair stretch" past a motel, a left at a tall red pine tree, and a right at a row of cedars. I got all that down just before he dozed off. I called the camp to tell them that I was going to track down Tom's relatives, but no one was picking up because they were probably still busy with Colour Wars. I left a message on the answering machine and went to my car.

I drove along the single-lane highway and was soon on that rut-filled dirt road that Tom had described. It seemed to lead nowhere. After a few minutes, I was so far off the beaten path, there was no one around to ask directions, no gas stations or pay phones. My cellphone wasn't picking up signals, and I was getting nervous. Eventually, after turning past a row of some trees, I stopped at a shack with a sagging porch. A grizzled man in bib overalls over his bare chest emerged. He stared at my car with suspicion. I got out and walked toward him. A woman came out on the porch and stared at me. Two naked toddlers were playing in the dirt. The man grunted, yes, when I asked if he was Tom's uncle. I told him about the accident but he showed no reaction. I left, shocked at what I had seen. *How could I have been unaware of such a terrible situation that existed so close to home? No one should have to live like this*, I thought, as I drove back to camp. *A nurse should know about this!*

As far back as Florence Nightingale, nurses have known how poverty causes illness and higher mortality rates. They understand the health effects of inadequate housing, sanitation, nutrition, and hygiene, and championed their reform. Tom's family was way off the grid and far beyond the protection of our social safety net. They had no running water or electricity and no access to healthy food, proper housing, health care, or education. How did they cope with our severe winters? What did they do when someone got sick or injured, like Tom? I had never come up close and personal with a case of such extreme deprivation. What a huge divide existed between the two sides of the camp's kitchen counter.

"Where *were* you?" Wendy pounced on me when I returned. I was so relieved I'd found my way back to camp that I'd completely forgotten they'd be wondering about me. Coach Carson joined her and said how worried they'd been, but they both sounded way more irritated that I hadn't been there to help on the busiest day of the summer. I explained what had happened, assuming they'd understand.

"You spent all day with a kitchen staffer and left one nurse all by herself to care for eight hundred campers?" Wendy said.

"How irresponsible! You jeopardized the safety of everyone at camp. Where were your priorities? What were you thinking?"

"That a boy needed me. I couldn't leave him. He's only fifteen."

"He's a hired worker. He's not one of ours. Your responsibility is to the campers under your care, to the parents who have paid us to keep them safe, and to us, your employers. Pills were missed at lunch and at dinner – Caitlin couldn't handle it all by herself. The MC is packed with kids who need your attention. You better get in there right away."

Kitch didn't say a word and Caitlin was quiet. She seemed miffed, though we chatted briefly about Colour Wars, but then she stopped, applied a layer of lip gloss, and turned away from me. Gone was her usually friendly demeanour and she wasn't calling me "girlfriend" any more. But she was a nurse, too; why didn't she understand the choice I'd made? I guess all she could see was that she had been left alone with a lot of extra work and that I had let her down. I later found out that not only had the MC been busy all day and the work non-stop, but in the middle of it all, Samantha had fainted once again. Kitch told me that when she returned to consciousness, she wouldn't talk to anyone or let anyone touch her, not even to take her vital signs. Kitch had called her mother and told her that Samantha's medical condition was now unstable. The camp could no longer take responsibility for her and he had no choice but to send her home.

Just as we were about to close up for the day, someone ran in to announce that the Blue team won. I didn't join the victorious celebrations, nor the evening entertainment at the amusement park that had been set up on the soccer field, complete with roller coaster and go-karts. I went to bed.

The next day Samantha's mother arrived at eleven o'clock in the morning, looking as well-groomed and glamorous as ever. Kitch told her that Samantha needed medical intervention and psychiatric treatment and that she could die from anorexia

nervosa, which is what he finally concluded she had. The mother
seemed far more concerned about getting back to the city in time
for a business meeting. She looked at her daughter and said to
me, "Sam's been given everything. I simply don't understand
how this could have happened."

Just before she left, Samantha looked at me and said in her
soft, wispy voice, "My mom never worries about me. She always
thinks everything is okay."

"Well, we're worried about you," I said, "and we know everything isn't okay."

I hoped now she would finally get the help she urgently needed.

That day Hailey was quiet, too, but it was unlike her. The night
after her parents left on Visitor's Day she had stayed in her cabin
and wouldn't come out. She went on a hunger strike in protest of
her "incarceration" at camp, but gave up by mid morning the
next day.

I offered no sympathy but did feel admiration for this feisty girl
and her rebellious spirit. Secretly, I was rooting for her, but there
was no way I would condone her self-destructive behaviour. That
very evening at dinner, she came up with a clever solution to her
problem. We were sitting in the dining hall when someone
shouted out "Hailey jumped!" There was a collective gasp and
then a hush.

The trippers, whose table was closest to the balcony, leapt to
their feet and ran over. Others quickly followed. People gathered
at the railing, looking down the sloping hill that led into the lake
below. At the bottom of the six-foot drop lay Hailey, among
fallen branches and twigs, and banana peels and apple cores that
the kids had thrown off the balcony. I ran down the stairs but as
I approached, my pace slowed. Her eyes were tightly closed and
she was breathing normally. My ICU intuition informed me that
she was okay. She hadn't done any harm to herself.

"Hailey?" I knelt beside her on the ground. "Open your eyes."

She kept them pressed shut. I could tell she was fully conscious. The old phrase *the lights are on and someone is home* came to mind.* Kitch soon arrived at the scene but also saw right away that Hailey was okay. Since he knew I had a connection with her, he backed right off. She had a few scratches and he would examine her later, but for now she was okay.

"Hailey," I said firmly. "Please get up."

This is your ticket home, I thought. I helped her to her feet, brushed her off, and watched her limp away, leaning on to her counsellor's shoulder. I went to tell Coach Carson what had happened and pushed for her to be sent home.

"You're going to put me out of business," he pretended to complain, but he recognized the seriousness of a suicide attempt, regardless of how half-hearted this one was. He knew she had to go. I kept her overnight in the MC but she was angry and wouldn't talk to me. In the morning her mother called.

"Is Hailey all right?" Eileen asked tentatively.

Then Douglas came on the line. "I understand you have our daughter in your custody. How could this have happened? Why wasn't she supervised?"

"I hate them," Hailey said to me when I got off the phone, "and, I won."

---

* In the ICU, privately, quietly, among ourselves, we occasionally utter variations of this coarse shorthand about patients we're worried about. Admittedly, the phrase sounds callous – though I've never heard it used that way – but it can actually be somewhat useful. When we say that *the lights are on but no one is home*, it captures something about a certain ambiguous, often-fluctuating disturbance in a patient's level of consciousness. It conveys the notion that the patient has a partial or limited awareness that is coupled with a significant underlying neurological impairment, which may be temporary or permanent. Lastly, the *lights are off and no one is home* denotes a rare and extreme situation. If the patient has suffered extensive brain damage and rescue attempts are deemed futile, then this version may even be a description, albeit a very superficial and cursory one, of the irreversible state known as "brain death."

"Hailey, would you like me to arrange for you to get help? I know you've refused therapy in the past, but would you go now?" I asked her.

"Can you say that the camp forced me? I don't want my parents to think I'm agreeing to anything."

I said goodbye and then did something I've rarely done in my long career. I wrote down my telephone number on a slip of paper and handed it to her. I told her she could keep in touch and call me at home if she ever wanted to talk to me. I usually keep my private life separate from my patients, but my experience with Hailey helped me realize that sometimes stepping across the divide is the right thing to do. What had helped me when I was Hailey's age had been the few adults who befriended me. I wanted to be that safe adult, that sympathetic listener for other young people, and I knew I had been, however briefly, for Hailey.

But she crumpled up the paper, threw it at me, and stomped off to her parents' car.

A few evenings before that first session of camp was over, the kids put on the long-anticipated production of *Wicked*, directed by Eric, with outstanding performances by talented children and staff. I went backstage to congratulate the cast members and Eric and his ever-present assistant Wallace but they were being swarmed by fans and I couldn't get close. The next morning, on my last Pill Patrol run, I caught up with Eric.

"I want to congratulate you on a *wicked* good performance," I said, having fun with teenage lingo.

"Can I tell you something on the down-low?" He looked at me. "I know I can." He drew a deep breath. "This is my last summer at camp. I haven't told my parents yet, but I'm not coming back."

In a flash I knew why. For some time I had sensed that Eric was gay. Why else had I instinctively held back from asking him who *he* was crushing on or had hooked up with as we drove around camp, gossiping? Why had I never teased him about joining in on the trippers' late-night parties? As for Einstein, I had a feeling that he was more to Eric than merely his stagehand. But Eric was so deeply in the closet, especially to his parents. He could never come out here at this camp. This was not an accepting or emotionally safe place for a gay person. One of the things camp teaches young people is what it is to be male or female. It can be a place to experience awakening feelings of sexuality, of which, to be sure, there are many variations. But at a camp like this there were only a few acceptable choices, and being gay was not one of them.

Eric thanked me and said goodbye. Though he didn't confide in me, I believe he knew I understood and would keep his secret safe.

On my last day at Camp Carson, early that morning, Caitlin and I went on our last hike. Again, I invited her to visit me in the ICU. "Sounds awesome," she said, but I didn't think I'd hear from her. She and Kitch never did warm up to me again after that incident with Tom.

There were certainly things I would miss about Camp Carson. I had many pleasant days there. I took one last look at myself in the MC's waiting room mirror. No, I hadn't lost any weight – the food had been too delicious – but I was fitter and trimmer. I now owned a pile of clothes that I'd never wear again, but they held good memories. I vowed to keep up my new commitment to exercise back in the city. As for all those funky hip hop moves and grinds that I'd learned? I probably should have saved them for the privacy of home, under the dark of night, but I went ahead and did a short demonstration of "Souljah Boy" for my kids.

Harry covered his eyes. "If anyone asks, say you don't know her," he deadpanned to Max.

"Who are you and what have you done with our mother?" Max wailed.

But I had gotten what I'd wanted out of camp. I had observed first-hand the pleasures to be had if you were a part of the fun and secrets, and also the perilous position you were in if you weren't. I had a lot of sympathy for the relatively few kids I'd met who simply weren't able to join in. Sometimes they were excluded from the group, but some excluded themselves. The group wasn't always at fault; there were kids who weren't able or didn't want to let themselves in. They needed more privacy, or more rest from the constant activity and demands of having fun. Fun could be exhausting. At camp, so much depended on your ability to cut loose, lose yourself, be silly. I loved the campers' utter lack of self-consciousness as they sang the "Funky Chicken" or "Little Bunny Foo Foo" or their full-on engagement in zany antics, like the counsellor who made announcements using a banana or a broom as a microphone; a table of girls all with orange-peel smiles; Eric and Wallace sauntering around with hollowed-out watermelons on their heads like green helmets. I delighted in watching their delight.

What I really understood was the connection of kids to their counsellors. As parents, we like to believe we have the greatest influence on our kids, but I saw the power of peers and, even more so, that of the counsellors whom the kids look up to. They are the ones the kids are watching. They are the ones they idolize and try to emulate.

I knew I'd never return to this camp. Camp Carson was far too big, profit-driven, and materialistic for me. That exclusive "members-only" feel I'd picked up on the first day stayed with me the entire time. Differences were, at best, tolerated, never embraced nor encouraged. All the same, I felt proud of the work I had done there. I helped a lot of kids go through the experience of a minor illness or injury and learn that they could be cared for or comforted by someone other than their own parents. I felt grateful to Kitch for all he taught me about the "care and feeding" of healthy children. I'd met many fine, talented children and young adults who would likely go far in life. They'd been given every opportunity to succeed, every advantage that money can buy. Among them there were also some terribly unhappy, depressed, and anxiety-ridden teenagers who weren't getting the attention or treatment they needed. In some ways their lives were stressful, and in other ways they were coddled and sheltered. They faced very few hardships and even fewer opportunities to take risks or solve their own problems. Most kids overcame the difficulties they encountered at camp by themselves or with the help of their bunk mates or counsellors. However, in too many cases, children were deprived of the opportunity to solve their own problems by adults stepping in to fix things for them.

I was thoroughly exhausted and ready to go home. I needed to recover from so much fun. Was there even a place for a grown-up like me at a camp like this? I was surprised when the Carsons invited me back. Despite Wendy's annoyance with me for leaving camp during Colour Wars and the minor disagreements I'd had with Coach Carson over the summer, there must have been enough about my work that they liked for them to offer me the position of coordinator of the Medical Centre.

"You'll run the show," Wendy said. "It's time we began turning things over. Eric will soon be taking over the business, as you know."

I didn't betray Eric's secret and although I declined, Coach Carson didn't think I could resist. "You'll be back," he predicted. "You're a camper now. It's in your blood."

My own kids had a blast at Camp Carson but couldn't say they preferred it over Na-Gee-La. They simply loved camp. The day before we left, Harry ran off to the forest to release the snake and the frogs he'd caught (kept in separate jars, naturally) back into their natural habitat. Max was pleased with the new word he'd learned: "Lacoste." He begged me to buy him one of those polo shirts with the tiny green alligator, but sadly for him, he had parents who balked at spending eighty dollars on a child's shirt.

The last night farewell campfire was a stirring ceremony. A chunk of charred wood – legend was it had been salvaged from last year's campfire, and from all Carson final campfires before that – was passed carefully around the circle. A display of inter-twined canoe paddles spelling out CARSON was set ablaze on the dock at the waterfront. It was a sweet moment.

After a few of the usual rollicking songs, including a final round of the "Cha-Cha Slide," the songs grew quieter and the kids became pensive as they stared into the flickering flames, their arms wrapped around each other, swaying back and forth. The last song was "Taps." The wistful mood it conjured felt strange in this usually jovial place. The children sat cross-legged around the fire. I could see my own two smiling boys sitting side by side with their friends, their arms entwined, leaning into one another as they swayed and sang the simple words.

Day is done, gone the sun,
From the hills, from the lake,
From the skies.
All is well, safely rest,
God is nigh.

Still sitting outside the circle, but singing softly along with them, I was momentarily jarred at the unexpected mention of "God." *Who said anything about God?* It seemed out of place here at this camp, which, for me, had been completely devoid of any sense of spirituality.

As the bonfire died down, my summer at Camp Carson came to an end and along with it, I decided then and there, my career as a camp nurse. It was time to get back to my work in the ICU with real patients. My camp days were done, *gone the sun.*

10

CAMP GOLDILOCKS

Sticky, heavy, humid – that's August in Toronto. A sign in the window of an industrial laundry caught my eye as I drove past on my way to work at the hospital.

Who wants to wash dirty camp clothes?
We do!

Too late – I'd already done load after load of laundry in my own washing machine at home after first dumping out my kids' duffel bags onto our back lawn to air out the rumpled, mildewed clothes; shake loose the sand, clumps of dirt, and little twigs; and set free the stowaway spiders and assorted bugs.

"They smell like camp," my kids had said gleefully, thrusting their noses into the heap to inhale traces of sun, wind, earth, and campfires. "Don't wash them," they begged.

There were also a few mysteries in those musty duffel bags. In Max's bag there was a red striped towel I didn't recognize. And who was Eli Lipton? Well, we had a pair of his swimming trunks. As for their toiletries, Max's bar of soap was bone-dry, the brand's imprint clearly intact on its smooth, untouched surface. I felt reassured about Harry's hygiene when I saw his gear, but then he told me that his stuff only *looked* used because his counsellors had gone around on the last night of camp dumping shampoo, squeezing out toothpaste, and roughing up the bars of soap to fool the parents.

Camp had changed my kids in noticeable ways. Both were stronger and more confident. They held themselves with more assurance and were definitely sassier, with traces of new attitude, probably picked up from their teenage counsellors. They were developing their own private lives and friendships that were separate from me. I felt like we needed to get re-acquainted.

The boys were also going through camp withdrawal. Irritable and restless, they wandered from room to room as if they didn't know where to put themselves. They couldn't handle the quiet after so many days filled with noise and laughter. After three weeks of constantly being part of the group, sleeping, eating, playing side by side with their friends, it felt strange to them to be on their own. After being outdoors every day, in the lake, the fresh air, with the wind on their faces, they were now cooped up in the city in the close, sticky heat, breathing the smog and pollution. I knew for sure they were missing camp the day I found them in the kitchen trying to roast marshmallows over the electric toaster.

August dragged on. We cooled ourselves off in chlorinated public pools, rode the subway downtown to visit museums and art galleries, and went on outings during which they kindly refrained from uttering the banned "b" word. But they weren't *bored* so much as longing to be outdoors with their friends, enjoying the freedom of camp.

As for next summer, it was a long way off and I knew one thing: my camp nurse days were over, contrary to Coach Carson's prediction.

At the end of August I got a call from Wendy Carson. She told me Samantha had been admitted to the hospital and was still there, that Wayne's and Alexa Rose's parents had already signed them up for next summer, and that Hailey had run off with her biker boyfriend and that her parents (who were now separated and had filed for divorce, as Hailey predicted) had no idea where she was. Wendy finally asked me if I would come back next year. I thanked her but declined.

A week later, when the kids went back to school in early September, I felt the relief of every frazzled parent. The school supplies store TV jingle expressed it perfectly: "It's the most wonderful time of the year!" I was happy to have them back at school but I did feel a pang as Max sailed out the door to what he jokingly referred to as "jail."

I had more understanding for kids like him who have difficulty being cooped up all day indoors, expected to sit still and quietly. In some ways, camp and school were diametrically opposed. There were many things you couldn't do at school that were allowed, even encouraged, at camp. I made a list:

- Make noise – even yell at the top of your lungs
- Dance, listen to loud music
- Daydream and stargaze
- Be messy, mess up, mess around
- Be silly
- "Waste time," putter around, or even be idle
- Try something new and screw it up, like wiping out on water-skis or making a lopsided clay pot
- Dabble in different activities and interests
- Throw your arms up in the air and shout, move around, and jump for joy

At camp, these are sanctioned, even encouraged, activities. Not at school.

I've visited schools, walked down corridors, and this is what I've heard.

- Stop talking!
- Settle down. Shhh. Be quiet. Use indoor voices only!
- Do as you're told.
- Walk, don't run!
- Settle down! Stay in your seats.
- Stop that! Don't do that!
- (And, worst of all) Sit still!

I never heard those admonitions at camp. School certainly can't be camp, but couldn't school take a lesson or two from camp? Camp does a lot of things right and is a satisfying environment for sociable, exuberant, active kids.

At school, children are expected to sit for hours on end. Their brains are exercised, their bodies so much less so. At camp, when I'd watched children in motion, their faces flushed and jubilant, smiling naturally and breathing deeply, they looked so content. I never once saw anyone look worried or anxious or heard any complaints about homesickness from kids when they were engrossed in play, actively moving, or creating something. I was beginning to think that "sitting still" was overrated.

I asked Ivan what he did during school vacation, growing up in South Africa where summer was in January and February. He told me about exploring the fields, forests, and streets of Johannesburg by foot and on bicycle, and how his mother only said "be home by dark." As for me, I had also had a great deal of independence, travelling all over Toronto on my own from the age of twelve. As a teenager I went backpacking across Europe and Israel. We both had had a lot more independence and freedom than our own kids do. We chauffeur them to organized activities and schedule every hour. So little in their lives is impromptu, spontaneous, or unsupervised. What does a child lose by all of this shuttling around and constant surveillance? What do they miss out on by not having the opportunity to explore the world, especially the *natural* world? Being out in nature is completely different from playing in playgrounds, parks, and backyards. How were our kids going to protect, much less save, our environment, if they didn't know it intimately and feel a connection to it? I was coming to the conclusion that in many ways camp was an ideal place for children.

By winter, I missed camp. Coach Carson was definitely right about one thing – camp does create memories to be enjoyed long after it's over. Images of those early morning walks, the crackling campfires, gorgeous sunsets, and singsongs burned brightly in my mind. I would also miss that little window I'd had into my kids' world.

"But you complained about it when you were there," Ivan reminded me. "Remember how homesick you were?"

Of course! I'd felt lonely and out of place. I thought about how hard I'd worked and all the nighttime interruptions. Why go back and have to learn a whole slew of kids' names along with all their nicknames? Why put up with the deafening mealtime food frenzy and running after kids who didn't bother coming for their meds? Why be exposed to the late-night antics of horny counsellors? I wasn't doing that again, but I had to find a camp for our kids. I didn't want a crazy, disorganized camp, or a big, fancy one, either. I knew I'd better choose wisely this time, because all of our flitting from camp to camp, making friends and never seeing them again, couldn't be good for anyone.

It was late April and I still had not made summer plans. I looked into camps and found a huge variety out there. There were day camps and overnight ones. Some camps had twenty kids and others sounded like little villages with fifteen hundred campers on sprawling acres of land. There were camps that specialized in magic, math, photography, sports, technology, and cyber arts;

camps for budding marine biologists and others for young film-makers. There were camps for every religion: Jewish camps of every style of observance, Christian bible camps that "teach the love of Christ to kids and have a blast doing it," as well as Islamic, Hindu, and Sikh camps. There were weight-loss camps, boot camps, wilderness survival camps, and even a grief camp for children who had recently experienced the death of a loved one. Fresh-air funds and other community charities provided a wide range of non-profit camps for kids who couldn't otherwise afford to go. Some of these were camps for kids with chronic ill-nesses such as asthma, diabetes, or cancer, or for kids with special needs. Some were for at-risk children and provided an escape from their homes where there was substance abuse or domestic violence. There were camps that had appealing names like Spring Lake, Pleasant Valley, Lake View; happy-sounding camps like Camp Surprise, Camp Cheerful, and New Horizons; and ones with deliriously over-the-top names such as Camp Happy Days, Summer Fantasy, and Kids' World. A handful of camps had Aboriginal-inspired names like Cherokee, Algonquin, Cree, and Mohawk, but I had to wonder if there were any real native influences at those camps, other than the fact that the land they were on probably belonged to those peoples at one time.

How did one choose a camp? I wanted to find the right fit for my kids, though truth be told, so far they'd been happy wher-ever I put them.

I asked my nurse friends who were parents what they were doing with their kids. Many had signed them up for day camps in the city; others were sending their children to hockey camps to improve their game. Some had summer cottages, where the grandparents would be looking after the kids. I was surprised at how many were going to let their children hang out at home, with no plans or supervision whatsoever. I wasn't so brave, but I still hadn't come up with an alternative. Soon, our options would be down to road hockey, video games, and the occasional trips to the zoo. Threats of the banned "b" word!

By June, with summer vacation only a few weeks away, I pulled out a file of brochures I'd been collecting. More and more I saw new definitions of "camp," quite different from the old-fashioned notions I still clung to. Take "Hospital Camp," whose goal was to interest teenagers in a career in health care. (Their on-line brochure stated that they held back the nursing component for the end in order to save the "best for last," but had so far managed to interest only one camper in a career in nursing.) Another camp listed a wide range of activities: "pottery, arts and crafts, tennis, dance and swim instruction, forensic science, canoeing and tennis."

Whoa! Beep, beep. Back it up. Crime scene investigation? What would that be, fingerprint examination, DNA analysis, and blood stain evidence for ten-year-olds?

There were theme camps such as "Nineteenth Century," where kids got to dress up in faithfully reproduced period costumes and learned to be milliners, cabinet builders, artisans, and blacksmiths. What about the "manners and etiquette" camp? (How badly behaved were the kids who needed that? If manners were the issue, their problems were way bigger than which fork to use.) And for kids whose behaviour was really obnoxious, parents could always send them to Dr. Phil's Brat Camp. Budding performers could go to camp to learn to be a DJ, a stand-up comedian, or a circus acrobat under the Big Top.* What about Cowboy Camp? "Bring your own lariat and be a real cowhand!" There was culinary arts camp, where kids could learn the rudiments of being a chef; Camp Millionaire, where campers would devise schemes to create financial freedom; and Camp Great Masters, where children would travel to Italy to learn the

---

* No, Harry, don't worry; I won't sign us up for that one. My circus days are over.

techniques of Michelangelo. At adventure camps, children could be princesses, wizards, pirates, or astronauts. It went on and on. Did summer fun have to be complicated and expensive? I needed a simple solution: a camp that was not too big, not too small, not too chaotic, and not too sophisticated. A camp that was *juuust* right. I needed Camp Goldilocks.

Just when I was getting desperate for a camp, I got a call from Rudy Schwartz, a man desperate for a nurse. He'd gotten my number from a friend. He was the camp director of Camp Solomon, the one type of camp I'd been avoiding: a faith-based camp. As far as I knew, religion and fun didn't mix.

Camp Solomon was a liberal, Jewish camp in the beautiful Kawartha Highlands of Northeast Ontario. It offered all the standard camp activities but religious education too. I wasn't sure about that. Playing as well as praying? My first response was no; not for my kids, and definitely not for me. What kid would want to sit through classroom lectures or go to prayer services?

After only a brief chat on the phone, Rudy was ready to sign me up. "It'll be a barter system: your nursing services for the camp fees."

That was a given. He was going to have to seriously sweeten the deal. I waited.

"What activities does your camp have?" I asked to break the silence, since it didn't seem like he was going to.

"The usual. Swimming, canoe trips, a ropes course, Colour Wars. The whole shebang but more than that."

"Like what, exactly?"

"Well, man, we don't have all the latest bells and whistles," he conceded. Rudy's hippie-speak and joking manner made me guess he was smiling at the other end of the phone. "But we have enough."

I fired a few more questions at him. "How many campers do you have?"

"Around 350." I heard him shuffling through papers on his desk. "Maybe 360 or so, I can't say for sure."

Compared to one hundred individuals at the cozy but crazy Camp Na-Gee-La, and the overwhelming eight hundred campers, plus a few hundred staff members at Camp Carson, this medium-sized camp sounded manageable. "How religious is it?"

That was the defining question. Oh, I knew all about the various streams in Judaism, the main ones being Orthodox, Conservative, and Reform. Or, as my father used to say, "crazy, hazy, and lazy." Rudy explained that Camp Solomon was modern, questioning, and egalitarian. There were daily prayer services and classes led by rabbis. The food was kosher and blessings were recited before and after each meal. He explained more about the lessons, which were based on the weekly Torah portion, and lastly, he described the highlight of the week, the celebration of the Sabbath.

It didn't sound like it had too many rules and prohibitions. *Judaism Lite*. Perhaps this was the Goldilocks camp I'd been looking for. A religious camp, yes, but open-minded. Neither fly-by-night and spartan nor ostentatious and fancy. It might be *juuuust right*. I agreed to meet with Rudy at his office the next day.

As I got off the elevator in the building where the camp office was located, I was greeted by a dog. He was a mangy mutt – beagle and Lab mix, I guessed – who must have had some sheepdog in him, too, because he herded me down the hall to his master's messy, cluttered office. I found Rudy sitting in a canoe on the floor beside his desk, smoothing the inside of it with some sort of a tool. He got up to greet me and introduce his dog, Ringo. Rudy was a short, middle-aged man with a long, silver ponytail. He was wearing blue jeans, a psychedelic tie-dye T-shirt, and unappealing white socks with sandals, standard camp style. Rudy's cramped, crowded office was filled with a jumble of camping gear, musical instruments, and equipment.

It looked like he was having a garage sale. There was a junked-up desk, a tangle of life jackets on the floor, a pile of unfolded tents, and guitars and guitar cases lined up against the wall, beside music stands covered in sheet music. The wall behind his desk was crowded with plaques, diplomas, and inspirational sayings, some hanging lopsided. A few caught my eye.

Be kind, for everyone you meet is fighting a great battle.
– Philo of Alexandria.

"Who's that?"
"An old Jewish sage."

God's message to humanity is brought to life through the child.
– Rabbi Leo Baeck.

"Who's that?"
"The founder of the Reform Jewish movement."

Who is wise? He who learns from every person.
Who is happy? He who is satisfied with what he has.
– Ben Zoma.

"Who's that?"
"Some medieval rabbi dude."
I tried to decipher a quote from the Talmud written in old-fashioned Hebrew, but I knew only a smattering of the modern, spoken language. "What does that one say?"
"Something to the effect that a father's job is to teach his son how to swim. I take it to mean that as parents we have a responsibility to teach our children how to survive. Yeah, that's what camp's about."
He told me about himself. He'd grown up in a strictly religious

family but had rejected the Orthodox way of Judaism. He and his wife – they'd met at camp – got into drugs and yoga and gone off to India to live in an ashram. Unfortunately, she had died of cancer a few years ago, but in his year of mourning, through the daily recitation of the traditional prayer for the dead with a small community of other mourners, he'd "found his way back." He paused to turn the tables. "How 'bout you?" He looked at me skeptically. "You don't strike me as a camp person."

How could he tell? I'd managed to fool Carson. I told Rudy about my previous summers as a camp nurse and my professional qualifications. What he didn't ask and I didn't mention, because it didn't seem like a requirement, was that I didn't go to synagogue, didn't keep kosher, and I wasn't about to start. I hadn't rejected Judaism so much as I'd never really embraced it, certainly not the rules or rituals of it anyway. My father had been an involved member of a Reform synagogue, but for him Judaism was a cerebral exercise. He loved to tussle over intellectual questions and debate issues but he didn't practise many of the observances. My mother told me repeatedly that she was against all organized religions and warned me against religion like it was something harmful. "If there were no religions, the world would be a better place," she often said. Surprisingly, in her last few semi-lucid years, she turned to the Baha'i faith, because, as she put it, "it's about love."

"Tell me about the campers," I asked.

Rudy picked up one end of the canoe and caressed the wood. He looked like he wanted to get back to working on it. "It's a diverse group. We have kids from wealthy families, from middle-class families, along with children who are subsidized by philanthropic organizations like the United Way. Kids who live in mansions, and others who live in public housing. We have children who are in foster care. Kids from interfaith households. Kids from same-sex parents. Kids from Jamaica, India and

Ethiopia, and China. Every summer we host a contingent of counsellors from Israel. Most kids are Jewish, but not all. Oh, I almost forgot." He put down the canoe. "I should explain about our inclusion program. We have campers with various needs and abilities and we help them integrate into camp life."

"Together with the so-called normal ones?" How well I knew how needy "normals" could be.

"The new term for 'normal' kids is 'typicals.' At Camp Sol we have some campers and staff who have special needs. We do everything we can to help every kid enjoy camp to the fullest of his or her ability. We have specialized staff to support our vision of inclusion."

"You mean to help the special needs kids?"

"Not just them. There are lots of situations at camp in which someone might feel they don't fit in, don't you agree?" I nodded. "Off the top of my head . . ." Rudy closed his eyes to better help him recall the kids who had special needs because he clearly didn't think of them as different from all the other campers. "We have a twelve-year-old coming for the first time this summer. He's been recently diagnosed with diabetes and uses an insulin pump. The head of tennis is a paraplegic. He's competed in the Paralympics and gets around that court pretty fast in an electric wheelchair. We have a few staff with Down Syndrome who assist the counsellors. We have kids with Tourette's and a few with varying degrees of autism." He scratched his head to help him come up with the others. "We've got a fair share of kids who may act a bit strange, but everyone finds a way to fit in. Oh, yeah, we have a kid who uses a wheel-chair and comes with an attendant who lives with him in the cabin with the other boys his age. I can't understand a word he says but the kids do."

"Aren't there camps for children with special needs?"

"Our parents say they don't want their kids segregated because of their medical diagnosis. The kids themselves don't see it as a problem. It's just the way they are."

"I guess it's good for them to be there."

"At first, that's what I thought, too, but I've discovered it's even better for us." He thought about it. "It has an interesting effect on the other campers. They step up and take on more leadership. I also think it makes them behave better."

"What about bullying? How do you handle it?" Since he didn't seem to have any questions for me, I interviewed *him*.

"Bullying isn't a big issue at Camp Sol. Maybe praying together with their friends makes kids a little less likely to be cruel." He went on to explain that they provided anti-bullying training for the counsellors and had a rule that a counsellor stayed in the cabin every evening, a time when bullying often occurred and homesickness peaked. "The main thing is that every child feel included. Camp Sol isn't perfect, but we work at it. On most days, it's pretty darn good."

"What about the prayers and the study sessions? Don't the kids complain?"

"They complain a lot," he said with a playful grin, "about the food and the mosquitoes, but I've never heard them complain about a day of rest. What's there to complain about? We can all use that. Camp can get pretty hectic, as you probably know."

In theory, a day of rest wasn't a bad idea. Like most nurses, I didn't have set days off work. They occurred willy-nilly. My "weekend" could easily be a Tuesday-Wednesday. My days off were spent recovering from night shift, shopping for groceries, or attacking my "to do" list of chores and errands that I didn't get to the rest of the week. But a *mandated* day of rest? I didn't know about that. I recalled how the counsellors at Camp Na-Gee-La had ridiculed religion. "Praying?" Mike, the director, had scoffed. "What's that all about? Is that like God's your imaginary friend?" Yet, I also recalled the discomfiting feeling I'd had

when "God" was uttered at that farewell campfire at Camp
Carson. For me, something had been missing at both of those
camps, but was it God? How would my kids take to going to a
camp where they would have to study and pray? Well, I may have
opted out of religion, but I hadn't turned away from spirituality.
"I guess it'll be good for my kids," I said to Rudy.

"That's Pediatric Judaism." He looked at me askance, like he
was suddenly having second thoughts about my suitability.

Well, perhaps a dose of religion would do me good, too. I'd
call it Medicinal Judaism.

Rudy went off on a new tangent. "When you think about it,
camp is a shock for kids these days. Sometimes I'm amazed at
how they cope with it at all." He started getting restless; putter-
ing around with papers on his messy desk, making me realize
our meeting was drawing to a close. "We throw a bunch of city
kids together in the middle of the forest, cut them off from their
electronic gadgets, put fifteen or so together in close quarters.
Some have never shared a bedroom before. For many, camp is the
first time they meet kids from another neighbourhood or from a
different school. It's a huge adjustment."

I noticed he hadn't mentioned "safety," even once, and I asked
him about it.

"If safety is what parents are after, they'd better keep their
kids home," he said dismissively. He picked up a wooden paddle,
walked over to his canoe, stepped into it, and kneeled down like
he was ready to push off from shore. "All of our attempts to keep
kids safe are creating the most worried, anxious, stressed-out
kids I've ever met. The only way to keep kids safe is to teach them
how to look after themselves. Those are survival skills." He
pointed back at the quote from the Talmud, hanging on the wall.
"We're all so safety conscious these days, yet no one's feeling any
safer. Camp's a place to learn how to take risks and confront difficulties, a place where kids can go wild, yet still be under our

wing." He smoothed his hands over the wood along the inside of the canoe. "Hey, man, do the math. When you add it up, the number of camp hours is greater than school hours, considering it's round the clock, weekends, too, especially if they stay for the whole summer. Think of the opportunity to impart some good values to our kids. Sure, there's fun, but we can do much more than keep them safe and entertained."

I liked Rudy and what he'd told me about the camp. The sight of that canoe was enticing to me, too. I could feel it luring me back in . . . to camp.

"Okay, I'll come, but on one condition."

"Shoot."

"I don't have to go to prayer services."

"Hey, no pressure, man," Rudy said, backing off, his hands up as he and Ringo walked me to the door. "Do your own thing."

"One last question," I said, just before leaving. "What about candy? What's your policy there?"

"Two tuck shop visits per week and lots of treats, but no candy or junk food from home. They don't need it and it attracts critters, especially bears. Camp Solomon is right in the heart of bear country." He said all that seriously but couldn't resist slipping back to his usual big, sunny grin.

11

SURVIVAL SKILLS

It was the summer of Crocs! It seemed like just about everyone had a pair of those stubby, rubber clogs that came in every colour of the rainbow. (To me, they looked more like toys than shoes.) Harry didn't want them but Max wanted a pair in every colour. He settled on two pairs – bright yellow ones that made him look like Donald Duck (at least he could be spotted all over camp) and turquoise ones that he promptly gave away to his new friend, Ryan, underneath him on the lower bunk.

No Crocs for me. This time I wasn't going to dress to fit in – and as it turned out I didn't need to. Camp Solomon fit me as easily and comfortably as a pair of Crocs. They say "three's the charm," and maybe it's true. At this camp, it didn't take me long to find my groove. One of the reasons was that here were people my own age to play with. They were adult staff, or "inclusion co-ordinators," who helped the special needs kids, as well as the ordinary needs ones, to cope with camp. There were also visiting rabbis, cantors, and educators, many of whom came with their young families. The babies in high chairs and toddlers running around outside the dining hall gave the place the feeling of family. I enjoyed having adult company and sitting together at our own table, and I think we lent a certain *gravitas* to the mealtime mayhem.

Like Max, I also made an instant new friend. Her name was Alice Gordon and she wore lavender Crocs. A public health nurse with two daughters at camp, she had also left her husband back in the city while she worked to cover the cost of camp for her children. Together with Louise Mandel (navy Crocs), the camp doctor, who came with her teenaged boys to camp, we were the health care team.

Not called the infirmary as at Camp Na-Gee-La, nor the Medical Centre as at Camp Carson, at Camp Solomon it was the Health Centre, or, as the kids called it, the Health Hut. The name itself gave it a positive spin. Nearby, Alice and I had our own quarters, clean, simple dorm rooms. It didn't take long to familiarize myself with the layout of Camp Solomon. Around the periphery, nestled in the woods, were the camper cabins, connected by paths that converged onto a main road that led to the central gathering spot, "the Tent," which provided shade, and with the flaps up, a breeze. The dining hall was a polygon-shaped building with windows on all sides that ran right up to the ceiling, providing a view of leafy green trees, a wide expanse of sky, and the clean, sparkling lake.

At this camp, morning pill call was handled differently than at Camp Carson. Campers were expected to come to *us* for their meds. The onus was on them and their counsellors to make sure they got their meds, rather than on us to track them down. They were good about coming and, perhaps because they wanted to get to breakfast, they usually arrived on time.

First to show up in the morning were two nine-year-old girls, Xiu-Ling Rosenberg and Frankie Colwin. Xiu-Ling was petite with long black hair, and Frankie was also small and wiry, pale with short brown hair, and glasses that magnified her eyes and always made her look startled.

Xiu-Ling noticed me reading her name. "It's *Zweeling*," she said helpfully. "I'm from China. My parents rescued me from being drowned by some village peasant, a.k.a. my biological father," she added cheerfully. "I have ADD and Tourette's but I'll let you know if I start ticcing 'cause I'll need the chewing gum my parents sent. It helps me." She took her friend's hand. "Frankie has ADD, too. Hey, what meds are you on this summer?" she asked Frankie, who told her. "I'm on the slow-release stuff now," Xiu-Ling boasted. "It has fewer side effects and stuff. Ask your parents to switch you over." They got their meds and walked out arm in arm.

Thirteen-year-old Sharon was in a bad mood. She had a headache and was annoyed to have to come to us for the medications she took at home independently. I explained that we had to keep meds locked up, but she was impatient and left as soon as she swallowed her pills.

We were just about to lock up when Bradley arrived at the last minute. He was on daily allergy pills but preferred to take matters into his own hands. "You may not see me from time to time," he cautioned as he slapped a baseball into his catcher's mitt over and over. *Thwack!* "I decide when to take my meds. Don't worry, I'm gifted, so I know what I'm doing." *Thwack! Thwack!*

"How will we know whether to expect you or not? Will you RSVP?" I asked.

"Oh, don't worry." *Thwack! Thwack!* He launched into the history of his allergies and all the signs and symptoms but we hurried him along so we could all get to breakfast. As we were leaving, we noticed that with all of his chattering, Bradley had forgotten to take his allergy pill, the one he had come for. "I'll take it to him," I said.

"No need. I have a feeling he'll be back." Alice pointed at the baseball he'd left behind on the counter.

When I entered the dining hall for breakfast, *camp* came back to me in a wave: the noise of hungry kids, their excited voices, the breakneck speed of eating, and the hilarious post-meal announcements. But at Camp Solomon, there was one difference. I learned not to dig in to my food as soon as I sat down but to wait until everyone arrived and recited a grace together before the meal.

After breakfast, the day's routine was also familiar. A morning clinic was held for anyone who had complaints of any sort. Most mornings, by the time Alice, Louise, and I strolled back to the Health Centre, coffee mugs still in hand, a small but vocal crowd had gathered. We handed out slips of paper for the kids to write down the reason they'd come and then decided in what order to treat them.

I went out to the waiting room. "Who's got the 'fly buzzing inside his skull?'"

A sleepy-looking boy closed his comic book and waved. "Yo. That'd be, uh, me."

I checked his ears and throat, took his temperature – Louise examined him, too – but since we couldn't find anything wrong, we offered him a fly swatter, which he declined, then sent him on his way.

Meanwhile, Alice had been busy with an anxious teenage girl who had a bump on her neck and who'd written "may have cancer." Alice put her arm around her and led her in for a thorough examination, then explained that the bump was a swollen lymph node. "They help your body fight infection," Alice reassured her. Next, she took the tall counsellor with "Big wart on foot. Been there for months" and taught him a slow-acting home-made treatment that involved duct tape. However, he chose to see Louise to get a prescription medication for a speedier remedy.

I took the boy who was "all stuffed up," and gave him a decongestant, nasal spray, and box of tissues, told him to wash his hands, and that he was good to go.

A boy who had "puked all night in cabin (throw-up tasted like dill-pickle potato chips)" was looking better, but I let him lie down for a rest.

Xiu-Ling and Frankie arrived. Xiu-Ling was crying and pointing at Frankie. "We were sitting in services and she hit me over the head with a prayerbook!"

Frankie looked pleased with herself. I examined Xiu-Ling's head and felt all over for swelling but found nothing. I placed an ice-pack on the sore spot. After a few minutes, I checked. "It's fine, now, Xiu-Ling."

"But there's a bump," she wailed, "and it hurts so much."

Alice and I looked at each other and tried not to smile. I placed the ice-pack back on for a few more minutes and returned to ask how she was doing.

"Bad. Very bad," she cried. She rubbed her head and glared at Frankie.

The morning crowd thinned out, but it picked up again as the kids starting coming for their lunch meds on their way to the dining hall. During a quiet moment Alice took the opportunity to search through the drawers for medication – anti-psychotics and behavioural drugs – that a fourteen-year-old boy named Eddie was supposed to be on. He hadn't shown up for his breakfast meds and now not for his lunchtime meds either. It wouldn't have mattered because she couldn't find the meds anywhere. Alice looked worried because already – it was only the first day of camp – we'd been hearing lots of buzz about Eddie and it wasn't good.

Seth, Eddie's counsellor, had been reporting to us that Eddie had been acting up, trash talking, and making racial slurs toward Sam, one of the other counsellors in that cabin, who was from Serbia. "Serbia is the skuzziest country in the world," Eddie had said to him. He'd been bullying a boy named Mitchell, calling him names, "pantsing" him (pulling down his pants) and threatening to give him a wedgie. He'd mocked a counsellor who had special needs, for his slow, careful way of talking. Alice called Eddie's parents to ask about the meds. His mother told her that Eddie's behaviour had improved so much lately that she and Eddie's father had agreed to let him go off his meds for camp. Alice looked worried when she got off the phone.

I continued handing out the lunchtime meds.

"Hi, I'm Chelsea." A tall girl with unruly blonde hair stepped forward, her hand outstretched for her pills. She talked at top speed and her loud voice was growing louder by the moment. "You'll be seeing a lot of me 'cause I'm on three-times-a-day meds – breakfast, lunch, and late afternoon, but not too late, otherwise, I won't sleep at night." She barely paused to take a breath. "You must be the new nurse. I heard there was a new one this summer. Hey, did you forget my name?" she practically shouted. "It's Chelsea and FYI I'm bi!"

"Biracial?" I asked. "Bilingual?" *Bisexual?*

"No, bipolar and I love it! I get mood swings." She leaned over the counter to read the menu posted on the bulletin board over our desk. "Oh, it's tacos for lunch!" She waved her hands up high over her head in jubilation. "Tacos are my most favourite food in the whole wide world!" She wrapped her arms around herself in a big hug. I couldn't help but wonder if and when Chelsea would dip down to the other end of the "pole." (And it didn't take long to find out. Only two days later, I saw her at the lake, sitting at the end of the dock, sobbing into her beach towel over a perceived slight – an unintended diss – from another camper. Luckily, her counsellor arrived on the scene and managed to coax her back to the group.)

Xiu-Ling and Frankie were soon back, for their lunchtime meds. They were giggling madly as they lined up with the other campers. Xiu-Ling had completely forgotten about her sore head but now complained about itchy bug bites. She scratched at her legs, showing me just how severe the situation was.

"I'm soooo itchy! I've got way more bites than Frankie."

"I hardly have any!" Frankie crowed.

"Why do I get covered and they don't come near you?"

"I guess the mosquitoes like me so they don't bite me."

"They like me better 'cause my blood is sweeter. Hey, I'm sweet, you're sour!"

On that first day of camp, right after lunch, I had gone to check on Daniel, the twelve-year-old with diabetes who was on an insulin pump. His care was complicated, so I asked to speak with his counsellor, and Tim stepped forward. He was a shy, serious-looking guy who listened carefully while I explained that every night at midnight Daniel was to be woken up for blood-sugar testing. If it was too high, the insulin rate would need to be increased; too low, and Daniel was to be given crackers and sugar cubes. If it was *very* low, he needed to bring Daniel immediately to the Health Centre. I described the early warning signs of hypoglycemia and how, in Daniel's case, it was very serious. Tim nodded but his quizzical expression worried me. We'd been counting on a counsellor to help with Daniel's condition and I wasn't sure about Tim.

"How will I know when it's midnight?" he asked slowly, thinking it through.

"You have a watch, don't you?"

"Yes, but . . ." He looked at it on his wrist. "I don't know how it works."

When I told Alice about this encounter, she explained that Tim was mentally challenged. He worked as an assistant counsellor, helping out in the cabin. Seth was Daniel's main counsellor and he would be responsible for helping Daniel manage his diabetes.

Oops! I was going to have to be a lot more sensitive. Someone with special needs didn't exactly walk around with a label, now, did they?

It was Alice's third year at Camp Solomon and I was envious of the friendly greetings she received from all the kids and how she knew not just their names and medical problems but their personalities and quirks, too. I'd never spent long enough at the other camps to have built up these relationships.

Alice and I spent the rest of that first afternoon going over charts. There was a handful of kids with chronic health issues: some were hidden, others were obvious and visible. Some problems were dormant with potential for flare-ups. There were kids who managed on their own and others who needed help from us. Sophie was a thirteen-year-old, born with spina bifida, a developmental birth defect that affected her ability to urinate. She had to catheterize herself and was prone to urinary tract infections. "We probably won't even see her," Alice told me. "Sophie is extremely private. She doesn't want the other girls in her cabin to know, only her counsellors. Don't even let on that *you* know." There was Beth, a CIT, who had been recently diagnosed with Crohn's disease.* Alice and I planned to check on her daily, assess her pain and symptoms, and give her medications. Drew was a teenager with a rare metabolic disorder that he'd had most of his life. He was on morning meds and needed once-a-day monitoring but otherwise was healthy and participated in all activities. Steven was a thirteen-year-old who used a wheelchair to get around. I had seen him motoring all over camp, accompanied by his attendant, Dave. Steven had an assortment of developmental delays and physical problems. Everyone seemed to know Steven as this was his third summer at camp. His mother insisted he be treated like all the others. "Please don't make him an object lesson," she'd written in a letter to us. "And when the kids act up and are disciplined, make sure he is, too."

---

* A type of inflammatory bowel disease characterized by bouts of painful abdominal cramping and bloody diarrhea.

We were still reviewing charts when Warren, a counsellor, suddenly rushed in with a frightened little boy in his arms. "Nathan can't breathe!" Nathan was gasping for air, chugging away at forty breaths a minute.* I jumped up and took out my stethoscope, but even before placing it on his chest I could hear how tight it was, full of high-pitched whistles and wheezes. There was very little air moving through his lungs and I knew his airways were likely constricted and inflamed. Alice grabbed an oxygen mask while I put a drug to open up his airways into a nebulizer, a device that aerosolized medication, and attached it to Nathan's face. We called for Dr. Louise to come immediately.

Nathan sat hunched over, working hard at breathing. Warren held his hand and Alice, Louise, and I stood by watching closely. When his treatment was finished, Nathan was breathing more easily but looked up at us with sad eyes. He seemed so alone in the world, even with all of us comforting him.

Alice showed Nathan how to use a small, hand-held inhaler for his medication. But he had difficulty managing that, so she switched him over to a different instrument called a spacer that was easier to use. Still, it was hard for him. It took all of his concentration and he squirmed, jiggled his stick legs, and twisted his feet around on the floor as he tried to master it. I sat down to read through his chart and quickly got a better understanding why all of this was so difficult. Nathan had serious developmental problems. In his chart, there was a sample of his handwriting. It was the barely legible scrawl of a child learning how to write but Nathan was twelve years old. He looked about eight.

He'd had an asthmatic attack like this at camp the previous summer but there were few details of his health the rest of the year. Alice filled me in on the horrific story of his early childhood. Nathan had been rescued from parents who had abused him, kept

---

* Around twenty per minute is normal.

him on a leash, and tied him to a chair. Two years ago he'd been placed with a loving foster family. He enjoyed coming to camp even though it wasn't easy for him to interact with other children and he was emotionally dependent on Warren – his counsellor last summer, too – who was completely devoted to him.

As they were about to leave, Nathan reached up to be carried. Tough, eighteen-year-old Warren wearing a black do-rag and multiple earrings slung him across his chest like a guitar and Nathan clung on. I said we wanted to check him again later but Nathan shook his head, no. He didn't want to come back.

"We want to prevent this from happening again," I explained, but as soon as I said that I could tell he didn't know what "prevent" meant.

As the days went on I got to know many campers well and a few parents, too, over the phone. Daniel's mother called every other day for an update on Daniel and for a report on his blood-sugar levels. There was anxiety in her voice and I tried to reassure her that her son was doing well and under Seth's close supervision. She frequently made minor adjustments to his diet or insulin regimen. Later, when I would convey these messages to Daniel, he would roll his eyes or look exasperated. "I like to stay on the down-low about my diabetes," he told me, only coming to the Health Centre if he had to change the site of his insulin needle or pick up his supplies. Usually, he came by himself, slipping in quietly so he wouldn't be noticed, but once, he brought a cabin mate with him. "I don't like needles," the friend said, giving an involuntary shudder as he watched Daniel give himself an injection of insulin into his abdomen. Daniel looked at me and I had a feeling we were thinking the same thing: He couldn't afford not to like needles. His life depended on them.

Every day after lunch was camp-wide rest time and everyone was supposed to be in their cabin, but sometimes I would find thirteen-year-old Dylan pacing around outside my door. "Can I help you?" I'd ask, but "No, I'm good," he'd say, and run off. I could tell he was trying to place me. I remembered very well where we'd met – the ICU where I worked – but decided to keep quiet about what might be a traumatic memory for him. I told him simply, "I'm here if you want to talk."

Mitchell was a more eager visitor who stopped by frequently with minor complaints or just to chat. He was thirteen, over-weight, and more at ease with grown-ups than with kids his own age. The Health Centre was a refuge for him. He came so often that we kidded him we were going to make him our mascot. Mitchell often looked sad so I asked him how things were going.

"Camp's awesome," he said with forced cheerfulness. "My cabin mates are cool, well, except for Eddie. No one likes Eddie." His face clouded over as he told me that Eddie picked on him, called him names like "fat-boy," "wuss," and "Mitchy Mouse," and said degrading things about his sister. Then Mitchell abruptly changed the topic and made disparaging jokes about his looks or his weight, such as he was so fat that when he got into the lake, the water level rose. "I've tried diets, but they never work," he said helplessly. He was worried about an upcoming canoe trip and if he'd be able to keep up, and what he'd do if he got hungry. On another occasion, he told me, "I'm starting to think I should go home." Mitchell settled into one of the couches and made himself comfortable. "I'm thinking maybe I won't stay for the whole summer." He said it like going home was an option, but we both knew his parents had signed him up until the end of August. "See, I hate the position I'm in. If I go home, I feel like a failure, but if I stay, I feel horrible. Camp isn't for me. There's no privacy and it's just go, go, go, all the time and, Eddie . . . well, he and I don't get along."

I felt a swell of affection for him. He enjoyed mountain biking and when I mentioned that, he visibly brightened. We talked about how Lance Armstrong had used his bike to conquer cancer and maybe he could do the same with his homesickness? Mitchell seemed to cheer up a bit with that idea and went off in a better mood, for now.

Another camper I was becoming fond of was Amy. She was a bright, creative twelve-year-old who had high-functioning autism. I'd seen her around camp, sometimes with her friends, other times standing alone, immersed in her own, very different world. Sometimes she'd stand and stare into the distance or peer down at the ground for a long time. Once I found her gazing into a single green leaf, chanting softly to herself, "back to leaves, back to leaves," over and over. Occasionally she came to us describing "weird sensations" in her body that bothered her. They usually went away on their own if we helped her take her mind off them.

Once her counsellor brought Amy in. "Amy didn't eat a thing at lunch," she said, looking worried, "well, only the parmesan cheese. That's all she put on her plate, a huge pile of parmesan cheese, but she just picked at that and kept rolling her eyes right back in her head, you know like this." She did a frighteningly good imitation. "It was freaking me right out – I mean, it was weird, even for you, Amy, no offence." She put her arm around Amy, which must have cued her to realize her counsellor was kidding, so after an awkward delay, she gave a little laugh.

Amy didn't usually volunteer much information, but that day, she did want to explain what was bothering her. "I was thinking about mud and when I think about mud, I can't eat." She gazed around the room, averting her eyes from us when she spoke. "I can only eat white foods and they can't touch each other." She spoke in chopped sentences and a monotone, saying each word in a sentence like it was on a list, every item of equal value. As if suddenly overcome with exhaustion, Amy moved over to the couch in her strange, floating way, stretched out and stared up at the ceiling, quietly describing its topography to herself. It was as if she had become the object of her rapt attention, just as I'd seen with the leaf, or another time with a handful of sand. Mud disturbed Amy greatly but she loved sand. I'd seen her sitting for hours on the beach running her fingers through the sand, chortling happily to herself. We decided to let her rest for the afternoon until she was ready to join her cabin again.

I was beginning to expand my notions of what to expect in a child; there were many different ways to be normal, and clearly there was a spectrum of normalcy. I enjoyed being at a camp that managed to accommodate a wide range of kids with a variety of abilities and to find ways to live and play together.

It was turning into a pleasant summer. Alice, Louise, and I worked well together and were a great team. Other than at meals, I didn't see much of Rudy, the camp director. He was either at the canoe docks with Ringo, his constant companion, or in his camp office, which was just as cluttered with equipment and repair jobs on the go as his city office had been.

Rudy was a quiet leader but he made his presence felt. I remember an incident in the dining hall. After each meal music was played, usually a pop or rock song, which was the signal to get up and clear the tables. As soon as the music started, the kids jumped to their feet and boogied around the room, returning dishes to the counter, scraping plates, and stacking the cups and cutlery. Then, once they were back in their seats, they launched into a longer after-the-meal prayer, this one accompanied by banging the tables, stomping their feet, clapping their hands, and making motions, each corresponding to a line of the prayer. It was fun to be in the midst of it all and I even found myself joining in from time to time. But one day, things got out of control. Kids were adding nonsense words and making rude gestures. Rudy got up and strode to the front of the room. When he spoke, his voice was so strong he didn't need to use the microphone.

"Stop!" he said sternly and silence fell. "This is a prayer, not merely a song. We're going to start over from the beginning. Pounding on the table is okay. Shouting is okay. Making noise is okay. But changing the words or making fun of it is not okay." Afterward, he kept the counsellors back. "Your kids are watching you. They take their cue from you," he reminded them. "If you show respect, they will, too."

It never happened again.

Most afternoons, Alice and I locked up and went for a walk along a trail in the woods, staying in touch with a walkie-talkie that one of us always carried. Alice was a true nature lover who appreciated the outdoors in a way I was still learning to. She was always looking around, seeing everything we encountered with a sense of wonder and delight, as if we had entered a museum full of exquisite and precious things. She showed me the delicate colours and intricate striations inside a strip of birchbark that had peeled off the tree. Once, she stopped me just in time from treading upon a large frog sitting on the path in front of us. It had huge, bulging eyes, a pulsating neck, and was so perfectly camouflaged I had almost missed it. Another time, she pointed out a bird that was chasing a persistent chipmunk away from its nest. "What chipmunk eats birds?" I asked.

"She's protecting her eggs," Alice explained.

"How do you see these things? I walk right past them."

"You're a city girl," Alice said with a chuckle.

You only see what you know. Kitch's words came back to me.

As we walked, Alice and I fell easily into intimate conversation as if we'd been friends for years. She told me about her marriage to a Jewish man and her conversion to Judaism. She hadn't converted at her husband's request nor to appease her in-laws but because she was sincerely drawn to the Jewish religion. She loved going to services at camp and felt the prayers and songs in a deeply spiritual way.

The daily services were held in an outdoor chapel in a clearing in the woods. I usually took that time to phone home to Ivan or to catch up with paperwork quietly in the Health Centre. But one day, when it wasn't in use, I went to the chapel by myself to take a closer look. Nestled in the forest, it consisted of a simple wood podium facing benches made of long, heavy logs, arranged in concentric half-circles. Interspersed among the benches were tall trees that provided shade and a canopy of leaves and branches. The blue lake could be seen through the trees. For a few minutes I sat by myself, enjoying the quiet and solitude that are usually so hard to find at camp.

Perhaps taking a few moments out of each day to express gratitude and to sit in quiet reflection did have a positive effect on all of us. Maybe it was, as Rudy had also suggested, that the presence of the special-needs children and staff brought out the best in the others. I think it also had something to do with Rudy himself. To Rudy, running a camp was a moral enterprise, not just a commercial business venture. The counsellors were a major influence, too. In many ways they were exactly like counsellors I'd met elsewhere – just as wild at night, just as mature or well-mannered, or *not*. However, counsellors here made an extra, concerted effort to ensure that each child was part of the group and no one was left out. These counsellors tried to be role models and leaders, not just babysitters or pals. On my first visit to a cabin, I saw a sign on the door, announcing, "Welcome to our crib!" Posted inside the door was a list of rules the kids had come up with under the direction of their counsellors:

1. Express yourself, but don't start drama.
2. Listen to one another.
3. Respect other people's space.
4. Don't touch anybody's stuff unless you ask first.
5. Stay clean (showers, flush toilets, etc.).
6. Tell someone if you are going somewhere.
7. No swearing unless absolutely necessary.
8. No violence or rude gestures like flipping the bird.

"Yeah, like that's all going to happen," I heard one kid say scornfully as I stood reading the list. I agreed those rules proba- bly weren't going to be followed to the letter, but putting them in writing seemed like a good place to start.

I saw other examples of counsellors leading the way.

A spider was spotted in the dining hall and after the initial screams died down, I heard a counsellor's calm voice. "Let's take it outside and put it back into nature. That's its home." They all trooped after her to help her set it free.

I liked the gentle, low-pressure swim test and the way the staff referred to the ones who "hadn't completed their swim test, *yet*," rather than saying they'd failed.

There seemed to be an unstated acceptance that not every child was sporty or good-looking or popular. At this camp, a child didn't need certain clothes, or to be "normal" or main- stream to fit in. Here, the attitude toward competition wasn't the sloppy love-fest of "everyone's a winner," nor was it awards and accolades only for the outstanding athletes. I saw kids who didn't get a lead role in the play or make a particular sports team and how their counsellors helped them roll with the punches. Here, there was simple, modest recognition for achievement and also for trying your best. The message was, you can be whatever kind of kid you are; you can find something at which to shine.

When we discovered that Jake, a fifteen-year-old, had a bad case of lice and told him he'd have to go home to be treated, he was so angry he punched a door with his fist. "Please don't make me leave. I'll shave my head," he pleaded. "I look forward to camp all year." But when he heard that his little sister Jenny had lice too, and saw her crestfallen face, he changed his tune. "Sure, I'll go home with you, Jennster," he said, then explained to me, "Our dad works a lot and he won't have time to take care of her hair." He put his arm around her. "Don't worry, Jenny-Benny, I'll pick out the nits."

As a parent, I'm lenient about bedtimes, negligent about homework, lackadaisical about unmade beds, junk food, and crumbs on the floor, but I'm a raging dictator when it comes to my kids being respectful, kind, and considerate. It's practically the only "rule" in our household. Somehow, this camp had created a culture where kindness was the expectation. It was even expressed in writing. On a wall of names of sponsors of the camp, I read the inscription under a photograph of the Solomon family patriarch, a twinkly-eyed, distinguished-looking man: "Be Good to Each Other."

And because I wasn't needed in the Health Centre all the time, I got out and met everyone. Rudy's daughter, Layla Schwartz, was the head tripper. She was studying environmental science at university and was exactly the kind of capable, take-charge person I'd want with me if I was out in the wilderness. *She'd get me home*, I thought. Layla referred to her specialty as "survival skills" and explained it to me. "It's learning how to find your way home when you're lost in foreign territory, tie the right knot to get the job done, build a secure shelter out of next to nothing, feed yourself with potatoes you roasted over the fire, and make do with what you've got." Layla knew a lot of useful information so I asked her about something I'd been wondering about. "What should I do if I'm in the forest and I see a bear?"

"Most important: don't make eye contact. Bears feel confronted when you look into their eyes," she said straightaway. "Get up on your tippy-toes to make yourself look as big as possible and spread your arms out. Also, make a lot of noise. Shout at it."

"What should I say?" I asked, giggling.

"Go away, you bad bear!" she answered, giggling along with me.

Layla had an assistant named Alon, a husky, muscular guy who had a gentle manner and was great with the kids, especially the ones who were nervous about going out on a canoe trip. For a first-year counsellor, it was considered an achievement to be a tripper, so he must have proven himself to have made the grade.

Another rising star was Matti, the head song-leader who was something of a camp celebrity. His irresistible music and charismatic personality attracted all ages.

Seth was a terrific counsellor who had his hands full that particular summer with a challenging cabin that included Daniel, the boy with diabetes, Mitchell, who was miserably homesick, and Eddie, who was causing a lot of trouble.

Even the rabbis added a lot of pizzazz to camp! Rabbi Emily came with her partner, Cynthia, and their baby daughter. The kids adored her – she was hip, into fitness, wore funky clothes, and had a sleek, chic haircut. Rabbi Danny played folk and blues guitar, knew hundreds of songs, and was an avid water-skier who helped many children get up on skis for the first time. The rabbis swam and canoed with the kids, played soccer with them, and even went out on canoe trips with them, sharing along the way lessons from the bible about respecting our environment.

As pleasant as that first summer at Camp Solomon was for me, there was a temporary blip of mild misery for a number of kids when an outbreak of upper respiratory infections started running through camp. They were getting colds and asthma flare-ups. You could see them everywhere you looked, sniffling into tissues and giving the familiar "salute," the upward rubbing of a dripping nose with open hand. Seasonal allergic rhinitis, also called hay fever, was in full bloom, too, with lots of sneezing, itchy, runny noses, and red eyes. Many kids were started on allergy meds, puffers, and antibiotics for secondary infections. We were going through lots of boxes of tissues, cough medicine, and throat lozenges and serving up plenty of hot broth, lemon tea with honey, and sympathy. "We need more portable sink stations for handwashing," we told Rudy. The bottles of alcohol hand-sanitizers were useful, but proper handwashing with soap and water was the best way to prevent infections. We discussed ways the kids could take better care of themselves. One thing we did was set up a do-it-yourself first-aid station outside the Health Hut and encouraged them to help themselves to Band-Aids, disinfectant, and ice packs so they could treat themselves.

But there was no doubt about it, the Health Centre had become a social hub. At times it was a real hangout, and not just for sick kids. Someone passing by during evening pill call would swear a party was going on in there – and sometimes, there was! First, the Flames, the youngest campers, arrived for their meds, still flushed and excited from their evening activity and looking nowhere near ready to settle down for bed. Soon after they left, the Pioneers and Builders arrived, also high-spirited and wound-up. Lastly the CITs came for their pills and stayed on to amuse us with crazy antics. A bunch of the boys who'd complained about a mysterious ailment they called "crotch rot" started a nightly ritual to treat it. They passed around a bottle of medicated powder and gave themselves a light sprinkling down their pants without even missing a beat in the conversation. Others came to show off their special talents. One CIT girl turned off the lights, aimed the examining-table light toward the wall, and made a rooster, a cobra, and an alligator appear on the wall with hand shadows. Another CIT was a Rubik's cube expert. Someone would jumble it up and after a mere glance at the cube he'd put it behind his back and solve the puzzle, without even looking.

By the time the CITs cleared out, the counsellors started dropping by. "Hey, let's go visit the nurses," I'd hear someone say outside the window. "Yeah, chill time with the nurses!" Seth always came in to see us. "What's poppin', Nurse Tilda?" He'd flash us a smile and put an arm around Alice and me. "Just checkin' up on you two troublemakers."

Alice and I would put out snacks like licorice sticks or popcorn. Matti and other song-leaders would bring their guitars and jam right there in the waiting room of the Health Centre, filling the place with music. They all sat around telling stories of the fun and funny things that happened that day.

"I love being a counsellor," one girl said, "but I had no idea it would be this hard. It's my first job and I feel so stressed. I never have any time to myself."

The others agreed and then shared the sweet moments they'd had with their kids.

"I piggybacked this kid around all day because he had a sore foot and when I put him down, he gave me this big hug and said, 'you're the best counsellor ever!' Like, wow, that rocked my world."

"We played basketball against another camp and they played dirty, but our kids didn't retaliate. I was proud of them and I want to find a way to reward them."

At times they needed to debrief or talk through sticky situations they weren't sure how to handle. They often wanted to run something by us, or get our take on a situation, such as when Bonnie, a first-year counsellor of a cabin of twelve-year-olds, said, "I don't know what to do about my girls. They talk about sex all day!" She looked more bemused than truly exasperated.

"Well, as long as they're just talking," I joked.

"Yeah, I guess, but they're sooo boy crazy. One girl had a boyfriend and told me they broke up last night. Twelve is way too young for that, but she was crying about it today like it was a major tragedy. Puuhhh-lease . . . I didn't know what to say to her."

"I know what you mean," another said. "The other night my girls were talking about blow jobs and if you should swallow or not! One of the girls said, 'Only if you really like the guy.' Can you believe this? It's unreal! I think they know more than me!"

"If they're not talking about sex, they're talking about their weight," Bonnie said. "One asked me if I thought she was fat. Well, she *is* a bit chubby, but I didn't tell her that, of course. What's the right thing to say?"

"My girls are still so innocent," said a counsellor of the youngest campers, the Flames. "I came into the cabin and found them trying on my bras. It was so cute."

They discussed the children as if they were their own, worried about the homesick ones, and pooled advice on how to break up a clique or deal with a bully. They shared tips on everything from how to get the kids to settle down at night to what to do if they felt a child might have an eating disorder.

Throughout the evenings, counsellors came and went, joining in the discussions, or sometimes just sitting around, listening in. I often looked over at Dave, Steven's attendant, who didn't say much but always seemed part of the conversations. I thought about the work he did with Steven, who couldn't walk and who got around in a wheelchair. Dave helped him shower, fed him, took him to the bathroom. He was doing a job not many would choose but he did it happily, even made it seem appealing. I thought of one day when Steven was upset. The hustle and bustle in the dining hall was too much for him and he felt overwhelmed. Dave had just brought him there but Steven wanted to turn right around and return to his cabin to get away from the noise. Dave felt Steven should be a part of the group and not exclude himself. Steven begged to leave but Dave sat with him, discussing it calmly. Together they came up with a plan. I knew that Dave could have easily exerted his will over Steven or given in out of pity, but instead he negotiated with him, one on one, as equals. It reminded me of times in the hospital when I'd imposed my will on my patients, insisting, for example that they walk farther after surgery than they felt they could or shooing visitors out of my patient's room if I felt that rest was more important than socializing. I believed I was in a position to know what was best for them, but it's an aspect of my role that I've never been comfortable with. I admired Dave's equanimity in handling a similar situation with Steven.

"Typical teenager," Dave said. "He's gotta rebel, but I'm not going to butt heads with him or dominate him. Anyway, he's a great kid," he said as if that was the reason Steven commanded his respect. "Steven's really into sports," he often told me, always emphasizing his strengths, not his disabilities. They did share a love of sports, even though Steven's participation involved watching games and memorizing stats, rather than actually playing.

Those late evenings, "just chillin'" with the counsellors, gave me a window into their world. They were on the front lines, day in, day out – and throughout the nights, too. They faced many of the same challenges that parents, even nurses, face.

One way they coped with the stress of their work was to let loose on their days off. They talked openly about those wild times in the local town, even tales of drinking, drugs, and sex, feeling no need to hide it from us. Rudy must have known the score because one day, early on in the summer, he took them aside to offer a friendly cautionary message, just before a group set out for a twenty-four-hour break.

"I know you work hard," Rudy had said in his relaxed, but authoritative way, "and I want you to enjoy your day off, but if you are somewhere, anywhere, at any time, and are drinking, call me and I'll come and get you – no questions asked."

They listened to him and I hoped they'd take it to heart.

And while they claimed that sex was on their campers' minds, it was definitely on theirs, too. Some nights, they let their guard down and opened up about their own love lives. One girl explained the particular challenges of a relationship with someone at camp. "I slept with him on our day off," she said about her boyfriend, "and then it was so weird seeing him afterward every day at camp and having to work with him."

"Everyone knows who everyone is sleeping with," they all told me, complaining about the lack of privacy, then eagerly telling me who was hooked up. But often, sex wasn't the most personal or revealing topic. When they dropped down deeper and spoke of their passion for music or extreme sports like wakeboarding and mountain climbing, their attachment to their tattoos and the meaning and messages embodied in those images, or their hopes and dreams for the future, I felt they were letting me in to their true selves.

Sometimes they worried about "life after camp" and how they were going to "make it big" or what they were going to do with the "rest of their lives," by which I soon realized they meant their twenties. Many had sincere aspirations to do "something to make the world a better place" but weren't sure exactly what. I didn't try to offer any answers to their questions or solutions, but simply listened, enjoyed their company, and treasured the connection I had with them.

As we headed into the third, and my final, week of camp, things were going well. Daniel, with Seth's supervision, was keeping his blood-sugar levels stable. The respiratory bug had run its course and most children were healthy again. Mitchell continued to show up for daily visits and to complain about Eddie. "He picks on me because I'm overweight," Mitchell said, but I wondered what would happen if Mitchell stood up for himself or gave it back to him. It was always Seth, or a cabin mate, who came to Mitchell's rescue.

There was no doubt about it – camp worked kids hard. The days were long and filled with strenuous activities. *A day at camp is like a week anywhere else*, Alice and I often said to each other. *So much happens at camp.* I'd seen this phenomenon before: by week three, the kids – and their counsellors, too – were completely rundown and worn-out. Sometimes, when children complained of a headache, or of vaguely "not feeling well," and when there was no real "diagnosis," I would lead them to a bed, cover them lightly with a sheet, and by the time I walked to the door to leave, they were fast asleep. All they needed was a break from the heat and noise and a chance to regroup. Invariably, when they awoke from the "treatment," they were refreshed and "cured."

One day a week there was a break from all that intensity. It started on Friday afternoon with preparations for the Jewish Sabbath. The frenzy of activities began to wind down. It became quiet, and as evening fell, we all gathered at the Tent. Everyone was scrubbed clean and shining, wearing their best clothes, many of the girls in skirts or dresses, some wearing jewellery and makeup. Perhaps the change in atmosphere and clothes put them on their best behaviour. As the sun set over the lake, everyone walked together to the dining hall from which wafted the aroma of freshly baked, braided bread. Candles were lit, blessings sung, and then we sat down at tables spread with white cloths and individually set places, not the usual rack of cutlery and stack of plates. A sprig of flowers was on each table and there was an exceptionally tasty meal of soup, roast chicken, vegetables, and dessert.

Afterward, the song-leaders set up their electric guitars, key-boards, and drums at the front of the room and placed ampli-fiers around the periphery. In no time, the dining hall was transformed into a dance hall and the entire camp burst forth into song and dance. With their arms entwined, all ages mixed, they moved together in a giant, coiling conga line that went around and around the room. They danced so hard, the floor-boards shook. They sang so loudly, the beat vibrated in my chest. With flushed faces and glistening bodies, they danced and sang into the night.

Saturday mornings were for sleeping in, except for the youngest kids who got up early and scampered around, generally left to their own devices. After breakfast there was a service that involved stories, skits, songs, and prayers that the kids wrote themselves. At lunch, siblings could sit together and Max invited Ryan – who still wore his turquoise Crocs – and Harry invited Becky, his friend from school, to join us, since they didn't have siblings at camp. Becky was a gorgeous girl, with a mane of dark, curly hair, and always a huge smile. She and I laughed about her camp hair, which was wild and free, versus her city hair, which she straightened and kept perfectly coiffed. After lunch, kids attended their choice of relaxing interest groups, such as yoga, music appreciation, meditation, drumming, cloud-watching, or nature walks.

As peaceful as camp was on those days, there was one time it didn't end like that. One Saturday night, as I lingered a few moments, enjoying the campfire, I saw Seth go over to add more kindling to the fire. At the same moment, Eddie got up, too. Something about his expression made me wary, but unfortunately I didn't act soon enough to stop what happened next. Eddie held a can of insect spray in his hand and aimed the spray right into the flame where Seth was kneeling. Instantly, the flames roared up, ignited by the combustible spray, and flared straight onto Seth's face, burning his arms and face and singeing off his eyebrows and eyelashes. I rushed them both to the Health Centre and kept Eddie under my supervision while Louise treated Seth.

"Hey, I didn't know that would happen," Eddie protested, putting his feet up on the desk and lacing his hands behind his head. "I had no idea."

Rudy called Eddie's parents. His behaviour was dangerous and we couldn't keep him at camp, he told them, but they begged for him to stay, promising they'd send his behavioural medications the next day by courier. Rudy said no, but he later relented at Seth's request. Despite the pain from his burns, and the anger he must have felt at Eddie's prank, Seth persuaded Rudy to give him another chance. "I'll make sure that kid straightens out and flies right," Seth promised Rudy. "There's something about him . . ."

"You like a challenge, don't you, man?" Rudy looked at him in disbelief.

I have to admit, I was skeptical that Seth could make Eddie improve his behaviour and surprised that Rudy had been swayed. As for Eddie, he didn't even want to be there.

"I hope they send me home," he said. "Camp sucks. I hate how they're always shoving religion down our throats. I'm an atheist."

My heart sunk. I'd just been warming up to it, myself. But what worried me more was that Eddie seemed to feel no remorse. He sat there, scowling and unrepentant. He made me angry, but

I kept my cool and went to check on Seth. When I came back, I saw that Eddie had gone into his chart and read Louise's note recommending he restart his medications. Eddie jumped out of the chair and began enacting a furious monologue, sneering and spitting in fury.

"Thanks, Mom, thanks, Dad, for putting me on meds that have ruined my life and made me the zombie I am today! It was always so important to you that I sit still and get good grades. It's easier to put me on Ritalin, isn't it? So fuck you! If you expect me to take that shit, it's not going to happen. This place is a fucking Nazi concentration camp!" He stormed out the door, unzipped his pants, and urinated on the door of the Health Centre, yelling out obscenities as he ran off. Seth started to go after him but I held him back.

I wondered if Eddie would ever agree to go back on his meds and privately, I was glad I wouldn't have to deal with this problem. My shift at camp was almost over. I was already think- ing of home and the amenities awaiting me there, comforts that, come to think of it, I hadn't missed this summer nearly as much as I had in the past. But the night before I left camp that summer, something happened that put all other problems into their proper perspective. We were working late when Layla came in with Alon, her assistant tripper. "It's nothing," I heard him say out on the porch. But when he walked in and we saw the scatter- ing of bruises on his arms and legs and noted his pale complex- ion, we knew right away that he was seriously ill. A few days later, at a clinic in Toronto, the diagnosis was confirmed: leukemia. Alon's life was put on hold as he faced chemotherapy, radiation, and an uncertain future.

The next morning, Alice and I reported to the nurses who were taking over from us. As I packed up my car, campers and counsellors came to say goodbye and give us hugs. One of them, Bradley, the boy who was never without his catcher's mitt, came

over to ask me, "You comin' back next summer?" We were standing in the sun and he shielded his face and squinted up at me.

"I'd like to," I said, unable at that moment to be more enthusiastic. I was preoccupied with the shocking news about Alon
and I couldn't think about next year. Bradley didn't know about
any of that and had no such ambivalence.

"I sure hope so," he said, waving goodbye. "Well, see you
then!" He stepped out of the sunlight and onto the shaded path
toward his cabin.

I was all ready to leave, but my kids hung back, crouched in
a huddle with their friends – Max with Ryan and Harry with
Becky, her dark curls covering her face – as they worked on
some problem with a pencil and paper. At last, Becky got up
and shouted out the answer. "Only 341 more days until camp
starts again!"

12

SEX TALK IN THE TENT

Of course I went back the next summer. I had finally experienced camp's magic and was hooked. I was a happy camper, now!

The evening before the first day – the campers would be arriving the next morning – Rudy gathered us in the staff lounge for a meeting. The counsellors sat on the floor and Alice, Louise, and I were on folding chairs at the back. First, he welcomed everyone back and shared his excitement about making this summer the best, ever. He ended his remarks with a word of advice. "Whatever your experience was with a child last year, good or bad, forget it. Give each kid the benefit of a fresh start. Everyone changes."

He didn't name names but Alice and I looked at each other and mouthed "Eddie." We'd heard he was returning and couldn't believe it. After the terrible incident with Seth, and Eddie's ongoing obnoxious behaviour and refusal to go back on his meds, he was sent home, but not before he stole money from the camp office, destroyed someone's radio, and defecated on Rudy's cabin doorstep. Despite all of that, his parents had managed to convince Rudy to take him back, albeit on a trial basis. One incident of bad behaviour, Rudy warned them, and Eddie would be sent home.

I looked around the room. It was nice to see familiar faces and to be one, myself. I saw CITs who had graduated to being counsellors, and last year's counsellors who had been promoted to unit heads or specialists in areas such as water-skiing or swimming. There were a few CITs who had been rowdy and had pulled some crazy stunts last summer who were now back as counsellors. Alice and I wondered how they'd managed to prove to Rudy that they'd turned themselves around. How had they demonstrated that they had the leadership potential he said he was looking for?

"It takes more than a pulse to land a job at Camp Sol," Rudy always said. "You have to have the right stuff."

But at that staff meeting, they did seem to have settled down. They listened quietly as Rudy spoke. One was even embarrassed when he was reminded of his past shenanigans and insisted he no longer be called his old, tough nickname, Bones, the moniker of some cartoon villain. Now, he'd be going by his real name: Eugene. "I have to set a good example for the kids," he said.

Looking around that staff lounge, I saw my favourite counsellor, Seth. Rudy's daughter Layla was back, as was Matti, the charismatic song-leader, softly strumming his guitar (it was irresistible to him) while Rudy spoke. Rudy told us about Alon who was still undergoing treatment. His family members were being tested to see if one of them was a match for a bone marrow transplant, a procedure that offered a chance of a cure. He wasn't well enough to come back to camp any time soon.

Well, the kids might have changed, but not Alice and me – not one bit. We fell right back into our summer friendship and easy partnership.

After the staff meeting, Alice, Louise, and I had a powwow with the senior counsellors to plan strategies to keep everyone healthy. We prepared first-aid kits and placed them in each cabin and reminded the counsellors about the do-it-yourself first-aid station, which campers and counsellors could use to treat anything itchy, sore, swollen, or bruised without having to wait for us. We taught them how to handle emergencies until we could get there. We discussed ways to reduce the incidence of infections and the consequent use of prescription medications, which had been so high the previous summer, the main ways being handwashing and good hygiene.

"One sneeze sends thousands of droplets into the air," Louise told them in a scary voice. "Touch a slimy nose, then touch someone without washing your hands, and – bingo! – infection."

Perhaps a small dose of fear – or at least vigilance – is a good thing when it comes to preventing infections. Well, it certainly got camp off to a healthy start.

When the kids arrived the next day, I quickly discovered that Rudy was absolutely right about how much children can change in a year. Some of them who had been on several meds were now on fewer, or lower doses. In many cases, their medical conditions had stabilized or improved. The most noticeable changes were in the teenagers.

Daniel was back. "Yo!" he called out to us as he dropped off a trunk of equipment for his insulin pump.

"How's it going?" I asked.

"I'm good," was all he said, eager to beat it out of there. "Expect lots of calls from my mom. She's still pretty hyper," he said as he joined his group.

He was more confident dealing with his condition, so much so that he didn't even want Seth checking and reminding him about his blood-sugar testing. If his mother called to make a change in his diet or the rate on his insulin pump, he'd say, "Yeah, yeah, I'll get on to it," and walk away. A year older now, he was going to be more of a challenge to keep a close watch while still allowing him his independence.

Another teenager who seemed to have made a change – more like a complete *transformation*, from hellion to angel – was Eddie. He looked pretty much the same, still small and thin, wearing glasses this year and multiple earrings. However, what *was* different was his smile, the reliable way he showed up each morning for his meds, and his good manners. Seth had asked to be his counsellor again, eager to reinforce the strides Eddie had made. I often saw Seth point at his eyes, then at Eddie's, and back to his own, to remind Eddie he was keeping tabs on him.

Sharon continued to suffer frequent severe headaches. She still felt frustrated to have to come to us for medication she took by herself at home. Since she was a year older now and very responsible, and to practise our philosophy of encouraging children to be more self-sufficient, we decided to let her keep a small amount of medication with her in the cabin to take as she needed. Sharon was pleased with the new plan.

I saw Sophie's chart, so I knew she was back, but I'd never actually met her. Now fourteen years old, she was the camper with spina bifida who catheterized herself throughout the day to remove urine from her bladder. She was managing well and still very private about her condition.

Bradley, who still had his baseball and catcher's mitt with him wherever he went, and who still took his meds at his "own discretion," came in and gave me a big welcoming hug. "I knew you'd show," he said. He was sweet, and thankfully had stopped his annoying habit of reminding us that he was "gifted."

Mitchell seemed pleased to be back. He kept up his role of cabin clown and still always made himself the butt of his own jokes.

I saw Amy around camp, either with her cabin mates or by herself, standing and staring at objects. Not as fixated on sand as she was last year, this summer she was fascinated with weather, particularly clouds, which she watched for hours and could describe in great detail. The most dramatic change about Amy was her looks. Her hair was now long and lustrous and her body had become curvaceous. Without even being aware of it,

Amy had blossomed into an attractive, even sexy, young woman.

Xiu-Ling and Frankie were back.

"I don't want to be in the same cabin with her!" Xiu-Ling said loudly, for all at pill call to hear. "All she wants to do is sit around all day and read. She's no fun."

"But you wrote on the form you wanted me to be in your cabin," Frankie whined. She turned to me. "She keeps dropping stuff from the upper bunk onto me. On purpose."

"By accident!" Xiu-Ling insisted.

"On purpose!" Frankie pouted.

"You're such a baby and you're so insensitive!" Xiu-Ling yelled at her.

"Yes, but . . . you're so . . ." Frankie stammered, trying to come up with a comeback. "You're so *sensitive*!"

"Ha!" was all Xiu-Ling said. She came over to whisper to me. "Between you and me, Frankie could use a higher dose of her meds."

I smiled at her and joined Alice who was handing out pills and welcoming new and returning campers.

Nathan was back. Much healthier this summer, he no longer needed to cling to his counsellor Warren; he now came by himself or with a friend every morning to take his inhalers and a daily pill to control his asthma.

Dylan, too, was back this summer. Now fourteen, he still occasionally paced outside my room and looked me over curiously. When I approached, he dashed off. I wasn't sure if he'd placed me yet. Two years ago, his father had died in the ICU and I had been his nurse. I remembered his horrible, painful death from liver cancer and the way his mother had fought so hard to save him, right up until her husband's last breath. When we did decide to stop treatment, because it was futile and of no benefit, she was furious. In the end, Dylan's father's death had not been a peaceful one. Seeing me must have brought back a flood of painful memories for him, but I wasn't sure he was ready to face them. I had decided to wait for a signal from him.

Alice and I kept up our daily walks. Conversation was just as easy between us, though sometimes we were simply quiet, enjoying that peaceful time in the early morning before the kids were up and the mosquitoes buzzed, before it got hot and we got busy in the clinic. We usually saw no one other than the occasional early-morning jogging rabbi or eager-beaver CIT who was into fitness. Sometimes we sat on the dock, enjoying the stillness of the lake, and watched the darting water striders on its surface. Alice taught me to identify hemlock, spruce, fir, and pine trees and laughed when I told her I'd always thought they were *all* Christmas trees! She pointed out a woodpecker poised at the side of a tree, a cedar waxwing eating red berries, and once, a regal blue heron. She caught sight of a family of minks with their silky, black fur and long tails, but I wasn't quick enough to see them before they scurried away into a cave of rocks near the lake.

One afternoon, a few days after camp started, Alice and I were just returning from a walk when a crowd ran up to tell us that Mitchell had been injured. We ran to the Health Centre where Louise was examining him. The first clue to what had happened was Eddie. He was in the waiting room with a big smirk on his face, sitting beside Seth who was steaming mad, but mostly upset at himself for not preventing the incident. "He sucker-punched Mitch," Seth said, "for no reason whatsoever."

"There *was* a reason." Eddie put his feet up on a table and Seth shoved them back off. "Mitchy Mouse was being his usual dorky self and he pissed me off, like he does everyday, but this time I'd had enough and thought, *You're going down.* So I tanked that dumb-ass kid right into next week."

I gauged the situation: Eddie's build was short and scrawny and Mitchell was hefty and solid. How much damage could Eddie have caused? But before Alice and I had a chance to hear from Louise about Mitchell's injury, Rudy came in and spoke sternly to Eddie. "Pack your things, young man. You're going home. I've called your parents and they're coming to get you." This time he made no mention of second chances, zero tolerance, or the golden rule.

"Whatever," Eddie muttered, as if he didn't care, but when he got on the phone and spoke to his parents he sounded more indignant than indifferent. "I didn't do anything," he told his father. "I have no idea why these people are on my case. They're insane. They must be on crack. The other kid's a truck. He's way bigger than me."

"You just lied to your parents," I pointed out when he got off the phone.

"Yup. I lie all the time. They say they *trust* me. Hah! Big mistake." He picked up a bottle of cough syrup from the counter. "Hey, this is the stuff they use to make crystal meth. I think I'll steal it." He made as if to pocket it before putting it back.

I tried to make conversation to pass the time until his parents arrived. "Do you have brothers or sisters?" I started off on what I hoped would be a safe subject.

"Yeah, an older brother, but he's the good one. My mother says he's going to turn out okay and I'm going to land up in jail!"

"Was there anything you liked doing at camp?" I was still trying to make pleasantries.

"Yeah," he grinned devilishly, "jerking off in the forest."

How's that working for you? I wanted to retort like Dr. Phil. I was infuriated at him but still felt the need to say something therapeutic and nurse-like. I could only come up with, "Eddie, you seem unhappy. Would you like to get help for your problems?"

"Oh, they sent me to a therapist but he was an idiot. I lied to him. I didn't tell him one true thing, only lies. My mother thought he was helping me deal with my issues. What a joke! There was no way I was going to tell that guy anything personal. The problem is my fucking family. They are totally out of touch with reality. Hey, they *are* a fucking reality show."

So much bravado, but anyone could see he was hurting. Yet, try as hard as I could to be non-judgmental, I couldn't hide my disapproval.

"I suppose you want me to de-fuck my language?" he asked, grinning.

I let out a sigh of exasperation. "Eddie, your language is the least of your problems."

Soon – but not soon enough – Eddie's parents arrived, apologetic and embarrassed. They were about to rush off, but Rudy took them aside.

"Eddie has serious psychological problems," Rudy said. "There is something terribly wrong with his behaviour. He needs help."

"Oh, don't worry, he's getting help," the father said, ready to leave.

"Whatever help he's getting is not enough." Rudy held fast, wanting to make sure his message got through. "He needs more. His behaviour is abnormal and totally unacceptable. He is violent and dangerous. We cannot give him the help he needs at this camp, but we wish him well."

The parents hurried off with Eddie in tow. Only Seth came to say goodbye.

"I didn't see it coming, so I wasn't ready," Mitchell chattered nervously. He sat up on the examining table grimacing with every movement. "I got the wind knocked out of me." He clutched at his side and breathed shallowly. I gave him a painkiller and took his vital signs. Despite his discomfort, he kept up the patter. "If

I'd been ready, I could've taken the hit like a man, but hey, that's the story of my life, I never see it coming." I listened to his chest with my stethoscope and heard air moving equally in both lungs. His colour was good so he was probably getting enough oxygen, but still, I felt uneasy. Mitchell wanted to return to his cabin, which was a good sign, so we let him go. He was enjoying the attention and was given a welcoming cheer by his cabin mates, to which he gleefully responded.

"Hey, guys, did you know Harry Houdini died from a punch in the stomach?" he announced. "Maybe that'll happen to me, too!"

After pill call that evening, I went to Mitchell's cabin to check on him. He was still wincing in pain. I took his vital signs and listened to his chest. This time I detected a slight decrease in air entry on his injured side, but his colour was good and vital signs stable. He might have fractured a rib, which could have punctured his lung, causing a leak. It could heal on its own but it could also get worse, drastically. Louise agreed and drove him to the hospital late that night, where they diagnosed a small pneumothorax, which meant there was an area of his lungs that had deflated and wasn't receiving oxygen. The doctor felt the "pneumo" would heal on its own without requiring a chest tube to reinflate his lung but did admit him to the hospital for close observation. Louise and Alice congratulated me for my good call and I have to admit, I felt proud of my well-honed skills.

Two days later Mitchell returned to camp. He was well enough to re-join his cabin but wanted to stay in the Health Centre and we let him. Most of the day, he lay in bed, reluctant to walk around. He asked if we could bring in a television and kidded that he'd probably get bed sores from lying around so much. We served him noodle soups and chilled fruit juices. Seth and the cabin visited every day, bringing him treats and even Muffin, a rabbit from the nature area (and at nighttime, Mabel, the nocturnal hedgehog, who was awake and eager to play).

Mitchell was enjoying our room service and being an invalid, but he was healthy now, and after a couple of days it was time to kick him out.

It's like that in the hospital, too, I thought. We nurses always say that when our patients start playing with the buttons on the electric bed to put it into different positions or complaining about the mattress, the food, or the "service," it's time to discharge them. It may seem harsh, but the whole point is to get better and go home, isn't it?

"Why don't you take a walk to the nature area and put Muffin back in his cage?" I suggested. "You have to start moving," I reminded him, but he complained that he was still in pain and too tired.

"Don't you want to get back on the bike? Remember how it made you feel better last summer?" We talked again about Lance Armstrong but Mitchell wasn't as inspired.

Try and help yourself, I wanted to tell him.

The next day Mitchell returned to his cabin but withdrew from his friends. He left swim class or sailing, even low-key arts and crafts, to visit us, each time coming up with some tiny or implausible ailment. He began to talk about going home.

"My parents say if I come home I'll spend the summer vegging out on the couch and gain more weight."

"Is that a possibility?"

He nodded and hung his head, guilty as charged. I put my arm around him as we walked back to his cabin.

"It's weird 'cause each year I think I'm going to like camp, and I'm, like, excited – well, excited-slash-nervous – but as soon as I get here, I can't handle it. I make the best of it on the outside, but on the inside I'm sad." He brightened. "The best part was the hospital. Now, *that* was cool."

A day or two later, Mitchell did go home. His parents came and thanked us for all we'd done. They were very loving toward their son but obviously disappointed. "We thought he'd at least make it through the first week," the father said to Rudy.

"I wouldn't worry," he said. "Camp isn't the right place for every child at all times. Let's try again next year."

Occasionally I put aside my resistance and went to prayer services. Alice was always there and the counsellors, too, sitting with their campers, setting a good example. I had to ask myself, what message was I sending by not attending? *It's good for you, but not for me. You need this but I don't.* Once I got there, I realized it was pleasant to be together with the rest of the camp, and the music was fabulous. Once, a visiting rabbi played the accordion. After a few guffaws at what everyone assumed would be a corny instrument, we all got into it, moving to the cool, old-world swing sound. Another day, the song-leaders sang prayers set to U2 melodies and one to Bob Marley's "Redemption Song." The children provided a lot of entertainment, too, reading aloud prayers and poems they'd written expressing gratitude for nature, friends, family, and camp itself. Some of their thoughts were touching and a few hilarious with the odd flub or blooper.

Alice always saved me a spot on the bench beside her but I preferred to stand at the side or the back of the outdoor chapel. There was a tree that had a deep cleft running down it right to the exposed roots and I liked to lean in there against the trunk. From that vantage point, I could look out at everyone and check out who had the sniffles or was coughing and who looked homesick. I watched Xiu-Ling and Frankie and tried to figure out if they were holding hands as best friends or scowling as mortal enemies. I double-checked that the brakes were locked on Steven's wheelchair because Dave often parked it on a slope. Once, I noticed a little boy squirming in a certain way that was very familiar to me. The bathroom was a far distance, so I led him into the woods nearby and found him a private spot. "Do you enjoy services?" I asked as we made our way back.

"No, but it's better than going to synagogue at home. How can I ever go back to that boring place?" he asked. "Even my dad falls asleep."

No, these services were not boring. They were relaxing, thought-provoking, and joyful. Even talking about God didn't seem as much of a stretch of the imagination, out in nature, in this beautiful setting.

"We each understand God in our separate ways," Rabbi Emily said one day.

"I don't know if I believe in God," a young boy spoke up, "but at camp, I feel God."

"Where's God?" one kid joked. "Beats me! Let's have a scavenger hunt for God."

"If ever you're looking for God," said Rabbi Emily, "you can always touch your pulse and say, Oh, there you are." She gave time for that idea to sink in. "Or, take a deep breath. That's God moving through you."

Sometimes Amy contributed to the discussion. One sunny day, she sat up and said flatly, "It's not raining today."

Rabbi Emily nodded. "Yes, Amy, go on."

"The sky is the colour of God."

One morning during services, as I stood off to the side, watching over everyone, my eye caught a movement in the trees surrounding the chapel. Then it stopped. It was big and black. A branch shifted. Leaves rustled. It was a bear, just a few steps away! I was the only one who saw it because of where I stood, facing the woods. I had to act fast to save the camp! I was panicking, but I tried to recall Layla's advice. Was it "Make a racket! Jump up and scream!" or "Keep quiet and stare him down"? My mind raced madly for a few moments until my ICU training kicked in. I became calm and rational and knew exactly what to do. I got up,

walked to the front, and whispered into Matti's ear. "Cut short
the silent meditation and go straight into the music." I mentioned a particularly loud number. I bent down and cranked up
the amplifier a few notches and cued Matti. Sure enough, as
everyone burst into song, the bear startled, turned around, and
lumbered off in the opposite direction. My scheme worked!
Goldilocks had fended off the big, bad bear! I ran to tell Rudy
but he wasn't the least bit concerned.

"Hey, man, you scared off Yogi Bear! He visits us every year.
He's never been a problem. Well, once he broke into the kitchen
and made off with a few loaves of bread."

He'd been more upset when the kids messed with the mealtime blessing!

"So, you're not worried about a bear at camp?"

"No, now that you're on top of it." He chuckled. "We can all
rest easy."

It was a swelteringly hot day – we had the air conditioner roaring
full blast and kids were dropping by all day to "chill," and, considering the temperature, we took that *literally* – when a counsellor came by with a special request. Could we have a "sex talk"
with two of her fifteen-year-old girls? A rumour was going
around that they'd been in a boys' cabin and gone too far.

For this matter, I deferred to Alice and Louise. As a public
health nurse and a physician, respectively, Alice and Louise were
experienced in counselling patients about sexuality. (Needless to
say, the topic didn't often come up with my critically ill patients
in the ICU.) However, Alice insisted I join the discussion. "We're
a team," she reminded me.

That afternoon, during after-lunch rest period, we met in the
Tent. Jasmine and Lee, two teenaged girls in halter tops, skimpy
bikini bottoms, and flip-flops, showed up with sour scowls on

their pretty faces. They'd been wrongly accused and misunderstood, they said. Now, they felt, everyone was against them and their reputations ruined, all because of vicious gossip.

"Why don't you start by telling us what happened?" Alice suggested.

"It was during the Carnival and we were shaving whipped cream off a balloon without popping it," Lee said.

"Don't forget the greased watermelon relay race," Jasmine added.

"Yeah, right, we got all messy and so we went into the boys' cabin – it was the closest one – to clean ourselves off, but we didn't take showers there. See, that's the rumour, that we took our clothes off. The whole thing has gotten completely out of hand and it's soooo embarrassing! We swear, nothing happened!"

Jasmine nodded her head in vehement agreement. "They're saying we took off our tops. There's no way we did that! We're just friends with those guys," said Lee, "*not* friends with benefits. We're not skanks! Everyone's talking about us and spreading lies. One girl said we were stripping for the guys and doing lap dances. How would she know? She wasn't even there. I thought we were friends! Well, forget that!" She flounced in her seat and looked away.

"Oh, you're all against us, too, I can tell," Jasmine chimed in. She was on the verge of tears. "This whole thing has been blown out of proportion. Are you going to call our parents?"

Louise spoke first. "You were asking for trouble. You put yourselves at risk by going into the boys' cabin by yourselves, and besides, it's against camp rules." She launched into the results of a study published in a medical journal that stated that 62 per cent of fourteen-year-old girls said they wished they'd waited until they were older to have sex.

"But we didn't do anything!" Lee wailed.

Louise switched gears and lightened up. "Did you ever stop and think maybe you were getting into more than you bargained for by going into the boys' cabin?"

Or, maybe exactly what we bargained for, their smiles at one another seemed to say. On the one hand they'd enjoyed themselves, but now they weren't so sure about this new bad-girl rep they were developing. *How confusing it is to be a young woman today with so many mixed messages out there!*

Next, Alice spoke. "You may be causing things to happen sooner than you are ready," she cautioned in her gentle way. "You have to know if you're ready for this." She spoke about her own daughters and her wishes for them to respect themselves and to wait until they were ready for intimate relations with the right person at the right time.

It was my turn and I wanted to contribute something useful. Louise had been the authoritative professional and Alice, the protective, concerned parent. Then there was me, who remembered all too well what it was like to feel those desires. It didn't seem so long ago that I'd done some pretty wild things myself, so it felt hypocritical to come down on them. Besides, I wanted to be the kind of grown-up who didn't stand in judgment, and who could help them sort out these complicated matters, but I wasn't sure how to do that. I'd read enough of those how-to-communicate-with-your-teenager books to know that offering advice was the worse thing. It only made them shut down, lose trust, and worse of all, it cut off the lines of communication. As a nurse, I've always been taught not to offer my personal opinion. We're supposed to merely echo back, in a neutral way, our patients' points of view and not influence them with our own values. However, here at camp, where I was both a parent figure and their nurse, that approach felt counter-intuitive. No, they didn't need judgment or information – "411" as they called it – but I wasn't sure what they *did* need.

"We're here, if you need to talk," was all I offered in the end. After they left, we congratulated ourselves.

"They really listened to us," Louise said.

"We kept the lines of communication open," Alice murmured.

"I guess we did a pretty good job," I said.

But later, as we walked to the dining hall for dinner, we happened to fall in behind Jasmine and Lee and overheard them talking to their friends.

"So, we had this major sex convo with the doctor and the nurses," Lee was saying to her friends, "and it was *soooo* ridonkulous!"

"*Soooo* lame," Jasmine squealed.

But how bad could it have been? The very next day they came back. I was working by myself when the two of them showed up. Jasmine was still pouting but Lee came at me in her assertive way. "We want to know what you really think. I mean, like, so what if we were making out with them? Is that so bad?"

If I said the wrong thing, they'd blow me off and I'd lose them altogether. *What to say? What to say?* I looked at their low-cut jeans and bare midriffs, their breasts spilling out of their skinny tank tops. *Okay, here goes.* "You both are very attractive —" I started.

"Are you saying we brought it on ourselves?" Lee snapped. "We have the right to dress however we like. It's a free country. This isn't Iraq, you know. We're not sluts."

"We didn't do anything wrong," Jasmine said, looking tearful.

"I didn't say you did," I countered.

"So, I take it you're saying, we should wait, before, ahh, doing anything more?"

"You're not ready for more," I said firmly. "Why not wait until you are?" I said the thing I'd want another parent to say to my own kids in this situation.

"I knew you'd say that," Lee folded her arms across her chest. "Talking to you is like talking to my mother. She always freaks out, too. C'mon, Jaz, we're done here."

I'd said nothing, but already I could feel those precious lines of communication shutting down.

"I sound like a seal," I heard a girl say.

I was in the midst of giving out the evening meds when I heard a strange sound. It was coming from Naomi, an always-smiling, very popular fourteen-year-old who'd never come to the Health Centre for anything before but was now sitting in the waiting room, surrounded by a group of friends while she had fits of coughing. In between bouts of a high-pitched, insistent, squeaky coughing spell, she joked around and giggled. If this had been the ICU and a patient suddenly started coughing like that, I would have placed an oximeter on her finger (an instrument we used to measure a patient's oxygen concentration). Had she been a patient in the ICU, the sudden onset of a harsh cough like this would have garnered her a stat chest X-ray and maybe even a bronchoscopy, which involved a tube placed down into her trachea and lungs, but here, that wasn't necessary – at least not yet. Even without an oximeter, just looking at Naomi's rosy complexion and relaxed manner, I was fairly certain her oxygenation was normal.

I went out into the waiting room. Her friends were joking around with her, making her laugh. "This is not a party," I said, ushering them out.

"I can't breathe!" Naomi said, waving goodbye to her friends. I brought her into the examining room and listened to her chest and heard adequate and equal air entry on both sides, but she was breathing rapidly. "I can't swallow and my chest hurts." Her hands shook. "Is this a heart attack?" Off and on she gave that strange-sounding cough.

"No," I reassured her. "Probably your chest is sore from coughing so much."

Louise examined her thoroughly and then we went aside to speak privately. "I think it's a panic attack," she said. "You were right to throw out the friends. We want to make sure there's no acting up for an audience's attention. For now, let's try giving her a small dose of sedation."

I gave Naomi a tiny pill under her tongue and let that take effect. After about twenty minutes, we checked on her. She'd fallen asleep, and while she slept there was no cough, shakiness, or fast breathing. She must have sensed we were standing at the foot of her bed because she startled awake. As soon as she did, the cough and rapid breathing started up again. "I feel like I'm going to pass out," she yelled. I stopped in my tracks. *Someone about to pass out does not have the strength to yell. Someone about to lose consciousness is too weak to speak.*

"My heart is racing," she said, trembling. "It's flip-flopping all around!" Her hands shook violently. She clutched at her chest and took big gulps of air. "I can't breathe."

Her strange cough seemed to be gone but her pulse was racing at 120 beats[*] per minute and her respiratory rate was also fast at forty-five breaths a minute. I gave her a paper bag to breathe into, to try to retain the carbon dioxide she was losing by hyperventilating.

"My chest hurts," she cried. "I'm going to pass out." Before we could deal with one problem, Naomi had moved on to the next. "The room is spinning. I'm going to faint!" she shouted. I took her blood pressure and it was a robust and normal 132 over 80.

Someone about to faint would have low blood pressure, I thought.

---

[*] A normal, resting pulse is 60 to 80 beats per minute.

"I feel like I'm losing control of myself," Naomi said. But her words sounded false like she was repeating lines she'd learned.

"I'm sure it must feel that way," I said quietly. I felt sympathy for her because I could see she genuinely felt upset.

"My feet are numb! They're tingling. I can't feel my feet. They're paralyzed." She suddenly closed her eyes and lay there motionless.

"Naomi? Look at me! Open your eyes," I told her, feeling slightly alarmed.

"I think I just blacked out there for a moment," she said weakly.

But she hadn't lost consciousness. She had been awake and, I was fairly confident, completely aware of everything she was doing. None of this was adding up. I found myself in the situation I've always hated: suspecting a patient was "faking it." It was an especially uncomfortable feeling to doubt a child. I knew Louise was also looking for something deeper by her line of questioning.

"Is something bothering you, Naomi? Are you homesick?"

Naomi looked at her fiercely. "I love camp. I've never been homesick, not even for a minute."

"Because, if you are," Louise continued, "that can bring on these kinds of feelings and they can be really scary when you're away from home and missing your family."

"I live for camp." She turned away from us.

Louise and I spoke privately. "I can't find anything wrong," Louise said. "I think it's pure anxiety and nothing physically abnormal, especially since her memory is intact and she can describe her symptoms perfectly . . ." Louise's voice trailed off and I caught her drift: after a true faint, a patient can't recall events immediately prior to losing consciousness. "Let's give her another dose of sedation and watch her closely. If she worsens we'll take her to the hospital," she said, and went to call Naomi's parents.

Just then, Naomi's brother Lorne, an older camper, arrived. He rushed over to her, sat at the edge of her bed, scooped her up into his arms and held her tight. As she clung to him, their two heads of dark, curly hair mixed together like a huge, luxurious wig. He soon left to let her sleep. Naomi would stay overnight in the Health Centre. Alice was on call so I said good night.

The next morning, Alice told me it had been a quiet night. Naomi had slept and was now smiling and making light of what had happened, even apologizing for worrying us. She was dressed and eager to return to her cabin. Louise examined her and cleared her to return to her cabin. We wrote it off as a weird, inexplicable one-off episode and since she was now well and happy again, we didn't give it another thought.

I always looked forward to Saturday lunch because it was family day and I could sit with my kids.

"Where's Max?" Harry asked as he joined me. He wasn't too happy about it but grudgingly agreed to this one meal a week with me and his brother. Max soon appeared, triumphantly bearing a dripping, overflowing bowl of Greek salad he'd scored for me, because he knew I didn't have the patience to stand in the long line for this popular item, even though it's one of my favourite foods.

My kids were growing up. Their maturity brought many such delightful acts of independent thoughtfulness but it also meant they were pulling away from me and each one becoming his own person. *They grow up so fast*, I thought, and camp makes it seem even faster. It was exactly what was supposed to happen, but it was bittersweet, just the same. It was a reminder that I was getting older, too, and that they needed me less, or perhaps in a different way. Harry, especially, guarded his privacy, and now shared so little with me. Impulsively one day, I'd pumped his counsellor, prying for some insider details. He was reluctant to be an informant but eventually caved and dished.

"Harry is quite an instigator," his counsellor said with obvious pride. "He led a raid on a girls' cabin last night but took his punishment like a man."

"I guess he's coming out of his shell."

"What shell? He's the noisiest kid in the cabin. Oh, and by the way, he's quite the chick magnet. A few of the girls are majorly crushing on him."

Whoa, back off, I told myself, now uncomfortable knowing information I'd asked to know. Harry would definitely not want me hearing this. I was beginning to see why it might not be such a wonderful thing to have your mom at camp.

Late one evening a few days later, I was sitting in my room reading, when a buzz and crackle came over the walkie. "Is the nurse there?" a counsellor's voice cried out. "Someone's having a seizure!"

As I ran to the cabin, I remembered Amanda and that terrifying trip to the hospital in the thunderstorm with Wheels a few summers ago. She'd had a cerebral bleed – a mild stroke – and I prayed this wasn't going to be anything serious like that. When I got there I found Naomi, lying stiffly on the floor beside her bed, her friends and counsellors around her. I knelt down beside her. "Where are you?" I asked. Her eyes were open and I could tell she saw me but she didn't answer. This wasn't a seizure, but something was definitely wrong. "What's your name?" I asked her.

"It's Naomi," someone said. I explained I needed Naomi to answer for herself, because I was testing her level of consciousness, to see how her brain was working.

"What made you think she was having a seizure?" I asked the counsellor.

"That's what Naomi told me."

But from what the counsellor described of what she herself had witnessed, Naomi hadn't had convulsions. She was not now in a typical post-seizure state. We brought her to the Health Centre where she immediately began to flail about and breathe rapidly. Again, I gave her a paper bag to breathe into and coached her to slow down. I worried that her hyperventilation could cause her to pass out and might lead to a drop in her carbon dioxide levels so severe that it would disrupt the acid-base balance, or the "Ph," of her blood chemistry. Calcium levels would then be affected, leading to tremors and spasms, a state called tetany. I had seen the condition of "metabolic alkalosis" in my critically ill patients but never in a healthy person.

Again, Lorne, her brother, rushed in. "Naomi! Are you okay?" She stared at him blankly. "Naomi, you're going to be okay," he told her. He turned to Louise. "Is my sister okay?"

"My neck hurts," Naomi mumbled. Louise and I looked at each other grimly. Sudden neck pain was a classic indicator of meningitis, a highly infectious, deadly disease.

"Naomi, touch your chin to your chest," Louise asked her. She couldn't. It was highly unlikely she had meningitis – there were no other signs and she'd probably received the vaccine – but just in case, we closed all the doors and put on masks and gloves to protect ourselves. If it did turn out to be bacterial, or meningococcal, meningitis, it would be life-threatening for her and dangerous for us, as well as everyone at camp who'd come anywhere near her. Anyone exposed to her would have to go on antibiotics.

Naomi's counsellor went with her in the ambulance and I followed in my car. In the ER Naomi had a CT scan to examine her brain and a lumbar puncture, which involved putting a needle into her spinal column, to obtain fluid to test for meningitis. When these tests were done I went in to visit her. She was now fully conscious, sitting up, giggling, and playing a finger game called Chopsticks with her counsellor. It was as if nothing had happened. Again, she apologized for causing us worry.

I knew all the dire things that still had to be ruled out: seizure, a cerebral bleed, a serious disease, or a tumour. The ER doctor decided to keep her overnight for close monitoring and more tests. Her counsellor slept beside her in a chair, her head resting on the bed, while I headed back to camp. I had to get some sleep or I'd be utterly useless to anyone, much less myself.

13

SABBATH CHAOS

By the time I got back to camp from the hospital, it was morning. I could see Xiu-Ling, Frankie, and Nathan, along with the rest of the kids, making their way down from the cabins for pill call. One girl had beat them to it and was already there, anxiously waiting. I knew her name was Sarah but she didn't take meds and wasn't one of our "regulars." When she saw me, she ran over. "I *have* to talk to you!" I unlocked the door and she followed in, close on my heels. "I just got my period. What a nightmare! I can't believe this is happening. My mother said I probably wouldn't get it until I turned thirteen but I'm twelve so I didn't bring anything with me."

"Congratulations!" I gave a big, cheery smile to offer a warm welcome to womanhood.

"I'm so not ready for this," she moaned. "Why couldn't I just have pneumonia?"

I gave her some supplies in a brown paper bag. She waited while I finished pill call then walked with me to the dining hall for breakfast. "Do you think anyone can tell?" she asked, looking around self-consciously. "I never thought I would get it before my bat mitzvah. When does menopause start?" she asked wearily before joining up with her cabin.

After breakfast, Alice let her call her parents to tell them the news. Her cabin was planning a party complete with a red cake, and Rabbi Emily offered to take her for some private time, just the two of them, together. Sarah was very pleased with all the attention, and was it my imagination or did she now carry herself a bit more confidently?

Alice and I sat for a few minutes over coffee before starting the morning clinic. "You should have woken me," she said when I told her about the emergency with Naomi and my long night with her in the hospital. "I could have helped you. I can't believe I didn't even hear the ambulance. I slept right through it."

"That's nurse sleep for you," I said and we shared a laugh about that. I've slept through a lot of things, myself. After most night shifts working in the ICU, my entire next day would be lost to sleep. There have been days when sunlight streamed through my bedroom window, the TV blared, and my kids played game after game of mini-sticks hockey right there on the floor beside me, but I slept through it all. (Once, Ivan ran the vacuum cleaner around the bed. I only knew by the carpet marks.) Yet, when I was on call at camp, even a soft tap on the door would wake me up and I'd spring into action. As for nights when I wasn't on call, I slept soundly, just as Alice had done.

Problem was, we were both getting tired. It was only the first week of camp, which was usually quiet, but already there had been Mitchell's injury, his high-maintenance convalescence, and Naomi's baffling emergency – not to mention the late-night after-hour schmooze sessions with the counsellors, which were way too much fun to turn away – and it was all taking its toll on both of us. Now, it was Friday and things would slow down and hopefully we'd get a breather. (Mostly, I didn't even notice what day of the week it was until Friday night arrived and the Sabbath celebrations began. It gave shape to the week and reminded us of time itself. Oh, for sure, pills had to be given at certain times and clinic hours were set by the clock, but at camp, I was aware not just of clock time, but of natural time, too. I'd seen the sun rise and the sun set. I noticed the phases of the moon. In the city, I rarely paid attention to such things.)

The next morning I couldn't come up with a single compelling excuse to not go to services, so I went. It was a hot day. The lake was still and only a gentle breeze rustled the leaves in the trees. There had been no further sightings of Yogi Bear but I stayed off to the side, on guard duty – and also so I could sneak away if I wanted to. By eleven o'clock, sitting in the outdoor chapel in our good clothes, we were sweating. I'm sure everyone wanted to jump in the lake to cool off. I tried to hang in there because, eventually, there'd be cake. After the closing song, they passed around slices of delicious yellow pound cake, which I'd only heard about but hadn't actually tasted because I'd never stayed to the end. I sat for a few more minutes and then slipped off, anticipating a mid-morning snooze. But as I neared my cabin, I saw a swarm of people gathered outside on the lawn of the Health Centre.

"It's closed!" I yelled out to them. "You guys are supposed to be in services!" I said as I arrived upon a scene of utter bedlam. (Luckily, no one turned the tables on me to say, *What about you?*) Three girls were stretched out, writhing on the grass, clutching at their chests, spluttering, coughing, and gagging. A friend told me what happened.

"Tammy was sitting in services, minding her own business, and she swallowed a feather that fell off a bird! Zoe thinks she might have inhaled one, too, and just the thought of it is making Paige freak out – and can you check me, too?"

A few other "emergencies" had gathered. A little girl waved a splinter-ravaged thumb at me, begging for immediate attention. A pale, skinny girl stood patiently, but with a desperate look on her face. She gave a little wave and mouthed the words, "I don't feel well." There was Dylan, pacing around as usual, but this time not running off when he saw me. "I need to talk to you," he said urgently. Sarah, the girl who'd gotten her period, pulled me aside to whisper frantically, "I can't get the tampon out! It's stuck in there!"

I unlocked the Health Centre and they followed me in.

"I'm seeing double," cried Tammy, the feather-traumatized girl, spluttering and coughing. She and her friends were also coughing and very flushed. It *was* a hot day. Could it be sun stroke? But all three of them at the same time made that iffy. I was pretty sure this gaggle of gagging girls was okay, but they were adding to the overall chaos so I sent them off to lie down and told them I'd be with them shortly.

Just then, Daniel sauntered in. His insulin needle had fallen out of his abdomen and he had to re-insert it into his arm, but his hands were dirty and he refused to wash them. He was rude to Seth who came in to help. Was this ordinary teenage crankiness or a sign of a dip in his blood sugar? In Daniel's case, even slight hypoglycemia could quickly lead to a medical emergency. "Please check your blood sugar," I told him.

"Yeah, yeah, I'll get to it," he snapped at me.

"I need to know the results," I said when I saw he wasn't doing as I asked.

"Daniel, just do it," Seth said, wearily.

Alice and Louise were still at services and hadn't taken their walkies so I couldn't call them, but I knew they'd come afterward. *You can handle this*, I told myself. Out of the corner of my eye, I noticed a boy standing off to the side who had a stream of bright red blood shooting out of his nose. *Now, this is an emergency!* I ran for an ice pack, slapped it in place, and applied pressure. As the flow settled to a steady drip on the floor, I took a few minutes to assess the situation. There was a lot of commotion but nothing I couldn't handle on my own – for now. As usual, the urgent and the trivial were all mixed up. But since there wasn't anything truly serious, a part of me just wanted to gather up all their achy, needy selves into my arms, then go and put on the kettle for a cup of tea for me and a round of instant noodle soup for them. I sat there, looking at their miserable faces, taking comfort in the old ICU nurse dictum: *If the patient is breathing, the rest is gravy.* I took a deep breath and thought it through: Bleeding took priority over anxiety, but anxiety trumped a splinter and also a tampon lost in outer (inner?) space. As for the skinny, distraught girl, the sad little boy, and all the others vying for my attention, I would get to them as soon as possible. "Sit down," I told the boy with the nosebleed.

"It tastes gross."

"Lean your head forward so the blood won't drip down the back of your throat," I told him. "I wish I had some cocaine," I muttered to myself.

That got his attention. "Cocaine?" he asked. "No shit! Are you a user?"

There was no time to explain that in the hospital ER they kept a small vial of cocaine that was used to constrict the tiny arteries deep inside the nasal passages. "You'll have to go to the hospital if we can't get the bleeding under control."

"Can I have the cocaine instead?"

I went to check on the three feather girls. They were stretched out on the beds, out cold. *Once again, the magic sleep treatment cures all.*

Someone tapped me on the shoulder. I twirled around. It was the pale, worried girl. "What's wrong?" I asked, immediately regretting my abruptness. She had been waiting so patiently. *It's easy to overlook a quiet one!*

"I don't feel well."

I put my hand on her forehead. She had a fever and it was a high one. I had even more reason to apologize for my irritability when I realized who she was. It was Sophie. Catheterizing herself made her prone to urinary tract infections and fever was a sure sign of one. "I'm sorry. You *are* sick." I showed her to a bed and covered her with blankets because she was now shivering with chills.

Back in the waiting room, I was given a note from the little boy who was sitting curled up on one of the easy chairs, his legs slung over the arm, his nose deep into a comic book. It had been passed hand to hand around the crowded room, until this message in teeny-tiny letters reached me:

I'm depressed. I want to go home.

This needed time and attention, but just then Xiu-Ling and Frankie arrived, which made me glance at my watch. I thought it must be lunchtime pill call, but it was too early for that. Xiu-Ling was ticcing furiously. Her eyes were blinking, she was stamping her feet, clearing her throat, spitting on the ground, and shouting swear words. Frankie stood staring at her, stunned at this shocking scene, her eyes wide behind her large glasses. "Why is she doing that?" she asked, but there was no time to explain. I handed Xiu-Ling a package of chewing gum she'd told me helped when this happened. I had talked to her parents and they'd told me just to wait it out, it would run its course.

In the midst of all this chaos, Alice and Louise arrived, saw what was happening, and got straight to work. Alice obtained a urine specimen from Sophie to send to the lab and Louise started her on antibiotics "empirically," meaning without proof of infection, but knowing the high probability in her case. Next, Alice peeked in on the three copycat girls, still sleeping off their feather trauma. Louise took the sad boy into her office to talk to him. Alice checked on Daniel, whose blood sugar was normal and who had rejigged his insulin device, while I finished up removing the splinter and then returned to the nosebleeder. "Stop checking to see if it's still bleeding," I said. "No! Not you, Sarah!" I said, seeing her shocked face. "I didn't mean you!" Alice took

Sarah into the bathroom to help with the retrieval of the lost tampon. Just then Amy appeared and said in her stiff and stilted way, "I can't stop thinking about my vulva."

"Your what?"

She leaned toward me and stared at my hair. "I'm thinking about my, you know, my va-jay-jay. I'm having . . . *sensations* . . . down there."

No, not now! No sensations now! It was likely sexual feelings that were unfamiliar to her and that she didn't understand, but this was not the time for conversation about such delicate things.

"My vagina is talking to me."

I desperately wanted to know what it could possibly be saying, but I held back from asking just to satisfy my curiosity. Luckily, I recalled that her mother told me that if she got "sensations," we should offer her Vaseline. "Tell her it's medicine," the mother had advised. I've never liked the ruse of a placebo but I was under pressure. "Here's your medicine, Amy," I told her uneasily. "Put it on, say, three times a day?"

She nodded, went into the bathroom, and then outside to sit on the porch.

Meanwhile, a counsellor came for the little boy who'd written the note. He'd walked out of Louise's office feeling better. "Can I borrow this book?" he asked.

"How will you return it if you go home?"

"Oh, I'm not going home," he said, smiling up at his counsellor.

I went to check on Amy who was now lying on the grass, motionless, staring up at the clouds. She sat up. "Can you get sick from an animal if you don't touch it or come anywhere near it?" She stared at my nose as she spoke.

I reassured her that no, she couldn't. "Are you feeling better, now?"

"Yes, I am feeling sunny, but cloudy, too."

Well, at least those *sensations* had subsided.

Louise, Alice, and I stayed in the clinic, working right through lunch. Each of us had seen this phenomenon before: a sudden, inexplicable surge in accidents, injuries, and general neediness, all at once. I've worked shifts in the ICU where the whole team was going flat out, full throttle, and in the midst of it all, we'd get word that the wards were crazy-busy, too, and that the ER was busting out. At some point, someone would chalk it up to a full moon. We'd shake our heads, laugh, and get back to work.

Dylan came forward now that things had calmed down. I motioned to Alice and Louise and they waved back to indicate they'd manage without me. I walked with Dylan down to the lake and we sat on the dock. In moments it all spilled out.

"You were my dad's nurse, weren't you? It finally hit me! You were with him when he died. I was trying to figure out where I'd seen you and it all came back to me."

"What do you remember?"

"The machines! It was like we were in the cockpit of a plane – all those dials and screens and stuff. I kept thinking he was the pilot and we were going down. My mom kept saying he was getting better but anyone could see he was a goner."

He had many questions and they rushed out all at once.

"My dad didn't squeeze my hand. If he heard me why didn't he give me a sign?

"He was so cold! When you put that warmed-up blanket on him that made him feel good.

"He was breathing weird. It was like he was choking, but was he almost dead by then or just right out of it because of the drugs?

"What drug was he on? Was he like in some la-la-land or was that a coma? Was it the drug that did him in at the end?"

I had no difficulty answering these questions even though it was over two years ago. I have an ability – most nurses do – to recall each patient's death, along with many of the specific details.

"Your dad probably heard you but was too weak to squeeze your hand. As you know, he had the tube in his mouth, so he couldn't speak to you . . . When a person is dying, the organs shut down and the blood moves to the body's core. That's why your father's body was cool and I put the warm blanket on him, to keep him comfortable . . . That gasping or choking sound is the normal breathing pattern of a dying person . . . The drug was morphine and I gave the doses I judged to be sufficient to keep him painfree and comfortable but not more than that, which might have speeded up his death."

I had a hunch about the question he really wanted to ask. "Dylan, are you wondering if your dad knew you were there with him?"

Dylan nodded. "Yeah, kinda. What do you think?"

"No one knows for sure but I always talk to my patients, even when they are unconscious or dying, even though I don't expect an answer. I believe your dad heard your voice and felt your presence, and then he was gone."

Dylan thought this over before he spoke. "At first, his death didn't affect me much. I was okay with it, but my mom and sister took it hard. My mom had a total breakdown. She can't handle it when I go away, but I need my space and camp is the only place I can get it."

I sat listening and looking out across the lake as he spoke. I wanted him to feel at ease, that he could take all the time he needed to share what was on his mind.

"I did everything to make my dad proud of me, and then he ended up in the cancer ward with needles and tubes stuck in him, and then in the ICU attached to monster machines." Dylan shook his head in disgust. "But, hey, I'm good now. I'm dealing. I have an awesome therapist. He says I can still have a relationship with my dad even though he's dead. It sounds unreal, doesn't it?"

"It makes sense to me."

"All I have to do is play his favourite song and it's like he's right there with me."

"What was your dad's song?"

"It's called 'Stairway to Heaven.' Have you heard of it?"

You had to ask, didn't you?

"Well, I'd better get back." He stood up to go. "My cabin's going kite-flying even though there's not much of a breeze." He felt the air with his hand. "Wouldn't it be great to be a kite?"

Naomi was still in the hospital. She was not coming back to camp. Her parents drove from their home in Montreal to be with her. Her doctors still couldn't come up with a diagnosis but she was feeling better and kept apologizing for "causing such a fuss and making everyone worry."

"It's bizarre," Louise said, "but I've seen this syndrome before. It's called *la belle indifference*. It's rare and occurs mostly in adolescent girls, usually well-adjusted, high-achievers like Naomi who have everything going for them. It usually starts with anxiety but quickly spirals out of control, as we saw."

"In between attacks, she was perfectly fine," I said, "even laughing about it."

Louise nodded. "Patients with this syndrome typically make light of their symptoms. The other feature is that each event occurs in front of witnesses and if they fall, they manage to protect themselves, so there's rarely an injury."

"What are her parents like?" Alice asked Louise, who had met them when she'd gone to visit Naomi in the hospital.

"Absolutely lovely. Beside themselves with worry, of course. There was also a younger brother and an older sister and they seemed to be a very close and caring family."

"So, it's hard to understand why . . ." said Alice, her voice trailing off.

We backed off and let it go. We knew and accepted the fact that there weren't always answers. Some medical mysteries never get solved. Many things get better on their own, without our doing, or understanding, anything.

Sex was on my mind. I'd been thinking a lot about it ever since the infamous talk in the Tent. I asked Alice, "Camp is a very sexual place, don't you think?"

"No, not sexual," she said, "but *intimate*, I would say."

It was a true and important distinction. Counsellors engaged in lots of friendly hugging and playful touching, but "not in a sexual way," as they pointedly, jokingly reassured us, among themselves and with their kids. Campers often walked hand in hand or with their arms entwined; counsellors held or carried their children and gave lots of hugs and pats on the back. Teen-agers were in the process of growing aware of themselves as sexual beings. Everywhere you looked, you could see them blossoming right before your eyes. There was no doubt about it: sexuality was in the air. And there was something else charging up the atmosphere at camp. It was particularly special because it's something you don't see often these days and it was a pleasant thing to be around: affection, even, at times, *romance*.

Many evenings when I walked past the dimly lit staff lounge, where the counsellors played ping-pong and listened to music, I would see some couples standing off to the side or lounging on the couches, their arms around each other. I'd seen them go off to the woods, hand in hand. Late at night they shared details of their relationships, and when they got beyond the posturing and braggadocio about the hot and heavy hook-ups and the devastating breakups, they opened up and shared their real feelings – their longings, their desire for intimacy, and their disappointments, too.

Recognizing camp as an ideal place to discuss these matters that were on everyone's minds, Rabbi Emily formed a girls-only group and invited Alice and me to join a session. (A male rabbi was planning a boys' group and then a co-ed one, too.) Rabbi Emily started off by explaining that the purpose of the group was for them to explore not just their *feelings* but also their beliefs and values. She called the group "Sacred Choices," a term which at first elicited derisive eye-rolling and groans. They might not have regarded these choices as sacred but I do think most considered them important. Perhaps "choices" was also part of her message. Rabbi Emily was the perfect person to lead this group because the girls liked and respected her. She was young and cool, spoke their language, and knew many of them personally from a yoga class she took with them at camp. She started off the first group by stating it would be an "open discussion about how we make the moral choices that define us."

You don't get that in sex ed class! I thought.

She assured them they could say or ask anything and it would be confidential. It would be a safe space to talk openly and honestly. They took her at her word and didn't hold back. At the first session, Lee announced she had a new boyfriend.

"Yup, and he's here at camp! Last night I had my first kiss!"

"Wow! Your first kiss ever?" someone asked.

"Well, no." *Get real*, her eyes said. "My first kiss with him."

"Is it true love?" one girl asked.

"Maybe," she said with a smile. "He may be the one."

"Was it a French kiss," someone teased her, "or maybe an Aussie kiss*?"

"No . . . just a regular one."

"How does he treat you?" Rabbi Emily asked. Her question seemed to stump Lee and she sat there, mulling it over.

---

* I'd learned the kiss lexicon at Camp Carson – that was a kiss "down under."

Another girl, whose name was Tara, spoke up. "My love interest doesn't even know I'm alive. I'm *so* crushing on him but I can't even say who it is."

I had met Tara a few days ago when she'd come to the Health Centre not feeling well. "I have the 'flu," she'd said weakly, sinking onto the couch. She was pale and clammy and said her body "ached all over." Every few moments, she doubled over with stomach cramps. I sat down beside her and placed my fingertips on her pulse. It was pounding. She looked at me. Her face was tragic. "There's a guy I like, but I don't even register on his radar." She covered her face with her hands.

"Do you spend much time with him?"

"No, and there's no way anything could ever happen between us." She revealed her crush was on Matti, the song-leader, and Tara knew that at twenty-two years of age to her fifteen-year-old self, he was an inappropriate choice, but what could she do? I truly sympathized. How well I recalled my own attractions to older men,* not to mention days spent lolling by the phone for a boy to call!

Many questions the girls asked surprised me in their sophistication. I had to wonder, whatever happened to good ol' cooties? What about the progression of first base, second base, etcetera? Were these girls really so experienced and brazen or was it all male-imitation locker-room talk? It was hard to tell.

"Do you think a PSD – a pre-sex-discussion – is a good idea?" one girl asked. "I've heard that sex is actually better if you get to know the other person first."

"How do you get it to stop at major kiss action and go no further?" another asked.

---

* Mr. Rawlings, are you out there? Remember me? Grade 10 Science? I stayed after school, hung around the lab, and memorized photosynthesis and the Krebs cycle all for you but you never once offered me a ride home in your burnt-orange Mustang! Biology? In those days I was pure *biology*!

"Maybe you have to show some restraint before it gets that far," Rabbi Emily suggested. "You do have the right to say no."

"Yes, but do we have the right to say *yes*?" Lee asked with her usual boldness.

Before Rabbi Emily had a chance to answer, another girl jumped in with her question. "What I want to know is, how well should you know the guy for just casual sex?"

Rabbi Emily smiled and answered. "At the heart of all of these questions is knowing who you are and doing what you believe is right. You can only do that after you've given it some careful consideration."

"I'm not sure if I'm into casual sex," one girl bravely confessed, putting forward a position that suddenly seemed both quaint and radical. "I want to be at least semi-serious with the guy before I go all the way." She looked around to gauge her friends' reactions. "I mean, does that sound uptight? I know it's kind of old-school."

It must have taken courage to express this view but it also emboldened others to speak up and express their belief that, for them, too, physical intimacy was special, something they wanted to save for when they were ready and with the right person.

"I agree," said another girl. "Sex without emotions does sound empty. I'm not a prude, but I don't want to be crude, either." She looked startled, then pleased when they laughed at her accidental rhyme. "I'm so not ready for it." She looked suddenly shy in front of her friends, but they nodded their encouragement.

The questions kept coming.

"Rabbi, what's a good age to start?" a girl asked, "I mean, for going all the way? And what about oral sex? It's not really sex, is it?"

"I heard you can get re-virginized, if you lose your virginity," said another girl. "Not that I need it," she hastened to add, "I was just wondering if it's possible, in case . . ."

"How can you tell if you're gay?" someone else asked. "Just curious," she added.

Rabbi Emily spoke in general about sexual orientation and then openly about her own experience of coming out and how she now lived as a gay woman, married to her partner, Cynthia.

As the discussion continued, I looked around at the group. The girls were beautiful – and I wasn't just thinking about their inner beauty. In their outward, superficial shapes, sizes, colours, and even with their so-called flaws – a lisp, a stutter, excess weight, pimples, braces: the things they thought were all anyone saw – they were physically beautiful. Their beauty came from their radiant good health and from their natural, unadorned looks. Being their true selves made them shine with loveliness.

Rabbi Emily began to wind down the discussion with a few final thoughts that she prefaced by saying were her own, personal opinions. "It's important to stay true to what you believe. Having boundaries defines yourself and bestows dignity and self-respect. It comes down to, what kind of woman do you want to be? Are you prepared to make choices that are right for you, even if they are difficult or unpopular? I believe that what each of us has to offer, both inside and outside, is a gift from God and that we should value it. We've each been given a body and a soul but it is up to us to be the stewards of ourselves and take care of our health."

She had given them a lot to think about – me, too.

It was a great summer. We on the health care team congratulated each other: most kids stayed healthy and the incidence of injury and infection and the use of prescription medications were way down. Our illness prevention campaign had been a huge success. It was hard to leave, but I was feeling rested and refreshed and it was time to get back to my job in the city. My kids were staying a few more weeks on their own and were looking forward to experiencing camp as it should be, without parents around.

"Harry came to see me off. "Camp is so sick, Mom."

By then, of course, I knew that in some circles, *sick* can be a good thing.

"This is the funnest camp, ever," Max said, wrapping me in a hug.

"C'mon, bro," Harry said to Max, pulling him away. "Say goodbye to Mom."

As they turned and walked off, I saw that my wish was coming true. So far the brothers were friends and looked out for each other.

Alice and I stood near our cars saying goodbye to each other. Matti came over, his guitar slung across his back, pointing down, à la Bruce Springsteen. He grabbed our hands and held them over our heads. "Ding, ding, ding," he called out. "Tied for first place we have two winners – the best nurses, ever!"

14

GONE VIRAL!

It was hard saying goodbye that summer, especially for Harry. His cabin had gone on their first canoe trip and the group of guys who went out came back as a clan of brothers. You could see it in the way they slung their arms around each other, the horsing around, and the private jokes. Even with plans and promises to stay in touch during the year, it probably wouldn't happen. Camp friends and school friends don't usually mix. Camp is a place and a state of mind that just doesn't jive with life back in the city.

That fall, there was no time for missing camp because Harry turned thirteen and preparations were underway to celebrate his bar mitzvah; we knew that if we wanted it to be a meaningful rite of passage, rather than merely a party, we had to do something about it. The first thing we did was start going to synagogue.

One Sabbath morning, who should I run into there but Eddie, last year's *enfant terrible*? He sang in the youth choir and after services saw me and came over to ask a favour. Sixteen, still thin but taller, Eddie wore ripped jeans and a black T-shirt and had a military-short, buzzed haircut. In place of multiple earrings he now had an industrial-type bar in the crunchy part of his ear. "Hey, maybe you can help me," he said. "I applied to come back to camp but got turned down. Could you speak to Rudy and give me a reference?"

"I don't think so, Eddie. You caused a lot of trouble last summer."

"But I didn't want to be there, now I do. My parents off-loaded me to camp because they couldn't handle me at home. They were going through their own shit."

"How are things now?"

"Well, for starters, my parents went splitsville."

"I'm sorry to hear that."

"It's better this way."

"I hope you're getting help for your problems."

"My *parents* are my problem, but yeah, yeah, I go to a shrink now."

"The same one you told me you lied to?"

"I *used* to lie, just randomly, but I don't any more." He looked at me to see if I bought that. "Listen, I had to lie 'cause my parents never trusted me."

"Should they have?"

"It's better to keep them in the dark. The MO in our house was *don't ask, don't tell.* My dad didn't think I knew about his affair, but I went into his computer and saw the e-mails – and they say they can't trust *me*! Hah! So, can you help me or not?"

I didn't know how to answer. Rudy had already turned him down and I didn't want to be the one to tell Eddie he wasn't counsellor material. "I'm pleased to hear you're doing well," I said, skirting his question for now.

"Well, it's been rough, but you just have to deal, you know? I'm still on meds and I know I need them, but I'd like to come back and be a CIT."

"You seriously injured Seth, and Mitchell, too."

"You know, someone told me I was a bully, and I'm like, you've gotta be kidding. I'm always the one being bullied. Oh, I know I did some bad stuff, the bug spray and other things, too." He looked closely at me to see what I knew but I knew enough. "I guess I used to be kind of a jerk, but I've changed."

"Well, I'm sure . . ." I demurred, "I guess it's possible . . ."

"Could you speak to Rudy and tell him that? Do you have any pull with him?"

Sure, people change. Didn't Rudy always say that? I would stand up for anyone who'd been wronged or fight for a cause I believed in, but I didn't see how I could go to bat for Eddie. "I didn't think you liked camp. Why do you even want to be a counsellor?"

"Because of Seth. He saw me as a person, not just some trouble-maker loser. I want to do that for some other kid, maybe a kid who has problems like I do – I mean, *did*. Oh, you probably think I'm whacko, a freakazoid, a psycho," he said quite cheerfully.

Those were compliments compared to what I had thought of him last summer. What I thought now I wasn't sure, but he still showed no remorse, nor insight into his actions. "I'll be honest with you, Eddie, there aren't many of us who saw your behaviour last summer who'd want you anywhere near their child, and as a CIT you'd be taking care of little kids."

"But, hey, I do volunteer work in a homework club. I'm getting straight A's at school and I sing in the fucking choir! What more do you want?"

You may sing in the choir, but you're no choirboy.

"Good luck," I said, knowing it wasn't much to offer.

"That's so unfair," he said as I walked away.

I called Rudy to tell him about my conversation with Eddie. He sounded heavy-hearted about his decision. He never wanted to exclude anyone, but "Eddie's too much of a risk," he said regretfully. "I can't take the chance."

Despite the fact that there was no longer any cachet to having your mom at camp (if there ever had been), and the growing realization that Harry didn't want me there any more (but was too nice to tell me), I went back for a third summer at Camp Sol. How much longer could I keep up this camp nurse gig? My time was running out to be a grown-up interloper in this child's paradise. I figured I'd better squeeze in another summer while I could.

Time was passing fast. That fall when Harry turned thirteen, he changed almost overnight, in all the ways he was supposed to, but still, it took me by surprise. His voice deepened and he got taller. When I went to lug his heavy duffel bag from the car to heave it onto the camp bus, he took it from me easily, along with Max's too, and slid them on. He now had muscles and heft to his body. When did all of this happen?

When I arrived at camp, Xiu-Ling and Frankie ran over to greet me.

"Hi, my name is Cookie," Xiu-Ling shouted and waved at me, "and this is Cupcake." Frankie curtsied. "And that's Lollipop, Brownie, and Candy." She introduced the other girls in their cabin.

"Me likey cookies," said Frankie in a baby voice.

"Me likey cupcakes," said Xiu-Ling. "Stop! You're making me laugh!"

"No, you're making *me* laugh!" Frankie squealed with delight, which made them all dissolve into sweet giggles.

Most of the old crowd were back – Alice, Louise, Matti, and Layla. Seth came by later to say "hey." He'd lost a lot of weight and had a beard that made him look much older and serious. He seemed preoccupied. His easygoing, jovial manner was gone. He was on medication now and wanted to keep that confidential. Of course, I said, and found a place in a cupboard to store his meds.

As for Alice and me, we slipped back into our daily routine: breakfast pill call, followed by the morning clinic, which usually carried on till after lunch. Somehow we always managed to get away for a walk, a swim in the lake, or a paddle in a canoe. The first few days flew by and the kids stayed well. At night, we continued to welcome the counsellors who dropped by to chill and relax – *chillax* – serenade us with music, replenish their first-aid kits, tell us what their kids had said or done that day, and occasionally, bare their souls. It went on late but they were irresistible to us. We'd never turn them away.

That summer they seemed to have a lot more on their minds: school, travel plans, and for some, the reluctant realization that their camp days were coming to an end.

"Camp is my security blanket," one wailed, only half joking. "I have to move on but I haven't a clue what to do for the rest of my life. I wish I could stay here forever."

Matti said this was his last summer at camp. "I've got to get a decent-paying job in the city. I want to make music, but realistically I don't think I can make a living at it."

"I won't be back for sure," Layla announced. That was a surprise, because I guess we assumed as Rudy's daughter she'd always be there. "I just got into law school."

Many had a desire to give back to their communities, through volunteer work or political activism, and to find ways to tackle the big issues: saving the environment and combating social injustices such as racism and poverty. I'd attended an open-mike session in the staff lounge where a group of them talked about their upcoming mission to Guatemala with Habitat for Humanity. So many of them had big dreams of doing noble work, but one night they also enjoyed a flight of fantasy about ideal jobs such as toy designers for Lego sets, greeting card copywriters, skateboard designers, and cosmetic labellers, coming up with "Campfire Crimson" lipstick and s'mores-scented perfume. They kidded each other about becoming celebrities or being filmmakers, actors, or rock stars, and a startling number wanted to do "something related to forensics."* More than anything, they all expressed a longing to be *known* for something and to make their mark. I had a feeling many would.

One morning, at the beginning of the second week, I came in for pill call and found Alice looking worried. She'd been up all night with Murray, a counsellor. "Around one o'clock he banged on my door, but when I opened it he was gone. He'd run off to throw up. He managed to stagger back in and has been vomiting non-stop ever since."

"Was it an upset stomach? Did he eat something that disagreed with him?" I asked with the annoying innocence of one who's had a good night's sleep.

"He'd just returned from a day off in Toronto participating in a karate tournament. He ate dinner with his cabin, felt fine afterward, but got sick during the night."

"Sick?" I asked.

"He's sick," she said, firmly, "*really* sick."

"How sick could he be?" *C'mon, impress me, I'm an* ICU *nurse!* "*Sick.*"

Sick is an important word and the inflection and tone are crucial. Even in the ICU where all of our patients are sick, when a nurse says a patient is sick in the way that Alice did, the seriousness goes up a few notches. I peeked in, took one look, and had to agree with her. The fit young man I'd seen doing kicks and

---

* Possibly because of the recent explosion of shows like CSI? In fact, so many mentioned an interest in forensics that I figure the crime rate will have to soar to keep them supplied with work.

punches in the martial arts studio was now a pathetic-looking, pale, clammy specimen, sitting at the edge of the bed, shivering, and clutching at his stomach, as he leaned into a garbage can to retch.

"I can't believe I didn't hear the commotion. Why didn't you wake me up?"

"You weren't on call," she said with a chuckle. Now, it was my turn to marvel at my own imperturbable nurse sleep.

Louise arrived to examine Murray. When she was done she came out of the room and stripped off the vinyl gloves she'd had the foresight to put on when she heard Alice's report. Louise was positive he had gastroenteritis – a stomach virus – which was very contagious. He would probably be better soon, but the main thing was to prevent its spread. Alice and I started scrubbing down all the surfaces in the Health Centre.

All that day and into the next night, Murray had a raging fever, and stomach cramps so severe he could only drag himself out of bed and crawl to the toilet, where he had uncontrollable diarrhea. I watched over him, dozing off and on, stretched out on the waiting room couch. It was about two o'clock in the morning when I heard the sound of running footsteps outside my window. I unlocked the door. One of the other counsellors in Murray's cabin stood there, trembling. "Help me," he moaned. "I'm dying." He turned his head away from me as an arc of vomit spewed from his mouth and hit the wall. He collapsed at my feet and lay there, writhing and moaning. Another counsellor who'd come with him had run off to vomit into a garbage can and was making his unsteady way back in. "What is this?" he cried. "I've never been so sick in my life."

I put on gloves and a gown and stayed with them while they went through agony, violently ill all night. By morning, they were taking turns running to the bathroom with diarrhea. Then, they stripped off their clothes, covered themselves with sheets, and flopped down on the narrow cots, one on either side of Murray, who was now peacefully asleep.

I went to wash my hands. On second thought, I decided to take a shower. Just before entering my room, I peeled off my clothes and dropped them in a heap outside my door to be boiled, bleached, and laid out in the sun later when I had the time.

After lunch, a little boy from Murray's cabin came over to me.

"I think I just threw up." He rubbed his stomach.

"You think so? You don't know if you did or not?"

"Something came out that looked like the bean burritos I just ate."

"Yeah, I saw it," his friend reported. "His yark was bright orange." He peered at the sick boy. "Hey, you look pale. Maybe you should eat some meat."

"Can I have a Tums?" the boy asked me. "That's what my mom gives me when my stomach is upset." He suddenly bolted off to find a garbage can, but – blat! – missed it entirely.

This was no upset stomach. This was a virus and it was spreading – fast!

"Can you give me medicine to make it better?" he called out as he ran off to the bathroom, but he didn't make it there in time, either. I went to get a mop.

Later that afternoon, I heard someone just outside the Health Centre groaning.

"Owww . . . my stomach hurts." I looked out the window and saw a little girl doubled over, vomiting on the ground. "I feel *sooo* yucky. I want to go home," she cried as her counsellor tried to soothe her. A few minutes later, another counsellor brought in a little girl from the same cabin. She dropped down onto the floor, sobbing and begging for her teddy bear that she'd thrown up on and that her counsellor had washed and hung outside to dry. Her counsellor held her and stroked her hair while the little girl threw up again and again. The counsellor herself looked pale and I had a feeling she'd be down soon, too.

By evening, the CITs started dropping. One boy lay on a cot while his girlfriend stood at the door. They looked like Romeo and Juliet, gazing at each other with desire, but forbidden to touch, or even come close. "I love you," she whispered.

"Love you too," he mouthed weakly as I pulled the star-crossed lovers apart.

This outbreak was escalating at an alarming rate. We could barely focus on measures to control it when we were so busy taking care of patients. We didn't even get to some of them in time and would come upon kids lying limply on their beds or even on the floor, too weak to get up. After the vomiting came diarrhea and extreme fatigue. Their eyes became red and sore from the strain of retching and their mouths were parched. We had to examine each person carefully so as not to miss any of the other things that can also cause nausea, vomiting, and diarrhea, things such as appendicitis, a bowel obstruction, or even ordinary heatstroke. I recalled Kitch's warning that stomach pain that wakes a child in the middle of the night is always serious.

Rudy called an emergency meeting of all staff.

"This is a very aggressive virus," Louise said.

"Tell me about it," someone mumbled, going outside for air.

"It's the bubonic plague," someone said glumly. "Everyone's gonna get it."

"This thing's gone viral," Matti said, putting down his guitar. He picked it up again and wiped it all over with antiviral cleanser before putting it away in its case. He was looking unwell himself. Even those who weren't sick were feeling queasy. They also were caring for sick kids and knew the chances were high they might get the bug, too. All we could do was try to contain it with frequent, thorough handwashing. Isolation at camp was going to be difficult and probably already too late.

"The bad news is that it is highly infectious and if you get it, you'll feel rotten," Louise said, "but the good news is that it is short-lived and you'll all recover."

"That's great," they said sarcastically.

"After two or three days of misery, you'll get better," Louise went on to say. "It's rough – I won't lie to you – but you'll all survive. What we're going to have to do is redouble our efforts to control it, or else it will turn out to be a disastrous summer."

Many were feeling like it was already. The burden of caring for sick kids and keeping the others well and preoccupied was wearing on them, but they soldiered on.

We beefed up the handwashing blitz. Rudy installed new, portable handwashing facilities and bottles of hand sanitizer were placed on each table in the dining hall. We ordered cases of rehydration fluids to replace lost electrolytes (salts and minerals) and glucose (sugar); gallon jugs of antiviral cleaner; boxes of vinyl gloves, disposable masks and gowns; and ten-pound bags of kitty litter to absorb messes and smells. Alice and I worried about vulnerable campers like Steven whose immobility put him at risk; a girl with Crohn's disease; a boy with a metabolic disorder; and most especially, Daniel, who had diabetes. And there were others, too.

Everyone was either sick or worried sick. The virus was the main topic of conversation.

"Am I going to get it?" so many children asked me.

"I hope not, but if you do, you'll get better. Keep washing your hands."

In the midst of all of this, ordinary wounds still needed bandaging, itchy bug bites needed soothing, and twisted ankles needed icing and taping. In fact, a minor injury that occurred back on the very first evening of camp was still keeping us busy with a time-consuming follow-up. It had been pouring rain and Xiu-Ling had run in ahead of Frankie, screaming that Frankie had fallen off the porch. Frankie limped in tragically, supported on one side by her dripping wet counsellor and on the other by Xiu-Ling, who'd run back to help her. Xiu-Ling was wearing a crazy hat that had a short pole on top to which was attached an open umbrella, and she kept her head cocked at an extreme angle in order to offer Frankie cover from the rain.

"How did this happen?" I tried to keep a straight face at this comical sight.

"She fell into the bushes and they were thorny," Xiu-Ling explained.

Alice and I cleaned her up and covered her scrapes. But every evening since then, she came back to us to have the bandages changed. Painstakingly, we removed them as Frankie whimpered. "Oooh, please be careful," she pleaded. "Ouch, ouch ouch!" We told her it would be easier if we did it quickly rather than prolong the agony but she wouldn't hear of such a drastic approach. It was the third night of the gastro bug, the place was packed with sick kids, and Alice and I had no patience for the drawn-out procedure. Besides, by then, her scrapes had mostly healed. Meanwhile, we were hopping busy: kids were being carried in, the examining rooms were full, the waiting room was packed, and there was a lineup out onto the porch.

I looked at Frankie's sad face. "Frankie, can you do it yourself, tonight, please?"

"No, no!" She shook her head. "I need you to do it and it's Cupcake, remember?"

"I'll do it, but only if you let me do it fast, *Cupcake*."

"Me no likey." She backed off, her eyes large behind her glasses.

"I'm sorry, but I don't have the time, right now." *For the Band-Aid ceremony.*

"I'll do it for you!" offered Xiu-Ling. "Please let me, Cuppy-Cake? You likey?"

I stepped back to watch this play out. *Let Cookie be the bad guy.* I watched Xiu-Ling distract Frankie with another silly joke and then in one smooth motion, ripped off the bandage. "Ta-da!" Xiu-Ling held it in the air, waved it like a flag.

Frankie was stunned, uncertain how to react. Should she cry out because it was supposed to hurt? Be furious at me for allowing Xiu-Ling to do this to her? Be angry at Xiu-Ling for tricking her? Or would Frankie make another decision altogether?

I busied myself, watching them out of the corner of my eye and thinking about these everyday choices: to cope or not; to be strong or to dissolve; to choose hope or despair, rise above it or sink down low. I readied myself to celebrate or console. Finally, Frankie made her decision. She burst out laughing, the surest sign of triumph! "Yay, Frankie!" a roar went up around the waiting room. She grinned at her achievement. Cookie and Cupcake went out arm in arm, laughing hysterically.

Once again, my nursing practice was teaching me how much more we can endure, and achieve, than we think we can.

Later that night, I was working, long after midnight, and Rudy showed up unexpectedly. At first, I thought he was sick, but he looked well. He sidled over to me with a sly look in his eye. "I have the key to the tuck shop," he whispered in my ear. "What's your pleasure?"

I gasped. Was he coming on to me? "Oh, no, I don't think so," I stammered.

"What'll it be? What do you crave?"

"I couldn't . . . possibly . . ."

"Your choice: Kit Kat or Twinkie? How 'bout a Crunchie?"

I burst out laughing for having misread his intention. Anyway, I desperately needed chocolate way more than sex!

The outbreak showed no signs of abating. More and more children were getting sick and counsellors, too. Somehow, Alice and I stayed well and kept going. *Nurses can't get sick*, or so the legend goes.

Camp had become a strange and uncomfortable place. Everyone kept their distance. No hugging or holding hands, no CITs sitting in each other's laps. Visitor's Day, which was coming up in two weeks, might have to be cancelled. Camp might even have to be shut down for the rest of the summer. Worst of all was the eerie quiet. The music stopped. Silence fell over camp.

15

CAMPFIRE NURSE

The crisis continued. Kids begged to go home. The mood was bleak.

Louise, Alice, and I were stunned at how fast this thing was racing through camp. Our efforts to contain it seemed to have no effect. There were new cases every day. Rudy was worried.

"They've all lost their sparkly eyes," he said in dismay. "Morale has never been so low."

When's it gonna hit me? counsellors caring for sick kids wondered. Most kept a sense of humour – especially the lipstick namer who came up with "Pretty in Puke Pink" and "Viral Violet" – but understandably, there was also grumbling and rumbles of discontent. "I didn't sign up for this," some said. A few packed up and left. "I can't take the chance of getting sick," said one. "I'm outta here." "Me too," a friend said. "This place is contaminated! It's teeming with pestilence."

"Yeah, *right*," said Seth. He was disgusted with those who jumped ship. "They'll never be able to show their faces here ever again."

Rudy got sick and retreated to his cabin with only Ringo for company.

By the morning of Day Four we reported the outbreak to the

public health authorities. They planned to come by later that day to investigate.

We studied the situation. There had to be a logical "chain of transmission," but if we couldn't discern the pattern we had no way of knowing if our control measures were effective. I came up with an idea. I ran to the arts and crafts shed and returned with a large sheet of cardboard, markers, and stickers in assorted colours. I drew a box for each cabin and put a red dot on Murray's cabin. *Murray was the first case.* For Day Two, I put two green dots for his co-counsellors and two more for the boys in his cabin. *That makes sense, they're in the same cabin.* For Day Three, ten yellow dots. *Those kids sit together in the dining hall. The sick CITs had been working with that cabin.* Today, Day Four, we had thirty-five purple dots and the web was getting more intricate. It was far from over. I only hoped it would end before we exhausted our entire range of colours.

Camp had come to a standstill. Activities were cancelled. The dining hall seemed particularly empty and mealtimes were subdued. Seth, Matti, Layla, and others got on the case. They picked up their guitars and played outside the cabin windows of the sick kids and entertained them with skits, pantomimes, and juggling. They started up a drumming circle, an activity that almost everyone could do, and it got kids with bad cases of cabin-fever outdoors again. In fact, the drumming group became such a hit that long after the kids went to sleep, the counsellors kept the beat going late into the night. They reinstated the dining hall music and not just the religious songs, but their own playlist, too. "Will Santana or Sly and the Family Stone pick up the mood better?" "Does Zeppelin go better with mac and cheese, or Judas Priest?" they asked one another, considering the various pairings with the same attention a doctor gives to choosing the appropriate antibiotic. Once again, the sounds of those classic bands, along with the upbeat tunes of Great Big Sea, OutKast, and

Dispatch, boomed out of the speakers. Those who were able got up and moved to the beat as they cleared the tables after meals. Like a restorative tonic, the music brought them back to life.

Two surprise leaders were Lee and Jasmine, last summer's "bad girls" who were now CITs. They even volunteered for the cleaning squad. "We're stoked," they said, "down for whatever." The squad roved around, mopping up messes, airing out cabins, and stripping beds. They probably didn't do this kind of thing at home but here they took it on with a cheerful attitude. They squealed with delight when we issued them a walkie, and with that in hand and spray bottles of disinfectant hooked onto their shorts, they patrolled the camp, doing their chores and keeping us in the loop along the way.

"Cleanup in aisle five" or "puke puddle alert," one would say over the walkie to summon the rest of the crew to bring the bags of kitty litter, brooms, buckets and mops.

"Nurse Tilda? Are you there? Over and out."

"Yes, Lee. I'm here."

"Hey, it's Jasmine. I'm down at the canoe docks with two little Flame girls who are spewing chunks!"

"Okay. Bring them in."

A few minutes later, I heard, "FYI: two other girls from the same cabin aren't feeling well. I think they're about to hurl."

"Bring them in, Jasmine, over and out."

"This is Lee. I'm all over it! Ten-four, Nurse Tilda!"

They didn't seem worried about getting sick themselves. They even offered to supervise our isolation ward, which had been dubbed "The Colony." They played an elaborate fantasy game with the children based on the TV show *Lost*, pretending they were survivors of a plane crash, stranded on a deserted island, having to band together to protect themselves from monsters, doomsday warriors, and evil island inhabitants. The male counsellors had their own style of fun, lining up garbage cans for duelling barf-fests, cracking lots of diarrhea jokes, and devising clever poop descriptions and fart charts.

In the afternoon the health inspector arrived. He strode in, carrying a briefcase like a detective, determined to get to the bottom of the case. First, he inspected the kitchen and found it spotless, quickly ruling out food contamination as a source of the infection. He examined my diagram charting the rapid, exponential spread and interviewed Murray, the first or "index" case, who had by then completely recovered.

"Continue exactly as you're doing," he concluded. "Disinfecting all surfaces, frequent handwashing, and minimizing physical contact is the only way to beat it." But as he got up to leave, he warned us, "If there's any escalation, you'll have to close the camp. As for Visitor's Day in a week and a half, I'd advise you to cancel it." He must have noticed our shocked faces because he added: "Go ahead if you must, but no touching."

Visitor's Day, without hugging or kissing? Unheard of!

Before parting, he offered guarded encouragement. "When the number of new cases starts to level off and you've hit a plateau, it'll be the beginning of the end."

We notified parents about the outbreak and the possibility of cancelling Visitor's Day. Some wanted to come and get their kids right away but we advised against it. They'd probably be feeling better in a day or two, and at home they'd be exposing family members, including possibly elderly grandparents or others who couldn't easily withstand a debilitating illness. Distraught, some mothers and fathers called daily. Anxiety was spreading like the virus itself. From his sick bed, Rudy composed a group e-mail.

"The children who have gotten sick are all recovering," he wrote. "If symptoms persist once your child comes home, please contact your doctor." *And your lawyer*, I heard him mutter. He must be joking! But no, Rudy was worried that some would try to lay blame.

"It's easy to criticize but it's no one's fault," I said. "These things happen."

"You're handling this quite calmly," he remarked.

"I guess my standards are different than most people's," I admitted. "Don't forget, I'm an ICU nurse." At least here my patients weren't *dying*. I never lost sight of how bad things *could* be, and there was another reason I could keep things in perspective: I had lived through something far worse – SARS.

It was 2003. A mysterious pneumonia was suddenly making people gravely ill. Some were dying. SARS was not the first time I'd worried about my safety and what dangers I was bringing home to my family, but it was definitely the scariest. Over the years, I'd taken care of patients who'd had infectious diseases such as hepatitis, tuberculosis, and HIV-AIDS, but SARS was different. The virus that caused SARS – short for sudden acute respiratory syndrome – travelled lightning fast and was transmitted person to person by incidental, casual contact. It was lurking in the air, potentially blown your way by the wind, a breeze, a breath, or a sneeze.

Overnight, SARS turned Toronto into a ghost town. Travel was banned by the World Health Organization; hotels and restaurants emptied out, streets were vacant. Many people were quarantined. It was a new disease, and at first even infectious-disease specialists didn't know what they were dealing with. People felt confused and afraid. At a party I went to during that time, guests jumped away from me and refused to shake my hand or come near me. Mothers cancelled play dates with my kids. Those of us caring for SARS patients, doing this hazardous but essential work, felt a punishing sense of isolation.

I'll never forget how dark and quiet the hospital was during that time. Only hands-on, front-line caregivers came to work. It was mostly nurses who kept the hospital open. Wearing two pairs of gloves, gowns, plastic face shields, and heavy masks, customized to fit our individual faces and impermeable to viruses, we worked in closed, negative-pressure rooms, caring for our patients. Overtop our masks we watched our patients, and in our eyes, patients sought assurance they would not be abandoned.

In a crisis a leader is needed, and Toronto had one. Dr. Sheela Basrur was the city's Officer of Public Health at the time and she led Toronto in the same calm, courageous manner that Mayor Rudy Guiliani guided New York City during 9/11. As more people got sick and mass hysteria threatened to erupt, Dr. Basrur reassured the public. She explained the need for the drastic quarantines and how they were the only way to stop the chain reaction. She acknowledged it was a serious situation, but not an emergency. "My job is to do the worrying," she said.

Dr. Basrur understood nursing. Like a nurse, she cared about the nitty-gritty, such as the proper handwashing technique and ensuring that we were equipped with the special masks, not the ordinary, one-size-fits-all paper ones. She was concerned that caregivers would become exhausted and unable to carry on. Then, just when the situation seemed to be coming under control, a second wave of SARS broke out. A nervous city became terrified, and again Dr. Basrur took control. Working around the clock, or so it seemed, she held daily press conferences in which she distilled complex information so it could be understood by everyone. In the end, in Toronto alone, there were over four hundred cases of SARS, the majority of them health-care workers. Forty-four people died. It was a terrible time, but many were left with a sense that it could have been much worse had it not been for the dedication of health-care workers and the leadership of Dr. Basrur.*

I tried to be that kind of leader, too. Together with Alice and Louise, we communicated openly with the counsellors, explaining

---

* Dr. Basrur resigned from her position in 2006 in order to undergo treatment for a rare form of cancer. When she died in 2008, nursing lost a great ally.

everything to them. We encouraged them to ask questions, express their frustrations, and let off steam. We acknowledged their efforts. During a lull one day, I spoke with Seth, who was looking mighty haggard. "How are you holding up?" I asked. He came in each evening, dropping by discreetly for his medication, but he didn't stop to chat or joke around like he used to.

"I'm good," he said, forcing a smile.

"It's been rough, hasn't it?"

He looked at me in surprise. "No, it's been the best summer ever. We've pulled together and are closer than ever. We're like family now."

Of course. I knew Seth loved a challenge. He was an extraordinary counsellor, an outstanding student and athlete, a terrific guy. He excelled at everything he did. I knew he'd gotten a full scholarship to university and I asked him how that was going.

"I dropped out. Couldn't hack it," he said blithely, but then sat down with me and told me the real story. "Something happened," he said, shaking his head. "I still don't get it. It was my birthday and birthdays mean a lot to me. I'd broken up with a girlfriend and none of my friends were around. I was alone in my dorm. It was August, right after camp, but before classes started. Suddenly, I snapped. I went over to the dark side. Nothing made sense. For days I couldn't even get out of bed. My parents came but they didn't know what to do. My mom cried and my dad kept telling me to pull myself together."

"What helped? You must have felt well enough to come to camp this summer."

"Camp was the only place I could be. What helped was being around people like you, Tilda. People who don't judge, who just listen, and don't tell me what to think or do. My parents are great but they give me advice when I just need them to listen."

"Are you lonely, Seth? When you're not with your kids, I always see you by yourself."

"My buddies know I need space. For awhile I was into mean-ingless hook-ups but no more. It was messing me up. At school, I dated someone I met on the Internet, but she'd never been to camp, so she didn't get it. I'm on my own right now and I'm cool with that." We sat together in silence for a while until he spoke again. "I've discovered you can go very far away and still make it back."

"How are you doing now?"

"I'm okay to be with kids, so don't worry, but I'm terrified the dark side will come back. I've got to make up the year I missed, so this will definitely be my last year at camp." He looked out the window as if taking it all in at once, this place he loved.

By the end of two weeks we reached the plateau the health inspec-tor spoke about. Lab tests confirmed that, as expected, it was a norovirus, the most common culprit in this type of illness. In total, twenty per cent of the camp had gotten sick and everyone recovered. It could have been so much worse.

The night before I left, we gathered around a huge bonfire. Other than the campers and counsellors who were still recover-ing, everyone was there. Matti led them in this song.

O Lord, my God,
I pray that these things never end:
The sand and the sea, the rush of the waters,
The crash of the heavens, the prayer of the heart.

I looked around the circle. Everyone looked happy. Even the sick ones who'd wanted to go home were smiling once again. They were all content within themselves and connected to their friends – this was camp happiness. They were glowing with it that night.

I returned to the Health Centre and gave out the evening meds. After I locked up and headed toward my room, I heard far-off rhythmic sounds. The music beckoned me and I retraced my steps to the campfire where the counsellors had gathered. I approached tentatively. (I didn't want to crash a private ritual as I'd done once before, accidentally intruding upon a band of bare-chested CIT boys performing a war dance.) They were sitting in a circle. Some of them were holding drums – tom-toms, bongos, djembes – and some had tambourines or maracas. In unison they beat a rhythm as compelling as my heartbeat, which suddenly welled up and throbbed inside my core. A girl got up and wordlessly handed me an instrument. *No*, I shook my head, *I'll sit out and just listen*, but she kept her hand outstretched. At last I took the instrument, waited for the beat, found my place to enter, and joined in.

Later, as I left the drumming circle, I felt quietly happy – and proud, too. Finally, I'd won my place at the campfire.

16

THE CURE FOR HOMESICKNESS

"You'll never guess who's back!" Alice threw out a teaser. We were busy unpacking supplies and organizing camper meds, getting ready for the start of a new summer. By her impish grin, I knew she was also gearing up for the fun to begin.

"Who?"

"Eddie! He's a counsellor, now!"

Unbelievable. Well, Rudy always said kids can change, didn't he? Later, I heard that Eddie was Max's counsellor and I felt uneasy about that but decided to keep quiet, watch and wait. I trusted Rudy's judgment and knew that if there was an issue with Eddie, it would be dealt with. I was getting better at letting go, at allowing my kids to solve their own problems and turn to others if they needed help. But it had taken me one more camp lesson to get that message.

I'd been strolling past Harry's cabin. It was quiet, a perfect time to sneak in for a peek – if his guitar was out, I'd know he was playing it; if his laundry bag was full, I'd remind him to send his clothes to be washed. If I could just get a glance at the skew of his flip-flops beside the bed . . . I mounted the creaky wooden steps and checked that the coast was clear. I knocked on the door, just to be sure. Harry's counsellor came to answer it. His eyes narrowed when he saw me. *A trespasser.*

Awhhh! Busted.

"What do you want?" he asked warily.

"Just dropping by, to, ah – visit." I squirmed.

He frowned. "Don't even think about it. This is Harry's space."

I slunk away, apologizing. "What can I do?" I said, helplessly. "He's my son."

"Yeah, but at camp, he's mine," the counsellor said, closing the door.

But later when I saw the counsellor, he tossed me a few crumbs. "Harry loves snakes. It takes a big heart to love a snake. He's friends with everyone. He knows right from wrong. What more do you need to know?"

What a comfort these connections give when we relinquish the illusion of control and learn to trust. I've heard there are now camps where the whole family can come along. "Have fun with your kids," the brochures say. But doesn't that defeat the purpose? The point of camp is to take those steps away and out into the world on your own.

At lunch, I looked around. Seth wasn't there and I missed him. Alice and Louise were back, Rudy, too, of course, but without Ringo. He'd been an old dog back when I'd first met him four summers ago and this winter he'd become unable to walk or even wag his tail. Rudy had done the kind, hard thing and taken him to the vet to have a comfortable death. He planned to get a puppy soon but had other things on his mind. He had a girlfriend now, a companion who shared his love of camp.

The first night we celebrated Alon's return to camp and his full recovery to good health. He was now head tripper, excited about implementing new "green" initiatives, such as reducing the camp's water and electricity usage and running a contest to reward the cabin that conserved the most energy.

I continued my own green awakening with Alice. One morning she stopped in her tracks, knelt down, and placed her hands gently around a large bug. She scooped it up and brought it close to show me: a shiny black beetle with long antennae and pincers that made it look like an alien from Mars.

"Isn't it beautiful?" she asked and now, at last, I could see that it was.

Most afternoons, we still managed to steal away for a swim in the lake. As I eased myself in, I commented on how cold the water was.

"Don't forget," she said, "a few months ago this lake was pure snow." I breathed in the clean smell of the air and water. "Thousands of years before that, it was a glacier."

Returning to camp was a homecoming for me. Even the noise and commotion were a familiar comfort. When I entered the dining hall, the roar engulfed me as I was immediately plunged into the midst of ecstatic, dancing bodies and a cacophony of voices, all whooping and hollering, cheering, chattering, and singing at the top of their lungs. I even joined in on one song and got up and waved my arms upward. "Oooh . . . ahh . . ." I said, swinging them back down in a swoop.

"Hey, man, you're really into it," Rudy said appreciatively, sitting down beside me on the bench.

Yes, their noisy exuberance was catchy. Why should we "sit still" or "be quiet"? *It's time to move!*

Alice and I looked at each other. How well we knew them, her smile seemed to say. Inside and out, their bodies and their souls, we knew every scrape, bump, bruise, and rash, as well as their worries, fears, and secrets, and dreams. *As nurses, we are so privileged to have this opportunity to get to know people on such an intimate level.*

At camp I learned how to care for healthy children. One malady I became skilled at treating was homesickness, especially after I understood that it's not always about missing home and doesn't only occur at camp: one can have a bad bout sitting at home.* At its core, homesickness is a yearning to be at home within ourselves. In fact, the cure for homesickness is camp itself, because at camp you can learn everything you need to know about finding your way home.

One afternoon, I had a surprise: Seth came to visit. He said he was feeling better. "I had to come back and see everyone, especially you, Tilda." He still looked wistful about camp but more hopeful about his future. "You know, I loved being a camper, but being a counsellor was the best time of my life. I'm looking into becoming a camp director."

We shared a chuckle about Eddie being a counsellor now and, from what we could tell, doing a great job. "Eddie's the best!" Max had run over to tell me – though that's what he says every summer about all of his counsellors.

Seth gave me a quick hug before leaving. "It's time for me to move on."

"You seem ready."

We hear so much bad news these days about young people in trouble, involved in delinquency, drugs, and violence. As parents we worry about the dangers and so many bad influences that are out there. Sometimes, we have doubts that the upcoming generation has the proper values or the right work ethic or sufficient motivation. Camp made me think otherwise. I met so many energetic and idealistic young people who want to do good work and give back to the community. One way they start is by being counsellors, giving the kids in their care all that camp has given them.

At the end of my last week at camp that summer, at the Friday evening service, Rudy started off by mentioning achievements,

---

* And let's not forget late-summer campsickness, too!

not only of individuals, but group ones, too: a cabin that had returned from their first canoe trip; another in which everyone had passed the swim test; a successful Colour War. Then, a tall, beautiful counsellor named Dani got up to speak:

This is my ninth summer at camp. There are so many things I love about camp: cabin bonding; stargazing; being with friends I don't see all year round (you know who you are); dancing in the rain; Sabbath cake; my summer as a CIT; meeting my cabin of girls as a counsellor for the first time; techno parties in the staff lounge; long, meaningful conversations that I would not have in the city; and seeing all of you, summer after summer. I will always and forever cherish the memories of our times together.

That says it all.
Yes, I'd probably come back next summer.
To be a camp nurse you don't have to be young, but you do have to be young at heart. At nearly fifty, I didn't feel old, but camp has made me aware of the passage of time – especially, its rush. *So much happens here. A day at camp is a week anywhere else. A week at camp is like a year*, Alice and I always said to each other.
When it was time to leave, I went up to the microphone to say goodbye to everyone at once. As I stepped down from the podium, they all rushed at me and swarmed me in hugs. Then I said goodbye to my sons and began the long, leisurely drive homeward. As I drove along that quiet, country road, I had an urge to turn around and go back, stay there forever, so camp would never end, not that summer, not ever.